Robert Browning:
A Shelley Promethean

Robert Browning:
A Shelley Promethean

None wrought his lips in truth-entangling lines
Which smiled the lie his tongue disdained to speak

Paul A. Cundiff

VALKYRIE PRESS, INC.

1977

First Edition

International Standard Book No. 0-912760-49-4

Library of Congress Catalog Card No. 77-77039

Published By

Valkyrie Press, Inc.

St. Petersburg, Florida

TO MARY

Also by the author

Browning's Ring Metaphor and Truth
(1972)

CONTENTS

PREFACE

The texts for this study have been Browning's *Complete Works* (edited with Introductions and Notes by Charlotte Porter & Helen A. Clarke, 1910), to which the Broughton-Stelter Concordance conforms, and Shelley's *Poetical Works* (Oxford, 1967). Without concordances for Browning, the Scriptures (James Strong) and Shelley (F. S. Ellis) the task would have been interminable. Without Professor Earl R. Wasserman's lucid reading of *Shelley's Prometheus Unbound* (Johns Hopkins Press, 1965) the interpretive errors would surely have been greater than they are.

Because Shelley's poetry is as excessively repetitive as Browning's, Browning's specific adoptions almost always have many parallels in word and thought. Therefore the Shelley references, whether single or multiple lines, require the reading of the context, often of a whole part or section. The warning does not consistently forestall the deception of Browning's bouncing about from part to part, poem to poem, but it pinpoints daring combinations of Shelleyan words and thoughts clearly adopted by Browning. Had he wished Browning probably could have quoted from memory any line in Shelley's poetry, but save for the ever-present *Queen Mab*

PREFACE

he usually had a particular poem in mind for each new effort.

Unidentified references in the synoptic Introduction are always identified in the textual paragraphs or, less cumbersomely, alongside the quoted poetry which gives rise to the reference. "God [Prometheus]" or "Christ [Prometheus]" calls attention to the probable identity until it becomes a reality. All typographical emphases, unless specifically noted, are added. Semicolons separate references within the poetic line and from the line number. Abbreviations of Shelley's titles conform to the abbreviations of the Concordance, the same for the Scriptures, and a few additional ones given here may prove helpful:

C-Eve — "Christmas-Eve"	PB —*Prometheus Bound*
E-Day — "Easter-Day"	PL — *Paradise Lost*
Epi Dram Pers — Epilogue, *Dramatis Personae*	
La S — *La Saisiaz*	PU — *Prometheus Unbound*
Para — *Paracelsus*	R & B — *The Ring and the Book*
Prom — Prometheus	Sord — *Sordello*

Paul A. Cundiff
University of Delaware
Newark

Robert Browning:
A Shelley Promethean

INTRODUCTION

Though it seems unbelievable, the poet Robert Browning lived and died an inveterate foe of Jehovah and a fanatical Promethean. His supposed return to monotheistic belief with a Christian bias, after a youthful adoption of Shelleyan atheism, was as pretentious as his defense of Platonic and Christian truth. The truth about which his poetry so earnestly speaks is the truth of paganism and Prometheus, not the truth of Christianity or the absolute truth of Greek philosophy. Its litany often impinges upon Shelley's exaltation of truth, but Browning's own unalterable thrust points toward Shelley's promise of a new Promethean day in which truth, beauty, goodness and love will turn the wilderness of Christian slavery into a flourishing garden of freedom, brotherly love and artistic perfection. The unrelenting debate between Fact and Fancy which Browning's poetry implicitly portrays as a glorious victory of Heart over Head is in reality a typical Shelleyan reversal. Explicitly it is a total victory for the human mind, displaying an indomitable Will to reassert the truth (Fact) of Prometheus' love and self-sacrifice, the falsity of a faith (Fancy) which enslaves the ignorant followers of Jesus Christ who himself denied his intellectual birthright by submitting to the will of Jehovah.

All has never gone quite well with Browning's eminence as a poet. He has been called an unregenerate pagan and a devout Christian, a barbarian and a visionary, a learned man and an ignoramus. His faith and optimism have been praised and denigrated, and serious claims of his being a great religious and philosophical teacher have been vigorously opposed by minds which discern the rankest inconsistency and disorganization. But Browning's remarkable deception has played no part in the appraisals, not even when he appeared to be the harbinger of modern poetry and imbued with a deep skepticism. Few poets have been quoted oftener than Browning, particularly by modern theologians and moralists, or taken more directly to heart, particularly by exponents of modern materialism. Disparate reasons alone for the quotations are convincing proof of the breadth of Browning's understanding of, the appeal of his sympathetic approach to, areas of thought as offensive to his nature as tyranny was to Shelley's nature. Yet through industry and machination if not always creative talent Browning was enabled to boast secretly during a long career of a crowning achievement: "A secret which this life finds hard to keep, / And, often guessed, is never quite revealed." "Could God be taken in default, / Short of contrivance, by you [R.B.]." "Ask him [Jehovah] if I was slack in use thereof [R.B.'s judging faculty]." "Not so filmy was the texture, but I bore it in my breast / Safe thus far."

Once the code in Browning's poetry is broken the narrative and descriptive elements buckle under the pressure of an intensive warfare. Imposed deception not congenital deficiency, the notorious obscurity and prolixity have little continuing function save for technicalities which can safely be ignored. Whenever the thought is derogatory to God, it is Jehovah about whom the poet speaks; whenever the thought is praiseworthy of God, it is about Prometheus. Add to this single ambiguity — GOD — Shelley's appropriation of the traditional Christ-figure for Prometheus, and Browning's Prometheus, now Christ, Master, Savior, Redeemer and Deliverer, makes the double entente almost impervious to detection. The only difference between Shelley's reversal of

Aeschylus' PROMETHEUS BOUND and Browning's reversal of Christianity is the secrecy Browning maintained. In each instance the scriptural attributes and characteristics of Jehovah are transferred to Prometheus, always openly by Shelley, always disguised in GOD by Browning; the evil characteristics of Satan, to Jehovah, that is, GOD in Browning, Jupiter in Shelley. Browning says that he would gladly give his life in open combat with Jehovah and his followers if he did not believe that the consequences of Shelley's Olympic struggle and failure with Church, State and Christian morality would be repeated. In vowing his life and talent to the defense of Shelley and the propagation of Prometheanism, Browning advisedly sacrifices almost certain defeat in his day for inevitable success in more receptive days. His willful declaration of secret and sacred warfare on Jehovah is never to be relinquished or relaxed. Wit, lightheartedness and mockery, he promises, are to be his weapons of retaliation, and his sole earthly care is the removal of a discredited Jehovah from man's mind in order that the human race may find peace again.

In PAULINE Browning's confession of apostasy is from Prometheus and Shelley. Thus his one genuine shame, after having been nurtured six years on the incomparable QUEEN MAB and other Shelleyan verse. The poet's extraordinary self-consciousness and tenacious intellect found no solace in a religion which demanded surrender of the Will, asking that adherents walk humbly before a supposedly all-wise God who covets demeaning prayer and praise. If Jehovah had the power to make man, a potentially godlike creature, Browning believes that he had the power, if it were not perverted, to make man a happy creature also. He was not to be bribed by Jehovah's slaves into becoming another great religious poet or by Jehovah's false promises of future reward into submission now. Instead of such degradation Browning will suffer ill repute to honor the beneficence of Prometheus. Only the first of Browning's spurious fellowships with Jesus Christ during his passion, the one in PAULINE is similarly modelled on Panthea's watch with Prometheus and as great a Christian sacrilege as Shelley's reversal of Christ's crucifixion. Here

Browning reveals, as he will again and again, a desire to be absorbed by Prometheus exactly as Panthea describes her absorption. Browning's unrestrained worship of Shelley's mental superiority, his love of man and hatred of tyranny preempts all earlier belief in his obvious but chastened praise of Shelley and clearly explains why he says that there is no wiser or more courageous genius than Shelley to join him, yes, after death in an ongoing struggle with Jehovah. For the present Browning will studiously pretend to be a follower of Jehovah in a masquerade which is dramatized as a hell-dress and adapted from St. Paul. Because he is deceitfully knit round, as with a charm, by the sin and lust and pride of Christianity, he will be free to expend wit, mockery and lightheartedness lavishly in the forwarding of Shelley's unparalleled thought.

Small wonder after John Stuart Mill uncovered the inordinate self-consciousness of Pauline's lover that SORDELLO and the unsuccessful plays became Browning's nemesis. But through them he did learn to apply a more subtle deception and he found guidance to the historical Paracelsus in whose misinterpreted life lay a more congenial deceptive medium. Like the young poet and his Sordello, PARACELSUS is obsessed by thoughts of self-consciousness, self-sufficiency and intellectual superiority, the sum of which accounts for his thinking himself sealed and destined for a great Promethean commission. Paracelsus also requires absolute freedom, holding that the imprisoning flesh must be pushed aside or cast into shade as a hindrance to proper flight of the spirit. And along with Sordello he initiates Browning's running complaint about a Jehovah-imposed machinery which alternatingly dispenses pain and pleasure, joy and sorrow, reward and punishment. So Paracelsus would understand why Sordello says to Jehovah, "Style yourself God alone; / Strangle some day with a cross olive-stone!" Indeed, on evaluating his religious experience which may be a dramatization of Browning's rejection of Jehovah, Paracelsus himself exclaims, "Hell-spawn! I am glad, most glad, that thus I fail! / Your cunning has o'ershot its aim. One year, / One month, perhaps, and I had served your turn! / You should have curbed your spite awhile." Paracelsus advises all to reject the glorious visions of Jehovah's untrustworthy love and to scorn the false consolations Jehovah sends by way of vast longings. One may be sure, he heatedly contends, that Jehovah never wastes the strength he deigns impart or tolerates the slightest delay in any charge before adding a new death of pain.

If there is not a second and perfect life to come, Paracelsus judges this life to be a poor cheat, a stupid bungle, a wretched failure. And for one, he protests against it and hurls it back to Jehovah with scorn. No more than Sordello does Paracelsus learn to live by Shelley's philosophic idealism and no less tragic are his attempts to storm the citadel of divinity. His willful acts have not been a sweet surrender to Demogorgon's law of Necessity; nor have those acts been tempered by the correct proportion of love and power. But with Shelley's "intelligent & *necessarily* beneficent actuating principle" to sustain him, Paracelsus may still rest secure in self-consciousness. He refuses to be awed by a shadow (Jehovah) mocking a reality, terminology which indicates familiarity with Shelley's Phantasm of Jupiter. For truth is within oneself and not to be effected by entry of a light supposed to be without. Anticipating death as a possible consequence of his first daring to KNOW, Paracelsus now wholeheartedly welcomes Death as the only entrance to Life. Like Aprile's attainment of Life in Death, his aspiration takes the same direction and encompasses reunion beyond the veil of death. Thus his courageous rise from deathbed and concluding remark to Festus that God's lamp (symbolic of a Promethean) will be pressed to his breast as he joins Prometheus. A distracting and deceptive foil, Festus is privy to the whole aspiration. Together they have been testing "a new creed," a way to the secret of the world, man and man's true purpose, path and fate. When Paracelsus fails, Festus always appears to encourage him. When Paracelsus would admit defeat it is Festus who rebukingly asks, "Your aims? the aims? — to know? and where is found / The early trust ..." (R.B.'s ellipsis). And when Festus demands that the dying Paracelsus be rewarded for his courage, will and mentality, he threatens otherwise to waive his own reward to become Paracelsus' slave elsewhere.

In CHRISTMAS-EVE AND EASTER-DAY, where Browning is thought to have reconfirmed his Christian faith, Mandevillean and Voltairean paradox is the game: one, pyrotechnics and a rationalistic speech by a Tübingen professor rather than a eulogy to Christ's birth; the other, the Last Judgment rather than a recognition of Christ's resurrection. How better could Browning honor his PAULINE avowal than in juxtaposing visions of a wise, benevolent Prometheus and of an unwise, parsimonious Jehovah, yet leaving the impression that Jesus Christ stands triumphant on the keystone of the famous double moon-rainbow and that whatever cruel God invades a "horrid" nightmare he cannot be Jehovah? Thus poised in overpowering light and color, Browning's spectral Prometheus is offered eternal worship in "ecstatic acquiescence," far removed from "thriftless learning / And Ignorance undiscerning." Even Prometheus' liberation, which Shelley modelled on Christ's transfiguration, is pressed into service and the famous "O, FOLLOW, FOLLOW!" is duplicated in the narrator's flight from Zion Chapel to Rome and then to Tübingen. As Asia and Panthea are fatefully drawn to the Cave of Demogorgon, so Browning's narrator fatefully "follows" the spectral creature, sucked along by the vacuum which an eddying vesture creates. Browning's displeasure with the Tübingen professor is not that Sonship has been taken from Jesus but that in the rationalistic reduction divinity has been denied to man altogether. Had the professor surmised that Christ "was also one with the creator" as are all men, he would have been in full accord with Shelley. The proper "God-function" is not to redeem men from the penalty of their errors, which are as insubstantial as growing pains, but to grant motive and injunction for practicing what they know already.

Browning's "unfailing" imagination excusably limped a little between PARACELSUS and CHRISTMAS-EVE AND EASTER-DAY, but in the completed SORDELLO he is able to score Jehovah "at whose defection mortals starve aghast / As though heaven's bounteous windows were slammed fast /

Incontinent" and to inform Walter Savage Landor of his Hercules-like ability to combat Jehovah and the falsity of Judeo-Christian theology. There he also incites his readers to gain the water of Life rebelliously before adding, "Then quaffing at the fount my courage gained, / Recall — *not that I prompt ye* — who explained . . ." (R.B.'s ellipsis). Remindful of "let me strive / To find [our best way of worship] , and when found, *contrive* / My fellows also take their share! / This constitutes my earthly care" in CHRISTMAS-EVE AND EASTER-DAY, the ardor explains why Browning judged mere verse to be small vent for his anticipated thought. The CHRISTMAS-EVE slur at Jehovah's parsimony in "Flung thee as freely as *one rose* / Out of a summer's opulence" and the vulgarity of "glut / Thy sense upon the world" are yet modest opprobrium compared with EASTER-DAY's "One magnific pall / Mantled in massive fold and fall / His [Jehovah's] head, and coiled in snaky swathes / About his feet: *night's black, that bathes / All else, broke grizzled with despair, / Against the soul of blackness there.*" Employment of such phantasmagoria — a fusion of Shelley's caricature of Jehovah in Jupiter and Milton's characterization of Death, the offspring of Satan and his daughter Sin — no longer intimates that Jehovah is an evil force upon whose demise the poet impatiently waits. The light into which only Paracelsus could look without blinkers may now rightly be assigned to Prometheus, for like Shelley's Jupiter, Browning's Jehovah is always clothed in darkness, blackness, shadow or cloud, ever suggesting secrecy, vapidity and evil.

Nowhere else in his poetry does Browning indicate greater delight in Nature than in CHRISTMAS-EVE AND EASTER-DAY. The narrator and the disputants are unrestrained Nature-worshipers. They pretend to believe that the gift of Nature is from Jehovah but they know that it was Prometheus who sacrificed himself to reveal the earth's secrets and to make them functional and enjoyable to man. In four emphatic confessions of pantheistic faith Browning's first mask states and restates a preference for worship outside all forms of organized religion, that is, under Nature's sky which he has cherished since youth. Having been endlessly taught by

Nature of "what love can do in the leaf and stone," he cannot imagine that "the Eternal First and Last [PU 2.3.95]," infinitely powerful and wise, would prove less good in bestowing whatever man requires. Thus his response to the most insignificant of Jehovah's restrictions: "I who thrill through every nerve / At thought" of what practicing Christians turn a deaf ear to. Or "Could God be taken in default, / *Short of contrivance*, by you," a bald intrusion by the poet himself. To Browning's second mask Nature's God, Prometheus, is eager to satiate man's every need and desire, whereas Jehovah is grudgingly indisposed to meet the simplest need of man. Ultimately denied heaven because of his paganism, Hard (Impossible)-to-be-a-Christian is joyously transported by the information that "Earth's exquisite / Treasures of wonder and delight" are forever his.

To renounce the world, to Browning's spokesman, is to renounce the Mind and this is the rationale of his assault on Faith. He recollects how much from books he may learn of earth's resources, her exhaustless beauty, and declares that "Mind, is best — I will seize mind, forego the rest, / And try how far my tethered strength / May crawl in this poor breadth and length." Though then warned that Nature and earthly beauty are mere antechamber to heaven's splendor, he escapes from Jehovah's tyranny in the established Shelleyan manner. So as a proponent of natural beauty and conduct he is not new to Browning's poetry but he and his colleagues in CHRISTMAS-EVE AND EASTER-DAY are possibly the most sophisticated and the most devastatingly scornful. Thus note should be taken that when Hard-to-be-a-Christian cries, "Mind, mind, / So miserably cast behind, / To gain what had been wisely lost," he boasts that Jehovah's heaven "had been wisely lost!" The pretended "anguish" cannot conceal the strong remaining courage, for its purpose — strangely associated with the poet's late departed mother — is to prove the paucity of Jehovah's providence and the indomitability of Browning's spirit. The reader naturally becomes less attracted to pious reluctance to speak while "standing in a cloud" than to "seeing that if I carry through / *My purpose, reason must aver / False after all* — the happy chance!" Scarcely different from the sardonic "How dreadful to be grudged / No ease henceforth, as one that's judged. / Condemned to earth forever, shut / From heaven!"

Often considered the most beloved of his religious poems, SAUL demonstrates how diligently Browning searched the Scriptures and Shelley to compose his most deceptive fabric of Christian overtones and pagan undertones. Ironically it is also in this extended effort that the poet leaves his thought and diction most vulnerable to detection, since he is emboldened to transpose Christ's "for my strength is made perfect in weakness" into Shelley's "Resist not the weakness." For Browning therewith empties Christianity of all its meaning and substitutes the independence of the human mind. As Shelley welded characteristics together until his Prometheus had all the aspects of Jesus Christ's recorded nature, so Browning interfused pagan and Christian matters until the Hebrew David could exclaim without detection, "See the Christ [Prometheus] stand!" By its implied reference to the Messiah or Anointed One a single ambiguous anachronism has deceived innumerable readers. Jesus Christ, who claimed to be the Messiah, is as far removed from SAUL as are his atonement, the Grace of his Father and a liberated Saul. No longer mystifying, it is the FACE of Prometheus which smiles on so many Browning characters, the HAND of Prometheus which sustains and guides so many. Fully informed of his mind's being a gifted part of the One Mind, the poetic David further knows that his Will is sufficient to the requirements of Demogorgon's "dar'st demand." Thus David's show of love and courageous "dares" confirm the Shelleyan truth of the absence of any barrier to the beneficent Prometheus and give him the warrant to seek and to find his Flesh in the Godhead. Precisely the same Browningesque aristocracy of mind which prompts Cleon, Karshish, Ben Ezra and the Grammarian prompts David.

Saul, for professed love of whom David would wrestle Jehovah's angel, serves chiefly as a reflection of David's own aspirations and a sounding board for Browning's denunciations of Jehovah. David says, "Leave the *flesh* to the fate it was fit for," but he is only pretending, for he then says, "Forget [do not believe] that man's *power* and his *beauty* forever take flight." Remember instead that as with the sun *nothing* has been produced in Saul's life beyond the measure of his own deeds. Self-awareness enough to "dare / Think but lightly [fearlessly] of such impuissance [weakness]" as permits him to surpass Jehovah's falsely proclaimed love and to pronounce approval or censure of all divine work, albeit by retaining the double entente GOD — Jehovah or Prometheus. If David has knowledge, it is confounded at wisdom (Prometheus') laid bare; if he has forethought, the meaning of the word Prometheus, it is purblind and blank to the Infinite Care (Prometheus). Believing that "all's love [Prometheus], yet all's law [Demogorgon's]," a perfect Christian and pagan syncretism, David will perceive Jehovah by these criteria, but all that he gains is an unanswering abyss when a mere dewdrop was asked. That is, of a permissive nature, for in spite of David's masterful dissembling the contrast between Jehovah's unloving rejection of Saul and Prometheus' infinite care accentuates the total catalog of the poet's grievances: arbitrary law vs. perfect wisdom, parsimony vs. beneficence, vindictiveness vs. munificence, dreadful might vs. loving power, tyrannical will vs. companionate will. Reminiscent of the evil Jupiter's being released on Prometheus, Saul's struggle seems to be directly with Jehovah, not with an evil spirit after the Spirit of the Lord departed: "To betoken that Saul and *the Spirit* have ended their strife, / And that, *faint in his triumph* [over Jehovah], the monarch sinks back upon life." It is the triviality of Saul's disobedient trip to the Witch of Endor which ignites David's smouldering will. Life's Dream, of which Shelley makes so much, is at best probative and worthy of endurance only because its end is the triumphant portal to new light, new life and new harmony, all vouchsafed in Shelley's apocalypse.

By hinting at magic from his earliest poems Browning gave the impression of being as deeply involved in magical if not arcane arts as his own Paracelsus. But this conclusion ignores the many times in which Promethean subtleties are subsumed in falsely implied magic. If the imaginary PIED PIPER is Prometheus or an envoy, as seems likely, he is nonetheless a most innocent and beneficent magical entity. If the imaginary PIPPA is a Promethean, as seems sure, she is nonetheless Nature's child and an angel of light. And though the gipsy witch who negotiates THE FLIGHT OF THE DUCHESS appears as anciently evil as the hoary cripple who supposedly but not really waylaid CHILDE ROLAND, she too proves to be beneficently assigned to guide the Duchess to the retreat awaiting all Promethean children. What the Duchess — all fire, life and gladness — drinks from the Gipsy Queen's eyes is Promethean "Life," the sum total of Shelley's universe. Everything in the wild setting and superstitious atmosphere of this barbaric tale contributes to the druidical circle the Duke's huntsman draws for the execution of his little lady's adventure. In exchange for her conventional Church and State imprisonment the Duchess is promised that not a power of life will be unemployed in satisfying her nature's need. And if she is inclined there "is the other fate in store, / And art thou fitted to adore, / To give thy wondrous self away, / And take a stronger nature's sway." Assured of her fitness by the Duchess' passionate eyes, the transformed witch reveals that the final and best part is merciful Death and reabsorption by Prometheus: "And like the hand which ends a dream [life], / Death, with the might of [Prometheus'] sunbeam, / Touches the flesh and the soul awakes, / Then —" Caliban, a neolithic savage, is less explicit about the new Promethean day, but like the Duke's serf and thrall Caliban would gladly search out "some snug corner / Under a hedge, . . . / And sleep a sound sleep till the trumpet's [mystic shell's] blowing / Wake me (unless priests cheat us laymen) / To a world where will be no further throwing / Pearls before [Christian] swine that can't value them. Amen!"

Disguised as the ruminations of a primitive mind on the nature of God, CALIBAN UPON SETEBOS dramatizes the characteristics of Jehovah which could not otherwise be made so ridiculous. Setebos is a counterpart of Shelley's Jupiter (Jehovah), the Quiet is the medium of Demogorgon, and Caliban is a masked voice for the poet's detestation of Jehovah and parody of the superstitiously ignorant Christian masses. Through Caliban's analogy of himself and Setebos

Browning presents a besotted Jehovah whose motiveless malignity is his sole redeeming feature. Loving not, hating not, Jehovah is fixed on keeping his underlings subservient, thus his practice of dangling false rewards for prayer and praise or inflicting dreadful pain and sorrow for the least infraction of degrading laws. Caliban's act of crushing each twenty-first passing crab makes Setebos a primordial god to be feared and gives Browning the chance to add that because of his thwarted growth Jehovah was entering a state of decrepitude from which he would doze and doze until he was as good as dead. Or should this not occur, since Caliban is presciently informed on Shelley's Demogorgon, the Quiet would some strange day catch and conquer Setebos (Jehovah). Reasoning thereby that since Setebos is omnipotent but not omniscient, Demogorgon's mighty law of Necessity is operative in Nature and bound to depose Jehovah eventually. The scenario even allows that as Shelley's Jupiter converted power surrendered by Prometheus into tyranny, Setebos converted his undeniably worthy, better, braver creatures into objects of spite and envy, playthings he both jealously admires and mockingly plagues. So He, Jehovah! There can be no mistaking any longer that Caliban's song gleefully ridicules Jehovah's inability to create a mate and renders easy Browning's deceptive way of delineating Jehovah's inferiority to Man: "What I hate, be consecrate / To celebrate Thee and Thy state, *no mate / For Thee.*"

Rather than being a defense of St. John's Gospel and an apologia for Christianity, A DEATH IN THE DESERT is an imaginary manuscript recantation of St. John's faith in Jesus and a spirited acceptance of Prometheus as the truly influencing savior and deity. Misled by lack of knowledge which the impatient young will be demanding and by failure to see that "Men should, for love's sake, in love's strength believe," Browning's John learns through his desertion of Jesus in Gethsemane that Truth can grow whereas Faith stands still. From out the blank profound of doubt, where John's mind has been grappling with fancy and fact, now rise stars of knowledge he would not conceal. With surprisingly intimate knowledge of how those who trust their minds and search for truth are benevolently guided and sustained by Prometheus, the comatose John has only contempt for individuals who are so ignorant as not to recognize that Jehovah's destructive might is vindictively willed. The first truth he had gained from recollection of the pagan "fable of Prometheus and his theft"; the second, from the heretical Cerinthus and his new shrewd commentaries. Thus a short step by Browning to the substitution of Prometheus' illimitable love, wisdom and self-sacrifice for Christ's refusal to challenge the tyranny of his so-called Father. The Christian doctrine of love, which was no more Jesus' alone than the air men breathe, does not make him Christ or raise him one whit above other loving men. Nor does Jehovah, "the nobler midge," fare any better when it is known that through unity of love and will man rises to the best and highest, achieving Demogorgon's Victory which is "God, in fine." Second in irony only to Browning's replacement of Christ with Prometheus on the moon-rainbow, the dying John joyously chooses the world as an historic fact and urgently recommends to his silent, disbelieving followers that they forget about false promises of eternal life and learn to become gods now.

Of course Pope Innocent is a Promethean and a pantheist; so are Pompilia, Caponsacchi and the barefoot Augustinian; and THE RING AND THE BOOK is Browning's magnum opus in advancement of Prometheanism. Described as one who had trod many lands, known many deeds and probed many hearts beginning with his own, the Pope is sagacious, resolute and prudent. Bringing his intelligence to bear, sitting with his thoughts, cheering his lips to benevolence and receiving "all his light" through a half-moon window, Innocent was first to bade leave in *peace* those Molinists "who may have other light than we *perceive*." To Caponsacchi he is "a strange Pope, — 't is said, a priest who *thinks*," and to Fra Celestino he is "an old good man / Who happens to hate darkness and love light." All of which explains Antonio Pignatelli's preference for the clean linen garb of his former self to the splendid vesture of his present papal self and Browning's preference for a Dialogue of the Mind, one voice always charged with reason, the other often with religious clichés.

To Man of the World, the Pope's alter ego, it is absence of "the manlier sin," not presence of the deadlier sin, and it is Nature which provides suave analogies seen in rougher, cruder form by the Pope. Incited by Guido's unmanly cruelty Nature shrieks to Pompilia, "Escape or die," after which Man of the World adds, "The spasm arrived, / Not the escape by way of sin." Truly Browning saw no diminution to Pompilia's purity in sharing her life with Caponsacchi, as witnessed by Shelley's echoes: "Where the earth reposed from spasms, / On the day when [Prometheus] and [Asia] / Parted, to commingle now."

The Pope and his Ancient Self (Ezekiel 8.12-6) are only slightly less impressed by Caponsacchi than Pompilia, once he is touched by her spirit. Even the foolishness of Pompilia's parents "is blanched / By God's gift of a purity of soul / That will not take pollution, ermine-like / Armed from dishonor by its own soft snow." Such was this gift of Prometheus who showed for once how he would have the world go white. Champions of truth (fact), Pompilia and Caponsacchi are thus miraculously rescued when "a *new* safeguard [Prometheus] sprang up in defence / Of their *new noble nature*." Though no bard will describe how Christ (Prometheus) prevailed and Satan (Jehovah) fell like lightning, why repine? "What does the [Christian] world, told [pagan] truth, but lie the more?" Canon Caponsacchi had better go wantoning, adopt the sword which springs from fire, than totally succumb to the Church's evil practices. Knowing that the Pope alludes to the wantonness of Shelley's Earth Spirit and the self-sacrifice of Prometheus' theft, Man of the World heartily agrees and scoffs at the Church for degrading pagan Venuses whom Roman citizens still honestly prefer into idolized Madonnas. While the Church condemns Caponsacchi's prolonged youth, he would rather chronicle the healthy rage. He knows that "there may have been rash stripping" and prompt self-display — "infringement manifold / Of laws prescribed pudicity," explains the Pope — but through pure and unselfish passion "for God's sake / He who is Pity [Prometheus]" Caponsacchi preserved the perfect beauty of body and soul.

Opposed to capital punishment the Pope answers once and for all how Browning felt about Guido's being beheaded. Man's spirit is part of Prometheus and indestructible beyond all culpability. Man of the World implies that Guido's ignorance in not securing a "change" of horses for escape was his downfall: "Guido is found when the *check*, the *change*, / The monitory touch of the tether [is] felt." But he talks about GOD and thinks about Prometheus who reminded friendly spirits that it was he, the Titan, who made his agony the barrier to Jupiter's vengeance as it was he who prevented Guido's murder by four scheming cutthroats: "me alone, who *checked*, / As one who *checks* a fiend-drawn charioteer, / The falsehood and the force of him who reigns [tyrannizes, PU 1.125] / Supreme." Therefore the Archbishop and his underlings draw the truly insensitive utterance from Man of the World, well concealed though it be by the Pope's "Huddling together [mother & sons] in the cave they call / Their palace." Browning would have the reader believe that the fierce indignation is directed at the hag and her three abortive sons huddled together. But Guido (dead) and Paolo (fled) are no longer available to cluster round an imaginary pitchy furnace in the impoverished palace. Such denizens as Man of the World speaks of are "now" clustered round with clerical threats of hell, and they are exactly as black as the Jehovah of EASTER-DAY. The offender which deserves no pity is the tyrannical Church, where miscreant priests fearfully await their last gasp of breath, if they are not prematurely pierced through with a bolt of deserved lightning.

In Browning's most famous simulated prayer — "O Thou, — as represented here to me ... Man's mind, what is it but a convex glass" — the Pope and Man of the World attribute their unconventional approval of Pompilia and Caponsacchi to the guidance of GOD. Actually the words comprise Browning's most lucid explication of Shelley's theory of the One Mind. Only thought or mind is immortal, or even existent, and as thought is the measure of the universe so Prometheus, the One Mind, is the God of the universe. True, the poet's syncretism is so cleverly wrought that almost every aspect of the Pope's Prometheanism is balanced by or disguised in a correspondingly acceptable scriptural allusion. To the Pope Pompilia's death is no tragedy at all: "[We] feel that life is large and the world small, / So, wait till life have passed from out the world." Not unlike Shelley's "Death is the veil which those who live call life: / They sleep, and it is lifted," although Caponsacchi more precisely catches the diction: "Death was the heart of life, and all the harm / My folly had crouched to avoid, now proved a veil / Hiding all gain my wisdom strove to grasp." Pope Innocent's touch of terror results from "these [intelligent] ones" who turn their backs on the Promethean future, for the talented ones should recognize, as did the ancient ones, that Prometheanism deserves to supersede Christianity since man's obduracy to good is the fault of his creator, Jehovah. Man of the World puts no such test to himself as the Pope's deceptive indecision, however, for within his circle of experience burns "the central truth, Power, Wisdom, Goodness, — God [Prometheus]." Eagerly concurring, the Pope asserts that the light which did burn will burn when "first things [pagan] are made new" again.

With considerable duplicity Browning incorporated the personality of the pagan Euripides, some of the most nearly universal of St. Paul's words and graphic allusions to PROME-THEUS UNBOUND in a frontal assault on Jehovah, on his laws and his followers who wallow in a "mire of cowardice and slush of lies." Pope Innocent's clear belief that man may applaud or condemn God's action is singularly muted by the ambiguous part given Euripides and by his opening deceitful words: "The inward work and worth / Of any *mind*, what other *mind* may judge / Save God [the One Mind] who only knows the thing he made." A rank alteration of Romans 2.28 which Browning knew would readily be associated with "For when Gentiles, which have not the law, do *by nature* the things contained in the law, these, having not the law, are a law unto themselves." If St. Paul was apparently so inconsistent as to allow that pagans were *by nature* a law unto themselves, how could it be detected that Browning was pointing toward "God forbid: yet, let God [Prometheus] be true, but every [disbelieving] man a liar"? For these memorable words were to be the text of a sermon Pompilia's confessor was to preach on the non-interference of a loving and beneficent Prometheus, the interference of an unloving and unjust Jehovah. Fra Celestino's diatribe follows Browning's longest account of the endurance of ancient pagan practices PRO CHRISTO (Prometheus) and precedes an assertion to his Catholic audience that he has "long since renounced *your* [Christian] world." Who could better conceal the poet's belief, not only that Pompilia was innocent in elopement as in her whole life but also that the Church doctrine of original sin was rightly abrogated by Prometheus? Especially since through the doctrine's repressive injustice beauty was made blank and innocence destroyed, strangled save for one Pompilia who was "plucked from the [Christian] world's calumny, / Stupidity, simplicity."

Browning's Promethean Euripides is fully answered by the Pope's wish for return of the thrill of dawn when the whole truth-touched man burned up assured the fire would, from his little heap of ashes, lend wings to the world's conflagration which Prometheus awaits before making all things *new*. So should the ghosts of the great dead, rapt from Christian glory of pain to Promethean glory of joy, feel the finite love blent and embalmed with the eternal life. But, deplore both Pope and Man of the World, we have become too familiar with the light. Faith now points the politic, the thrifty way. What is required for the propagation of Prometheanism is a formidable danger, unlikely in a world where ignoble confidence and cowardly hardihood make the old heroism impossible. "Unless," the Pope hopefully interjects, it be the mission of the age ushering in his death to shake "this torpor of assurance from our creed / Re-introduce the doubt discarded, bring / That formidable danger back, . . . / And man stand out again, pale, resolute, / Prepared to die, — which means, alive at last." Thus, and thus only, may "Man's God," that is, the Church's God, be corrected by the living God's God in the mind of man. Not to be denied a conclusion as apocalyptic as that of PROMETHEUS UNBOUND, Browning's Pope carefully distinguishes between soft culture, which he rejects, and the spirit of culture, which he indorses for the advancement of man, all in order to conclude on Shelley's

Emperor of the World (Prometheus) and the return of the Golden Age of paganism.

From first sight of each other Pompilia and Caponsacchi are disposed to reject the material world, blaming their unhappiness and deprivation on its organizational tyranny. When Pompilia approaches Caponsacchi and the escape carriage, the blackened night is charged with the expectant atmosphere of Asia's return to Prometheus. On the flight she gains the same strength from holding another woman's baby that Asia gains from the ever-loving Earth Spirit. Only just awakened to the new, novel faith Caponsacchi is solely dependent on Pompilia's love, which is as effusively unselfish as Asia's for Prometheus. And in their separation Caponsacchi vividly reflects the sadness and longing of Prometheus for reunion with Asia. Each ascribes the new grace of life to the self-sacrifice of Prometheus, and neither can well bear the delay in passage from this dream world through the veil of Death to Life. Like the young Browning the child Pompilia was made magically aware of the beauty, heroism and romance of the pagan world in contrast to the drabness of religious chapels. Playtime to Pompilia was distinguished from hasty trips to damp and dismally lighted San Lorenzo because of an exciting wall tapestry at home overflowing with mythological and legendary figures. She and Tisbe knew all about Diana, patron goddess of mothers and slaves, and when a cavalier (Guido) was expected Pompilia remembered Tisbe had said that the slim young man with wings at head, wings at feet and sword threatening a monster was a cavalier, confirming their familiarity with Perseus' rescue of Andromeda and possibly the "resplendent mirror" lent to Perseus by Athene. Otherwise, why does Pompilia name her son Gaetano after a *new* saint without knowing that it was Cajetan, the overseer of Luther at the Diet of Augsburg, who said a pope should be "the *mirror* of God on earth"? One may suspect that Pope Innocent and Pompilia had consulted on "Man's mind, what is it but a convex glass."

Pompilia pretends to have been blind to so much, even the love-letters Guido falsely conceived, but her innocence is blunted by the astuteness of "such *wormy* ways, / The indirect, the unapproved of God [Prometheus] : / You cannot find their author's [Jehovah's] end and aim, / Not even to substitute your good for bad, / Your straight for the irregular; you stand / Stupified, profitless, as cow or sheep that miss *a man's mind*." Resorting ever to pagan imagery she wondered whether Caponsacchi would answer her appeal for help, but at dusk she "started up, *was pushed* [by Prometheus], . . . / Out on the terrace . . . / Where the *deliverer* [Caponsacchi] waited." She believes that Guido had no right to make her and Caponsacchi "*unself* ourselves, / Be other man and woman than we were," and she understands one of Shelley's subtler passages on the difference in minds (PU 3.3.39) when eulogizing the glory of Caponsacchi's nature which "*shot* itself out in white light, blazed with truth / Through every atom of his act with me." Thus her last breath shall be spent in dispersing the stain and mist from a lustrous and pellucid soul. So that when she is gone people needing assurance will know that in Caponsacchi Prometheus has a servant, man a friend, the weak a savior and the vile a foe.

When Guido entered her room at the inn, Pompilia did attempt to thrust aside the "Ice-block" (PU 2.1.60) between herself and the Sun, lay low the "neutralizer" of all good and truth. And if it were sin, she adds, "Never obey voice / Of the Just and Terrible [Demogorgon], who bids us — 'Bear!' / Not — 'Stand by, bear to see my angels bear!' " (PU 4.573). She is positive that it was on impulse to serve God (Prometheus), not to save herself or her child unborn. Because Caponsacchi restored her soul, she has gained, enjoyed, suffered and got foretaste of better life beginning where this ends. Therefore before she withdraws from earth and man to compose herself for Prometheus, Pompilia shall end her breath in being true to her soul. It was truth which singed the lies and withered off the legal and Church protection of Guido. "You see," Pompilia asserts, "I will not have the service [to Prometheus] fail!" To Caponsacchi's heart and hand she would have sprung over the threshold (hell) posted to exclude her heaven. He was fated to call and she to respond. So, to be sure, he would not marry if he could, since marriage on earth is a counterfeit, a mere imitation of the inimitable in which she and Caponsacchi, like angels, shall "know themselves into one." Let him await Prometheus' instant men call years, hold hard by truth and his great soul. For through such souls alone Prometheus stooping shows sufficient of his light for them in the dark earth to rise by. And having done "out the duty" before Caponsacchi, Pompilia rises.

Alternately emotional and rational Caponsacchi has learned a great deal about Prometheus before he testifies in Browning's poem. He tells the Court that he has paid enough in relegation and that as a rehabilitated priest he has the right to speak truthfully about Pompilia: "The glory of life, the beauty of the world, / The splendor of heaven, ... / The glory, I say, / And the beauty, I say, and splendor, still say I, / Who, priest and trained to live my whole life long / On *beauty* and splendor, solely at their source, / God [Prometheus], — have thus recognized *my food in her*." It was the Church which invited him to be a fribble and coxcomb; it was Pompilia's beauty and strange sad smile which caused the Church to ask if he were turning Molinist: "Sir, what if I turned Christian [Promethean]? It might be. / The *fact* is, I am troubled in my *mind*, / Beset and pressed hard by some *novel* thoughts." When Caponsacchi expected to face Guido with the forged letters, "There at the window stood, / Framed in its black square length, with *lamp in hand* [symbolic of Promethean], / Pompilia" instead. She instantly admitted that good true love would help her so much, and Caponsacchi accepted his own *fact*, his miracle *self*-authorized and *self*-explained. As he recognized her at potency of truth she by crystalline soul knew him. God [Jehovah] and man were no help now. Dangerous or no, Death meant to spurn the ground, soar to the sky, die well and you did that. Thus Caponsacchi deduced that life and death are means to an end, that passion uses both, "indisputably mistress of the man / Whose form of worship is self-sacrifice." To the Church's cry "Leave that live passion, come be dead with me," Caponsacchi responded but not by ignorantly feasting on hips and haws while the thing of perfect gold, the apple's self, was scorned.

When Pompilia was forced to chide Caponsacchi for his

delay or wavering in the rescue, Caponsacchi boldly promised, "Lady, waste no thought, nor word / Even to forgive me! Care for what I care — / Only! Now follow me as I were *fate*!" So began the flight with Pompilia, whose very "breath or look of hers, / Which poured forth would present you one pure *glass*, / *Mirror* you plain, as God's [Prometheus'] sea, glassed in gold, / His saints, — the perfect soul Pompilia. Men, / You must know that a man gets drunk with truth / Stagnant inside him!" Truth so intoxicating that when Pompilia asked why Caponsacchi smiled at the great gate with the eagles and the snakes (Islam 193), he replied that he had an impulse to say to the residing prelate, one wise in ways of preferment: "What, still at work *so gray and obsolete* [PU 4.31]? / Still rocketed and mitred more or less? / Don't you feel all that *out of fashion now*? / I find out when the day of things is done!" As the hours of heavy travel wore on, however, the joys of being a new Promethean were eclipsed by Pompilia's weariness and bad dreams of Guido. So Caponsacchi prayed: "Oh, if the God, that only can [cf., SAUL 270], would help! / Am I his priest with power to cast out fiends? / Let God [Prometheus] *arise* and all his enemies / Be scattered!" Thus charged, by morn there was *peace* but by night of the next day all the *calm* was again gone, Pompilia was exhausted and delirious, and Caponsacchi was back at prayer: "Too deep i' the thick of the struggle, [not to] struggle through! / Then *drench* her in repose though *death's self* pour / The plenitude of quiet, — help us, God [Prometheus], / Whom the winds carry [PU 4.5.48]!" Suddenly there was Castelnuovo and the sweet lady was saved. Yet "in they broke / O' the chamber *late my chapel*" and there she lay "wax-white, seraphic, saturate with the sun [Prometheus] / O' the morning that now flooded from the front / And filled the window with *a light like blood.*" Facing Guido that "opprobrious blur / Against *all peace and joy and light and life*" (PU 4.577-8), Pompilia started up and cried, "I am God's, I love God, God — whose knees I clasp, / Whose *utterly most just reward* [Love, Hope 6] I take, / But bear no more love-making devils: hence!"

It was the last time in this life that Caponsacchi saw Pompilia though he could not have her dead, "that erect form, flashing brow, fulgurant [lightning-like] eye, / That voice immortal . . . / That vision in the blood-red daybreak — that / Leap to life of the pale electric sword [fire] / Angels go armed with, — that was not the last / O' the lady!" By no chance did they "rush each on each"; God (Prometheus) willed it so. The spark of truth was struck from out their souls, told Caponsacchi there was no duty like daring to be good and true, leaving the shows of things to the Lord of Show (Jehovah) and Prince of the Power of the Air. Misinterpret as the misapprehending ignorant will, Caponsacchi nonetheless advises: "For Pompilia . . . / Build [Promethean] churches, go pray! You will find me there, / I know, if you come, — and you will come, I know." "Sirs, I am quiet again. You see, we are / So very pitiable, she and I, . . . / Pompilia will be presently with God [Prometheus] ; / I am, on earth, as good as out of it, . . . / She and I are mere strangers [to the world] . . . [I live to] see her learn, and learn by her, . . . not by the grandeur, God [Jehovah] — / But the comfort, Christ [Prometheus]. . . . / Just as a drudging student trims his lamp [Promethean], / Opens his Plutarch [Greek & Roman pagans]." Thus does Caponsacchi dream of fighting dragons to save or rule the world, smilingly awaken and depart the old solitary nothingness of the Church: "O *great*, just, *good* God [Prometheus, PU 4.576-8]! *Miserable* me [PU 1.107-11]!"

If Browning did not plan LA SAISIAZ as a swan song he at least never compacted his reasons for being a Promethean and an antagonist of Jehovah more tightly. Nor could he have chosen a natural setting dearer to Shelley's heart than the spectacular view of Mont Blanc. For it is in MONT BLANC that Shelley most effectively and most beautifully advances his doctrine of Necessity. Like the snow which falls silently and secretly on Mont Blanc, Demogorgon acts only as he must act. And as the snow is destructive in its glaciers but life-sustaining in its resulting waters, so Demogorgon's tolerance of Jupiter-Jehovah may seem destructive while his liberation of Prometheus spells freedom. Hence Browning's distantly reached Mute Mont Blanc, dared and done: "But, the triumph crowning all — / There's Salève's own platform facing glory [Prometheus] which strikes greatness small, / — Blanc, supreme above *his earth-brood*." A dozen times Browning exults over having dared to climb Mt. Salève for this uncommon sight, and each time he intends to revalidate Demogorgon's "All things thou dar'st demand" and Prometheus' unquestioned supremacy. More than a dozen times he deifies Nature, exerting no precaution over "Earth's exquisite disclosure, heaven's own God [Prometheus]," and he draws confidence in intellect and self-consciousness from renowned residents of the area such as Voltaire, Gibbon, Rousseau and Byron.

Doubtlessly the sudden death of Ann Egerton Smith at La Saisiaz (The Sun) grieved Browning but that event only contributed to a summing-up the poet had been contemplating. So as Browning emulates the expansiveness of Shelley's love, the memory of Elizabeth Barrett modulates his thought. For Browning unfailingly associates the adequacy of love with the inadequacy of faith or Fancy, this time Elizabeth's sighing "We believe": "I take the cup of comfort . . . / Taste and try each soft ingredient . . . — slow, / Sorrowful, *but how decided*! needs must I o'erturn it — so!" Like his Paracelsus Browning does not pretend to modesty. He boasts credit for awakening Elizabeth to the knowledge of life, credit for the distillation of life's losses from her Christian faith, as unhesitatingly as he boasts credit for establishing self-assurance in the reticent Ann Smith. Thus the above material is prelude to a stepped-up warfare on divine governance which entails Jehovah's total being: "As the power, expect performance! God's be God's as mine is mine!" (300). "No, as I am man, I mourn the poverty I must impute: / Goodness, wisdom, power, all bounded, each a human attribute!" (347-8). The inescapable repetition, which permits a syncopated assault on faith in Jehovah, not only ridicules hopes and fears, rewards and punishments, but also enables Browning another chance to contrast his Promethean courage with Christian cowardice: "If a spirit of the place [Mont Blanc] / Broke the silence, bade me question, promised answer, — *what disgrace* / Did I stipulate 'Provided answer suit my hopes, not fears!'"

Only in SAUL does Browning approach the directness of allusion to Shelley's reversal of the scriptural "My grace is sufficient for thee: for my strength is made perfect in weakness." Never elaborating Shelley's subjective idealism in broader details, Browning presupposes two essential points (218): 1) he, Browning, *is*, knows; 2) he, Browning, perceives a force outside himself. Call one soul, he adds; call the other God (the One Mind). Since these are the only Facts for him, all else which may be added is surmise, mere faith or Fancy. Of course he is guided by Shelley's ritualistic "Nothing exists but as it is perceived." All of which leads to "What before caused all the causes, what effect of all effects / Haply follows, — these are fancy," "mere surmise not knowledge." "Cause before, effect behind me — blanks! The midway point I am, / Caused, itself — itself efficient: in that narrow space must cram / All experience," "that is knowledge" (225-64). Browning's purpose is to confirm Shelley's unrelenting insistence that "it is infinitely improbable that the cause of mind, that is, of existence, is similar to mind." Browning substitutes the rush for Mont Blanc's snow, and the rush knows the source of the stream on which it floats no better than the snow knows the universe in which it falls. But Browning's patience is at low ebb and in LA SAISIAZ he is determined to say as openly as he dare that he can not support a God who withholds any favor from man, exactly what he has opposed in Jehovah since the day he decided that love and justice are eternally incompatible.

To Shelley and Browning it is the arts and science which provide a two-way communication between Prometheus and man, and it is in Browning's surreptitious eulogies to various art forms that he most genuinely reflects Shelley's demand for freedom. At last it becomes clearer why Browning's aversion to Gothic architecture, a Church product; why his lack of sympathy for a copyist of Virgin, Babe and Saint, Pictor Ignotus; why his praise of Giotto's independence and aspiration, not of his quality to adore and glorify; and why his pretense that pagan art perished because it had no farther to reach. Shelley's exalted opinion of the arts and science, his insistence upon birthright and Self-empire and his severe indictment of Jehovah for restricting man, particularly genius, provide an exceptional insight into Browning's mind. That his animosity became paranoiac as discouragement overtook his avowal is not surprising. Shelley's vivid models and Browning's bursts of anger evidence a common distress at not being more influential in dethroning Jehovah in the minds of readers and a common tendency to absolve the failure in the sheep-like acquiescence of Jehovah's followers, in the unmitigated nescience of the masses. Having lived and suffered, loved and hated, Browning has learned and taught that there is no reconciling wisdom with a world distraught, goodness with triumphant evil, power with failure in the aim. Yet moving beyond his experience which is the only knowledge, Browning does once again extrapolate human pain and pleasure and once again conclude that they are the products of a wicked machine devised by an unloving and miserly Jehovah. Clearly the poet's problem was death to which he could not make adjustment unless offered assurance of a second life. Extinction of self-consciousness he would not entertain, and its avoidance may best explain his Prometheanism. Like Shelley Browning placed Genius and Self-empire within close range of absolute Beauty, Truth and Goodness, well knowing that to Fate, Time, Occasion, Chance and Change all things are subject but eternal Love.

Disdainful of Fancy's addition of heaven and hell to God, soul and earth as facts or realities, Reason agrees that there is nothing else to desiderate. In the one-sided debate Fancy accepts Jehovah's joys and sorrows, hoping and waiting for what he sees not. It is therefore he, never Browning the other speaker, who lives a life of nescience simply. As the postulates Heaven and Hell deny the poet the chance to consider life a probation-space and are repudiated, so Good and Evil, the sixth postulate, deny him the chance to reject rewards and punishments and are summarily repudiated. Without uninhibited choice Browning could not conceivably be responsible for whatever he does; he might as well be ordered not to breathe. Yet only Weakness and Strength seem more deeply ingrained in Browning's eschatology than Hope. In fact, hope is his ultimate mainstay, thus his long observed optimism. In a perfect syncretism he plays Shelley's hopefulness against St. Paul's "Hope that is seen is not hope": "To suffer woes which Hope thinks infinite; ... to hope till Hope creates / From its own wreck the thing it contemplates" (PU 4.570-4). *Athanasius contra mundum.* Browning against the world, why should he dare to hope more than they, the blinded to Prometheus' love and power? Because of the gifted few who dart magnetic might into the earth's central heart! Symbolic of Wisdom, the Light from Rousseau is like a fiery flying serpent; from Byron, a phosphoric fame swathing blackness' self with brightness; from Voltaire, a darting wit that sparkles in and out the boughs; and from Gibbon, a central solid knowledge kindled in the core. Under Nature's sky for architrave, in trust and not despair, Browning brandishes the dazzling beacon-light, the giant torch fed by the combustible resin of genius, all concentrated in one mighty flame.

In his last two volumes Browning utilizes unpublished poems or miraculously pulls all the stops, daringly casting to his conditioned readers an unbelievably concerted effort before death to strike one blow more at the arch foe. Whether REPHAN and REVERIE are late creations or from unpublished poems of Browning's creative prime, they are powerful protests to be compared with the deceptive genius of CHILDE ROLAND. All that the angry IXION now requires for clarity is the substitution of Browning's name for Ixion. The object of Ixion's scorn is the same GOD whom Browning parades through the resistance of all his heroes and opposes with the gifts which made Prometheus' self-sacrifice so glorious. IXION thus begins and ends with a prediction of man's triumph, each time symbolized by a Promethean rainbow juxtaposed to spasms of pain once ghastly borne, now glorified. So it is blind faith in man and pitiless power in Jehovah which introduce Browning's most exposed proselytical appeal, itself a paraphrase of Demogorgon's ringing last words: "Strive, mankind, though strife endure through endless obstruction, / Stage after stage, each rise marred by as certain a fall!" In remarkable ways IXION is Browning's own PROMETHEUS UNBOUND, for there he re-lives Prometheus' curse of Jupiter-Jehovah and Demogorgon's fulfillment of the curse.

IXION is also Browning's TRIUMPH OF LIFE — which is Death — and probably his closest reproduction of Shelley's thought and words. Unconcerned by the distortion of their metaphysics neither poet could believe that Jehovah possessed a soul. Shelley's Prometheus says that at Jupiter's fall his "soul, cloven to its depth with terror," shall "gape like a hell within." Browning believed it and never wearied of enunciating it. At best Paracelsus' inexhaustible energy, David's illimitable love and Ben Ezra's exalted genius are only symptomatic of the unplumbed depth of Browning's animosity toward Jehovah and of his Shelleyan hope. Like his Lazarus "the man's fantastic will was the man's law." In making Good and the means of Good irreconcilable, in rejecting Love for Justice, Jehovah willed his fate and shall eventually sink with the godship. Browning (Ixion) shall rise to a "Purity all unobstructed!"

BALAUSTION'S ADVENTURE, ARISTOPHANES' APOLOGY, RED COTTON NIGHT-CAP COUNTRY, PRINCE HOHENSTIEL-SCHWANGAU and THE INN ALBUM could have been selected to reveal Browning's deception as readily as the poems studied here, but they have fascinated far fewer of the poet's Christian and secular apologists. They are nonetheless as saturated with Shelleyan diction and imagery, as fully invested with the poet's adoption of Shelley's ideas and as dynamically charged with self-awareness, advocacy of freedom, victory of Death, tyranny of Jehovah and benevolence of Prometheus, no heroine of which is other than a duplication of the pagan Pompilia. Thus from the total panoply of deception rise many unasked but pertinent questions, particularly about Browning's favorite friends. For example, his friendship with Sir Frederick Leighton, painter of so many pagan subjects and designer of Elizabeth's tomb, and his dedication of the *La Saisiaz* volume to Mrs. Sutherland Orr, sister of Sir Frederick and only official biographer of the poet, may indicate more than concern over a son's profession or loneliness of a disconsolate widower. Many critics have known that the aging Browning led the Hiram Corsons up three long flights of steps in the Palazzo Rezzonico to show them his bedroom ceiling on which Pen had painted a most vigorous conception of Shelley's Eagle and Serpent wreathed in fight. Now they may not choose to dissociate the pioneer introduction of Browning's poetry into America from Professor Corson's reported conversational meals with the spirit of his dead wife, his weekly séances in Philadelphia and his faithful attendance with Daniel Willard Fiske at the graveside of the poet. Now, they may also find less tantalizing mystery in destruction and commissioned destruction of manuscripts, alteration of dates, shuffling of poems in collected editions, cryptic love letters, defense of nude paintings and of Euripides, preference for women, flirtation, perverse arguing and self-defense, primitive religions, tricky and excessive punctuation, obscuration, prolixity and a thousand other ambiguities. Now, Browning may be seen as perhaps the truest Promethean the literary world has known. The crowning irony of the poet's extravagant hoax may be his probable knowledge of the "scanty [unfilled] space" near Chaucer in Westminster Abbey.

PAULINE
1833

In his first published poem Browning exhibits familiarity with a scriptural and a Shelleyan quotation which have distinctly opposing meanings. The scriptural words were gradually to be identified in subsequent poetry and warmly associated by readers with the apparently sympathetic if not avowed Christian nature of the poet. The Shelleyan words have yet to be identified and shown to be truly the controlling but hidden motivation of the very great bulk of Browning's poetry.

> My grace is sufficient for thee: for my *strength* is made
> perfect in *weakness.*
>
> * * *
>
> Resist not the *weakness*,
> Such *strength* is in meekness
> That the Eternal, the Immortal,
> Must unloose through life's portal
> The snake-like Doom coiled underneath his throne
> By that alone.

Conceivably the initial curiosity was simply about Power, even a personal desire for power, but Browning was rarely thereafter to create a poem in which Weakness and Strength were not to operate as symbols of human and divine effort. More frequently than Shakespeare, Milton, Shelley or the Scriptures Browning employs the word Power (82 poems), and whenever Power is mentioned or implied Weakness and Strength are concomitants, ever spurring him on to further elaboration of theories which inscribe his life. Not counting variants beyond Weak (156) and Strong (183), Weakness and Strength appear together in twenty-nine of Browning's disputatious poems; as separate entities they appear three hundred fifty-seven times (Strength 276, Weakness 81). Naturally the two words are appropriated in many ways, but the more intently Browning responds to St. Paul's quotation

the more likely he is to reveal irritation and to add fresh sub-
stantiation to a counter proposal. In *Pauline*, for example,
the emphasis falls on Weakness which is incurred by recognition of "His [Shelley's] soul's *strength*" (409). Yet it is not
the weakness a young poet's critics are waiting to reprove:

So, my *weak* voice may well forbear to shame	(423)
What seemed decreed my *fate*: I threw *myself*	(pagan; PU 1.492)
To meet it, I was *vowed* to liberty,	(Intell Beauty 61)
Men were to be as gods and earth as heaven, . . .	(PU 4.164-5)

And, though this *weak* soul sink and darkness whelm,	(PU 3.1.76; 1010)
Some *little word* shall light it, raise aloft,	(Cenci 2.1.63, PU 1.396)
To where I clearlier see and better love,	
As I again go o'er the *tracts of thought*	(Shelley's "Mind")
Like one who has a *right*, and I shall live	(Birthright, PU 2.4.39)
With *poets*, calmer, purer still each time	(Genius)
And beauteous *shapes* will come for me to seize,	(PU 3.3.60)
And *unknown secrets* will be trusted me	(PU 3.3.35, 49-63)
Which were denied the *waverer* once; but now	(Heb 10.23,
I shall be priest and prophet as of old.	Hom Merc 275)

In addition to being independent of the body and potentially
as strong as Shelley's admired soul, the Weakness "breathed"
(710) and not "concealed" (54) in *Pauline* is of an unexpectedly joyous nature which does not shame in weak voice
or despair in weak soul. In fact, it is through Weakness that
Browning, confessedly the speaker, anticipates priesthood,
prophetic insight and right to be in communion with the gods.
And provided he is unyielding in holding to love and his
birthright of wisdom, his Weakness may call freely, inexhaust-
ibly on the history of thought, the work of poetic Genius
and the potency of Love to assure him success.

In the opening one hundred forty lines Browning tells
Pauline, whose quixotic functions characterize both Shelley's
Panthea and Browning's Imagination, that he would have
been spared a deep shame (28, 62) had he sat by her from the
first, nothing doubting of her uninhibited existence. For
Nature points at "one whose quivering lip / Was bathed in
her enchantments, whose brow burned / Beneath the crown
to which her secrets knelt, / Who learned the spell which can
call up the dead, / And then departed smiling like a fiend /

Who had deceived God [Prometheus]'' (18-23; 2 Cor 11.14).
Soon awakened to a law (35, Jehovah's) which binds fancy's
wing and imperils unrestraint, Browning reasoned that Christian praise of his genius and expectation of his becoming
another great religious poet were too dearly bought to
surrender his Will to another:

```
           that I am sad and fain                        (81)
Would give up all to be but where I was,
Not high as I had been if faithful found      (among Christian adorers)
But low and weak yet full of hope, and sure           (PU 2.3.93)
Of goodness as of life —                              (denial of evil)
```

Consequent to his disillusionment in Christian rules and regulations, all that Browning now asks, in confession of his
departure from paganism, is a renewal of the joys of his
naturalistic childhood. His least concern is the disheartening
reply made to a rich young man of great probity, "Why
callest thou me good? there is none good but one, that is,
God" (M't 19.17). Only "the waving mass / Of climbing
plants heavy with bloom and dew, / The morning swallows
with their songs like words" are permanently worthy of his
and Pauline's thoughts.
  Believing at first that in the exchange of pantheism for
Christianity his soul would remain strong and free as ever
(92), Browning soon discovered that in floating "from its
sphere / Of *wild* dominion into the *dim* orb of self" his soul
had conformed to that dim orb, reflecting all its shades and
shapes and staying where it alone could be adored. Thus in
returning to Pauline Browning takes his first step back to
paganism. Restoration of his old claims (26) and of being recrowned among the faithful pantheists, however, he would
never have ventured to hope for (141) except that the glow
he felt at Shelley's "award" (Epipsy 223) assured him all was
not extinct within. Yet until he unlocks "the sleepless [PU
1.4-5] brood / Of fancies" (6-7) from his soul — falsities of
Christianity — it is vain to hope to sing; some woe would in-
evitably light on him. A first indication of Browning's dis-
satisfaction with being a mere "singer," of a more compelling

desire to advance Shelley's glorious cause, this qualified restoration becomes a reality in lines 99-123. For it is here that Browning conjures up the SPIRIT OF THE EARTH (PU 3.4.1-96) with the express purpose of repentantly saying to Shelley, "I am still a god — to you." Indirectly he has been saying it all along in a scattering of sucks, shriek, wither, fiend, decay, peace, pant, fain, "so good, / So calm" and "Ah vain, vain," all Shelleyan in substance and frequency:

Sun-treader, *life* and *light* be thine forever!	(151)
Thou art gone from us; . . .	
But thou art still for me as thou has been . . .	(162)
But thou art still for me who have adored	(168)
Tho' *single, panting* but to hear thy name	(alone; PU 3.3.125)
Which I believed a spell to me alone,	(PU 2.3.88)
Scarce deeming thou wast *a star* to men!	(thematic for Shelley)
As one should worship long a *sacred spring*	(Mont B 4, pagan)
Scarce worth a *moth's flitting,* . . .	(Epipsy 220)
[later to find] it does ever spread	(187)
Like a sea's arm as it goes rolling on,	
Being the pulse of some great country — so	
Wast thou to me, and art thou to the world!	
And I, *perchance, half feel* a strange regret	(wholly feel)
That I am not what I have been to thee: . . .	
Yet, sun-treader, all hail! From my *heart's heart*	(Epipsy 385; 201)
I bid thee hail! E'en in my wildest dreams,	
I proudly feel I would have thrown to dust	(Islam 4381)
The *wreaths of fame* which seemed o'erhanging me,	(Christian)
To see thee for a moment *as thou art.*	(in spirit)

Much more than a youth's paean to Shelley, Browning's worshipful words are punctuated with evidence of undying devotion. The poet considers himself "of mould" (165) with Shelley's numerous spirits and as one with Shelley in pantheistic praise of the whole world. He sees Shelley as the "fountain-head" (179) "of some great river washing towns / And towers," awaiting some great change which can hardly be less than the new Promethean day. Thus in his wildest dreams of Christian fame, however sincere or insincere his apostasy from Shelley, he would proudly have thrown all away to see Shelley in the spirit:

And if thou livest, if thou lovest, spirit!   (206)
Remember me who *set this final seal*   (Epipsy 133-41)
To *wandering* thought — that one so pure as thou   (PU 2.3.5)
Could never die. *Remember me who flung*   ("wreaths," Gisb 216)
All honor from my soul, . . .   (in considering Christianity)
Remember me who praise thee e'en with *tears*,   (Epipsy 141; 219)
For nevermore shall I walk calm with thee;   ("remember me," Gisb 13)
Thy sweet imaginings are as an air,
A melody some wondrous singer sings, . . .
And here am I the *scoffer*, who have [now] probed   (at Shelley; 236)
Life's *vanity*, won by *a word* again   (Christianity, see 488, 943-7; Love)
Into my own [free] life — . . .
                   my [briefly] *lost soul* too soon   (to Christianity; 245)
Sinks to itself and whispers *we* shall be   (returns; R.B. & Shelley)
But *closer linked*, two creatures whom the earth   (PU 1.571)
Bears singly, with strange feelings unrevealed
Save to each other; or two *lonely* things   (PU 2.3.5)
Created by some *power whose reign is done*,   (Jehovah)
Having no part in *God* or his bright world.   (Prometheus)
I am *to sing* whilst ebbing day dies soft   (of Prometheus)
As a lean scholar dies worn o'er his book.

After indicating that his apostasy from Shelley was brief, half-hearted and shameful, Browning links himself with Shelley permanently and promises to sing out his life as a lean scholar in advocacy of Prometheus and his glorious freedom. So when readers identify the two creatures, "but closer linked," as Pauline and her lover, they respond as the poet deceptively planned it. For Browning is really thinking of "a legioned band of linkéd brothers, / Whom Love calls children" and of oracular vapor "which *lonely* men drink wandering in their youth." Both of which references, along with "wandering" in line 208, reflect Shelleyan thought as approvingly as "reign" reflects his Jupiter's (Jehovah's) tyrannical and limited rule and "bright world" reflects his Prometheus' loving and beneficient care. As Browning was later to assure Walter Savage Landor of his ability to combat Jehovah, he now assures Shelley of his Will, thus Power, to see his aspiration through:

I am made up of an intensest life,   (268)
Of a most clear idea of *consciousness*   (Shelley's self-awareness)
Of self, distinct from all its qualities,
From all affections, passions, feelings, powers;   (Q Mab 6.212-9)
And thus far it exists, if *tracked*, in all: (PU 3.2.29)
But *linked*, in me, to *self-supremacy*,   (PU 1.571; PU 2.4.42, 4.578)
Existing as a centre to all things,
Most potent to create and rule and call
Upon all things to minister to it;
And to a principle of *restlessness*   (Q Mab 9.2)
Which would be all, have, see, know, taste, feel, all —
This is *myself*; . . .   (R.B.'s totality, PU 1.492)

And of my powers, one springs up to save   (281)
From utter death a soul with such desire
Confined to *clay* — of powers the only one   (Shelleyan)
Which marks me — *an imagination which*   ("'tis like thy light, /
Has been a very angel, coming not   Imagination!" Epipsy 163-4)
In fitful visions but *beside me ever*   (like Pauline)
And never failing me; so, *though my mind*   (Mind, Epipsy 174)
Forgets not, not a shred of life forgets,
Yet I can take a *secret* pride in calling   (unrevealed)
The dark past [paganism] up to *quell* it regally.   (well/flow, rare)

Gifted with spiritual sensitivity and physical insensitivity, Browning takes inordinate delight in his self-consciousness, his sense of self-supremacy and right to be ministered unto, and his restlessness and unfailing mind, all characteristics possessed by Shelley and functionally honored in his poetry. Browning would see, know, taste, feel, possess all, since any deficiency would be an unwarranted denial of his birthright. But it is Browning's Imagination of which he is most proud and confident, for he can thus call the dark past up with the splendor of a mighty fountain or sacred spring, a good example of his frequent reversal of contemporary meaning ("quell," PU 1.787, 4.157). Because Browning's mind must dissipate its restless and fierce energy in an unearthly cause, he has had one "lode-star" (292, Epipsy 219), "a need, a trust, a yearning after God [Prometheus]," whose "brightness" (251) here distinguishes him from Jehovah's darkness. All a "feeling" (196) he has but lately analyzed, Browning now realizes that he has ever neglected Jehovah's laws as well as abhorred those who obeyed them. He has always "felt as

one beloved and so shut in / From fear" (300) of any punishment. Thence he actually dates his trust in signs and omens,
seeing GOD (Prometheus) everywhere, not just in appointed
places (churches).

Only to "a sad after-time" can Browning attribute his back-
sliding, his doubt in Prometheus (304), since through all the
experience he continued to feel Prometheus' presence and to
trust "in a *hand* to lead me through / All danger" (307-8). As
a true Shelleyan, Browning therefore faults his *"weakest
reason* and resolve [Will]," before warmly describing the first
formative influence of his life: his father's library, generously
weighted with pagan and unorthodox religious literature, and
his father's kindly guidance in the beauties and freedom of
"the dark past" and "wisest ancient books / All halo-girt with
fancies of" (320) Browning's own making. Becoming a part
of each tale through his unfailing imagination, Browning lived
"a god *wandering* after beauty, or a giant / Standing vast in
the sunset," or "an old hunter / Talking with gods" in unsurpassed clarity of time, space and fashion. Never new day
broke so clear as "those / On the dim *clustered isles*," where
Browning stood by the naked Hermes who bound his forehead with Proserpine's hair.

Thus endowed to dream (336) Browning thinks it strange
that he "should e'er have stooped to aim at aught beneath —/
Aught low and painful" as Christianity. Yet always strong
within "was a vague sense of power *though folded up*" (Hom
Merc 586), of indwelling and ruling pagan spirit:

<pre>
            I lost myself   (from Prometheus, not Jehovah; 345)
And were it not that I so loathe that loss,   (shame, not guilt)
I could recall how first I learned to turn
My mind against itself; and the effects   (tried Faith, Epipsy 273)
In deeds for which remorse were vain as for   (unworthy)
The wanderings of delirious dream; yet thence   (from Christian ethics)
Came cunning, envy, falsehood, all world's wrong
That [be-] spotted me; at length I cleansed my soul.   (lost)
Yet long world's influence remained; and naught   (Christian)
But the still life I led, apart once more,   (from Christian rule)
Which left me free to seek soul's old delights,   (Shelleyan)
Could e'er have brought me thus far back to peace.   (in Prometheus)
</pre>

Browning can no more understand why he would be deceived by the low and painful regulations and restrictions of Christianity than does his Paracelsus later, though in *Paracelsus* the "wavering" between Prometheus and Jehovah is probably a diversionary tactic rather than a reasonably true confession of apostasy as is Browning's above. As Prometheus' peace returned to Browning (357) he "sought to know

What other *minds* achieved. No fear outbroke	(Genius; 384)
As on the works of mighty bards I gazed,	
In the first joy at finding my own thoughts	
Recorded, my own fancies justified,	
And their *aspirings* but my very own.	(PU 3.1.17)
With them I first explored *passion and mind*, —	(Shelley's Mind)
All to begin afresh! . . .	
I was no more a boy, the past was breaking	(395)
Before the future and like fever worked.	
I thought on my *new* self, and all my powers	(restored)
Burst out. I dreamed not of *restraint*, but gazed	(Shelleyan freedom)
On all things: schemes and systems went and came	
And I was proud (being vainest of the *weak*)	(PU 2.3.93)
In *wandering* o'er *thought's* world to seek some one	(PU 2.3.5; 4.103)
To be my *prize*, as if you wandered o'er	(Ph'p 3.14, Q Mab 9.5)
The White Way for *a star*.	(Shelley)

Always a star to Browning, and the brightest in the firmament, Shelley here represents the highest attainment of the human mind and rationally becomes the choice for Browning to follow. So through his "new self" Browning will join an insurrection against "eldest faith [in Jehovah], and hell's coeval, fear" (PU 3.1.10), which Shelley imputes to the unextinguished spark of man's soul and Browning finds flaming in the aspirings of mighty bards:

And my choice fell	(404)
Not so much on a *system* as a *man* —	(inseparable in Shelley)
On one, whom praise of mine shall not *offend*,	(PU 1.603)
Who was as calm as beauty, being such	
Unto mankind as thou to me, Pauline, —	
Believing in them and devoting all	
His *soul's strength* to their winning back to peace;	
Who sent forth *hopes* and longings for their sake,	(PU 2.4.59)
Clothed in all passion's melodies: such first	

Caught me and set me, *slave of a sweet task*,　　(Q Mab 9.76; PU 2.2.56)
To *disentangle*, gather sense from song: [and find] . . .　　　(PU 4.569)
A key to a new world, . . .　　　　　　　　　　　　　　　　　(415)
How my heart leapt as still I sought and found　　　　　　　　(417)
Much *there*, I felt my own soul had conceived,　　　(in other minds)
But there living and burning! . . .
So, my *weak* voice may well forbear to shame　　　　　　　　(423)
What seemed decreed my fate: I threw *myself*　　　　　(R.B.'s *all*)
To meet it, I was vowed to liberty,
Men were to be as gods and earth as heaven,
And I — ah, what a life was mine to prove!

First, perhaps deceptively, Browning emphasizes only the man Shelley, "his soul's idol" (540). Definitely deceptive, after joyously accepting the fateful task of disentangling Shelley's system of thought for the "key to a new world," Browning pretends that this exhilarating experience lasted only an hour, requiring that he take consolation in Plato, a theorist with whom Shelley probably had more disagreements than agreements. Yet Browning was all too willing to be caught by Shelley and set "slave of a sweet task," that is, "the sweet desires within obey [Demogorgon's law of Necessity]." No longer a boy Browning had now wandered over the thought of the world, confirming both his own similar powers of mind and what, like Shelley, he had deduced about the slavery of Christianity or any institution which infringed upon man's freedom. He was thus prepared to choose the system he felt his "own soul had conceived" and to promote it with all the fierce energy of his being. "Many a thought did [he] build up on thought" (48), for in his urgency to assist Shelley in "winning back to peace" all mankind, there was "no rest for *mind*."

Inspired by "the orb of Shelley's conceptions" (419), Browning initially planned, perhaps openly, to support Shelley's advocacy of a paganistic peace and freedom the world had tragically lost. So when his theories were made firm (443), Browning left them to learn "mankind, its cares, hopes, fears, its woes and joys," and to devise a life whose end compriseth every joy. "Yet all his search was vain" (457). First went his hopes of perfecting mankind, then his faith in man, freedom, virtue and his own motives. "Human love went last," but he

> felt this *no decay*, because new powers   (PU 4.550; 462)
> Rose as old feelings left — *wit, mockery,*   (his life's scheme)
> *Light-heartedness;* for I had oft been sad,
> Mistrusting my resolves, but now I cast
> Hope joyously away: I *laughed* and said   (sardonic)
> "No more of this!"

No more of what? Only a reference to the text at this point will reveal how completely Browning distorts the time-sequence of individual events. He is now back to "Sad confession first, / Remorse and pardon and old claims renewed,/ Ere" (25-7) he can be recrowned by Nature. He is again talking about his period of apostasy from Prometheus and his remorse. He knows and ignores or contemns the report that Jesus Christ made no allowance for old claims, much less for their restitution:

> My soul, where naught is changed and incense rolls   (470)
> Around the altar, only *God is gone*   (Prometheus)
> And some *dark spirit* sitteth in his seat.. . .   (Jehovah)
> And I said "I have nursed up energies,   (481)
> *They* will prey on me." And a *band* knelt low   (of Christians)
> And cried, "Lord, we are here and we will make
> Safe way for thee in *thine appointed life!*   (R.B.'s poetic career)
> But look on us!" And I said "Ye worship
> Me; should my heart not worship too?" They shouted
> "Thyself, thou art *our king!*" So I stood there   (Mask 71, poetic king)
> Smiling — oh, *vanity of vanities!*   (Christianity, see 237, 943)

Escaping an offensive evangelical partisanship, Browning once more felt "myself, my powers" (491) and determined while youth and health sustained him, in spite of all life's nothingness, that no grief should ever dampen his lightheartedness again. Only this life's scheme — "wit, mockery, lightheartedness" — was the veil between despair and joy, so like the morn which wasted not a sunbeam Browning would wear himself out in secret defense of Shelley (cf., G Angel 22-35).

Thus Browning explains how he regained control over his spirit which earlier had been "freed" for flights to Christian fame (504). Because Genius is only joyous when working on

some trusted goal, men should never part "with truth's
[Prometheus'] peace / For falsest fancy's [faith's] sake"
(509-10):

so, *pain*	(517)
Is linked with pleasure, for I ne'er may tell	(Shelleyan)
Half the bright sights which *dazzle me;* but now	(as a singer only)
Mine shall be all the *radiance:* let them fade	(Epipsy 223)
Untold — others shall rise as fair, as fast!	(bright sights)

For when all is said and done how vain the vaunted influence
poets have over men compared with the one individual who
discards "shadowy hope," Christianity, to "encircle men with
praise and love," Prometheanism. How vain also the deceiver
who, in choosing "radiance" as reward for defending Shelley,
incautiously gives away a whole cluster of Shelleyan words
and thoughts from "Epipsychidion":

Then, from the caverns of my *dreamy youth*	(217-24)
I sprang, as one sandalled with *plumes* of fire,	
And towards the *lodestar* of my own desire,	(R.B. hyphenates)
I *flitted*, like a dizzy *moth*, whose flight	
Is as a dead leaf's in the owlet light,	
When it would seek in Hesper's setting *sphere*	
A *radiant death*, a fiery sepulchre,	
As it were a lamp of earthly *flame*.	

To Browning and Shelley "radiant death" meant spiritual reunion with Prometheus, and to Browning "radiance" meant
success in advancing Shelley's beauteous dreams of Love,
dreams which would come true in more enlightened days
than those through which Browning was fated to struggle:

'Tis a fine thing that one *weak as myself*	(531)
Should sit in his *lone* room, knowing the words	(Pr Athan 1.33, PU 2.
He utters in his *solitude* shall move	3.5; PU 1.14, 2.4.17)
Men like a swift wind — that *tho' dead and gone*	(R.B.)
New eyes shall glisten when *his* beauteous dreams	(Shelley's)
Of love come true in happier frames than his. . . .	(Islam 2658-63)
And my *soul's idol* ever whispers me	(Epipsy 268; 540)
To dwell with *him* and his *unhonored* song:	(Shelley)

Unenticed by the temptation of momentary fame and persuaded the climate of acceptance would be as unfavorable to
his open defense of Shelley's thought as it was to Shelley

himself, Browning "foreknows" (meaning of "Prometheus")
that he "would press / First in the struggle, fail again [like
Shelley] to make / All bow [who are] enslaved [to Chris-
tianity]" (542). Then he would again "sink" in despondency,
knowing that the curse would be:

To see our idols perish; we may *wither*,   (PU 2.4.100; 546)
No marvel, we are *clay*, but our low fate   (Epipsy 338)
Should not extend to those whom *trustingly*   (preferred to faithfully)
We sent before into time's *yawning gulf*   (Epipsy 231)
To face what *dread* may lurk in darkness there. . . .   (Jehovah, see 41)
         Naught makes me trust some love is true   (554)
But the delight of the contented *lowness*   (weakness)
With which I gaze on *him* I keep forever   (Shelley)
Above me; *I to rise and rival him*?   (Prom, Para & Pomp also rise)
Feed his fame rather from my heart's best blood,
Wither unseen that *he* may flourish still.   (also 111; Shelley)

Most thoughtfully Browning resolves at age twenty to
wither unseen in order that his idol Shelley may flourish and
that departed Private Prometheans be not left alone in time's yawning gulf to face Jehovah's wrath. Defying all past glory (563)
which comes to Genius, he sets himself to live this life so that
through wit, mockery and lightheartedness he may fulfill his
cause unsuspected. And then, as he has twice before frag-
mented his regret over desertion of Shelley, Browning for a
third time returns to a probing self-analysis. It is indeed the
wildest freedom which Browning covets, the fullest assertion
of self-consciousness, and the rarest selfishness in that he
wants "one joy" (608) insatiable and his alone in which his
whole Myself is absorbed. Somewhat marred by its repetitive-
ness in subsequent Browning characters, the poet's first expression of being "vowed to liberty" deserves to be visualized
in its original freshness and applied to his own nature. No one
needs to be reminded that such absolute independence is dissociated from and condemned by genuine Christianity.
Thus the unsuspecting have been misled by Browning's false
evidences of the Christian's goal to expand his love and to
deepen his trust (faith). They have also been deceived by the
poet's two-pronged presentation of his soul's unalterable
tendency to flight, suggestive of a desire to be with Jehovah

but indicative of Browning's restless spark of divinity. Similarly the poet's flinging away his youth's chief aim is suggestive of a reformed Christian life but indicative of Browning's briefly becoming enslaved to Christianity. And the poet's seeming selfishness to taste one joy all alone is suggestive of a former sinful nature but indicative of Browning's trust in his self-sufficiency and self-supremacy. The unsuspecting would have done better to note that Browning's self is insatiable; his restlessness, passion; and his craving after knowledge, "the sole proof / Of yet commanding *will* and *power*" (621-2). Too great a catalog to keep repeating from poem to poem, lines 577-728 enumerate in detail the "schemes and systems" Browning thought conducive to the restoration of Shelley's fame and Prometheus' throne. Chief among these are his plans to draw on the inexhaustible power of Will and Love, to exalt Reason and self-consciousness, to trust in a sure knowledge of and affinity with Nature, to display the unjust and unloving attributes of Jehovah, and to circumvent the unbearable imprisonment of the spirit by the flesh.

In spite of life's implanted hindrances, multitudinous though they be, Browning must never grieve "whom wing [of imagination] can waft / Far from such thoughts" (655-6). He will be gifted with a wondrous mind (669), and when calm settles in he is prepared to turn his experience to greatest gain:

I have made *life* my own.	(Shelleyan; 700)
I would not be content with all the *change*	(PU 2.4.119)
One frame should feel, but I have gone *in thought*	(Shelley's Mind)
Thro' all conjuncture, I have lived all life	
When it is *most alive*, where strangest fate	
New-shapes it past surmise — the throes of men	(Hellas 207)
Bit by some *curse* or in the grasps of *doom*	(Jehovah's; Demogorgon's)
Half-visible and still-increasing *round*,	(PU 1.470)
Or *crowning* their wide being's general aim.	(PU 1.399, Hellas 89)

These are wild fancies and claims, Browning readily confesses to Pauline. But he feels "as one breathing his *weakness* to the ear / Of pitying angel." Thus taking assurance from the Prologue to Shelley's *Hellas* and the Chorus of Greek captive women, Browning visualizes the "new shapes" man "still may weave, / New gods, new laws receive." Like his Paracelsus, Browning is confident that his spiritual urge or energy is sufficient to guarantee success in a secret mission of promoting the true God, Prometheus.

When Browning employs a word or thought from Shelley's poetry, particularly in *Pauline*, which was an experiment the poet dared not republish for thirty-five years, he nearly always endangers his deception by appropriating additional words from the same general context, capitalizing all letters of a telltale word or punctuating the total deception with an exclamation point. Thus close on a lament of not being "immortal," spoken to Pauline, Browning abruptly asks God, "What is this 'sleep' which seems / To bound all?" (812-3). And before he can finish the sequence (811-59), which is obviously based on Asia's curiosity about Death and THE EARTH's answer, he is driven to incorporate an elliptical "only ONE . . .", which is also obviously based on Shelley's "*One only* being shalt thou not subdue." Therefore Browning's four subsequent passionate appeals to GOD are clearly appeals to Prometheus, not Jehovah:

<pre>
              My spirit *wanders:*   (805)
Hedgerows for me — . . .
                    [to] keep   (807)
Thought in — I am concentrated — I *feel;*   (Shelley's top constants)
But my soul saddens when it looks beyond:
I cannot be immortal, taste all joy.
</pre>

Within the Browning lines "immortal" appears innocently enough and, by immediately changing the addressee and paragraphing, the poet no doubt believed his reference safe. But just above her admonition to Asia — "Thou are immortal" (PU 3.3.111) — THE EARTH says, "Strength for the coming day, and *all* its *joy* / And Death shall be the last embrace." Just below the admonition she says, "*Death* is the veil which those who live call life: / They *sleep* and it is *lifted.*" So Browning's next lines:

O God, where do they tend — these struggling aims?   (Prometheus)
What would I have? What is this *"sleep"* which seems (cf., PU 4.58-60)
To bound all? can there be a *"waking"* point   ("lifted")
Of *crowning* life? The soul would never rule; . . .   (radiance)
The last *point* I can trace is — rest beneath   (PU 3.3.41, 138; 818)
Some better essence than itself [the soul], in *weakness;*   (PU 2.3.93)
This is *"myself,"* not what I think should be:
And what is that I hunger for but *God*?   (Prometheus)

Browning not only borrows and approves Shelley's belief
that Death is a veil which, when lifted, ushers man from
physical existence into the realm of spiritual being; he also
advances Shelley's belief in man's spiritual "spark," his *weakness*, which longs to rejoin Prometheus of whom it is a portion. As the appropriation of Shelley's "sleep" is further confirmed by "Which star the winds with *points* of colored
light," so the use of both "spark" and disbelief in Death-as-
an-end is confirmed below:

My God, my God, let me for once look on thee   (Prometheus; 822)
As though naught else existed, we alone!
And as creation crumbles, my soul's *spark*   (PU 3.1.24)
Expands till I can say, — Even from *myself*
I need *thee* and I feel *thee* and I love *thee*.   (Prometheus)
I do not plead my *rapture* in thy works   (pantheism)
For love of thee, *nor that I feel as one*   (physical demise)
Who cannot die; but there is *that* in me   (spark)
Which turns to thee, which loves *or which should love.*   (diversion)

Browning's expression of trust in his own spiritual expansiveness, despite its weakness, and in God's power to grant
absolute audience to any loving soul seems unevasive. But he
had every reason to make obscure the implication of "creation crumbles," since his rapturous words probably convey
Browning's most direct "demand" for absorption of his total
Myself by Prometheus and too closely parallel Panthea's
memorable words to be accidental: "The overpowering light /
Of that immortal shape was shadowed o'er / By love; which,
from his soft and flowing limbs, / And passion-parted lips,
and keen, faint eyes, / Steamed forth like vaporous fire; an
atmosphere / Which wrapt me in its all-dissolving power, . . . /
I saw not, heard not, moved not, only felt / His presence flow

and mingle through my blood / Till it became his life, and his grew mine, / And I was absorbed" (PU 2.1.71-82). As with David's desire in "Saul," Browning's desire to be absorbed, or at least to be alone with the deity "as though naught else existed," is of course a denial of the unity of Jehovah's person. But the surrender Browning describes and yearns for is essential to the adjoining lines which express the dedication of Browning's life to the advancement of Prometheus, the dethroning of Jehovah:

Why have I *girt myself* with this *hell-dress*?	(2 Cor 11.14; 831)
Why have I *labored to put out my life*?	(self-sacrifice)
Is it not in my nature to adore,	
And e'en *for* all my reason do I not	(with)
Feel *him* and thank *him* and pray to *him* — now?	(Prometheus)
Can I forego the trust that *he* loves me?	(Prometheus)
Do I not feel a love which only ONE . . .	(R.B.'s ellipsis)

"Hell-dress" shrewdly disguises Browning's way of saying that his opposition to Jehovah is irrevocable: "And no marvel; for Satan is transformed into an angel of light. / Therefore it is no great thing if his ministers also be transformed as the ministers of righteousness." Thus Browning's assurance of secrecy, as he says below, through a "charm" which knits him round in the pretension that his sympathy lies with Christianity and its emphasis on sin, lust and pride. But Browning's "only ONE . . ." completes the breech of the charm of pretension, for it is Prometheus, in his curse of Jupiter (Shelley's Jehovah), who cries,

Fiend, I defy thee! with a calm, fixed mind,	(PU 1.262)
All that thou canst inflict I bid thee do;	
Foul Tyrant both of Gods and Humankind,	
One only being shalt thou not subdue.	

Earlier Prometheus also says to Jupiter,

Monarch of Gods and Daemons, and all Spirits	(PU 1.1)
But One, who throng those bright and rolling worlds	
Which thou and I alone of living things	
Behold with sleepless eyes! regard this Earth	
Made multitudinous with thy *slaves*, whom thou	(followers of Jehovah)
Requitest for *knee-worship, prayer, and praise,*	

as is later to be said about him, "From the conquest *but One* could foil" (PU 4.34). None too soon, judged by his ellipsis, Browning pretends to change the subject but he is still addressing Prometheus, precisely as if he were Jesus Christ, even to the pale complexion, the suffering of the crucifixion and the propitiation. Ingeniously Shelley had prepared Browning's way by an appropriation for Prometheus of every aspect of the life and death of Jesus Christ, including the thematic words of and in explanation of his life and the thematic words which are descriptive of the Messiah in the Old Testament. Both Browning and Shelley were fully informed of the tradition which had made Prometheus a Christ-figure, and they both judged Prometheus to be far worthier of the title than Jesus because of Prometheus' many demonstrable gifts to mankind and his refusal to become a slave to Jupiter (Jehovah):

Do I not feel a love which only ONE . . .	(R.B.'s ellipsis; 837)
O thou *pale* form, so dimly seen, deep-eyed!	("pale feet," PU 1.51)
I have *denied* thee calmly — do I not	(in considering Christianity)
Pant when I read of thy consummate power	(PU 3.3.125)
And *burn* to see thy calm pure truths out-flash	("fire," PU 3.3.151)
The brightest gleams of *earth's philosophy*?	(Alastor 71, Epipsy 213-16)
Do I not *shake* to hear aught question thee?	(in anger)
If I am *erring* save me, *madden* me,	(PU 3.3.129, 126)
Take from me *powers and pleasures*, let me die	(PU 4.79, 131)
Ages, so I see *thee*!	(PU 4.65; Prometheus)

Of all the appealing and thematic words Browning adopted from Shelley, "feel" is one of the most frequently honored, not however because Feel expresses emotion or intuition but because Feel, like Myself, represents the totality of man's responses, always intellectually ordered. So when Browning feels "a love which only ONE . . ." offered, he immediately associates his All with the suffering of Prometheus' impalement or crucifixion. To him it was an incomparable self-sacrifice, totally responsible for the eventual removal of Love's opposite — Jupiter's hatred and tyranny. Thinking particularly of Prometheus' "I speak in grief, . . . / I hate no more, / As then ere misery made me wise" (PU 1.56-8),

Browning knows that these words gave THE EARTH reason for saying, "Subtle thou art and good, ... thou art more than God, / Being wise and kind" (PU 1.143-5). To Browning as to Shelley, Beauty and Truth and Goodness are the brightest gleams of earth's philosophy, and "in that *best philosophy*, whose taste / Makes this cold common hell, our life, a doom / As glorious as a fiery martyrdom" (Epipsy 213-6) Browning planted his trust. All of which accounts for the introduction of "erring," which in a double entente permits Browning to imply a genuine Christian act, even to the willingness to sacrifice one's pleasure to God's glory. "Save me," another Christian concept, is also doubly directed, but it does not fare so well in the poet's deception once linked with "madden me," which identifies pagan rather than Christian theology and exploits a speech by THE EARTH:

<pre>
                There is a cavern where my spirit   (PU 3.3.124)
Was *panted* forth in anguish whilst *thy* pain   (Prometheus)
Made my heart *mad*, and those who did inhale it
Became *mad* too, and built a temple there,
And spoke, and were oracular, and lured
The *erring* nations round to mutual war.
</pre>

Hence Browning is not speaking of "erring" against Jehovah's will or word but of maddening errors which resulted from oracular vapor cast up from THE EARTH's anguish at Prometheus' excruciating pain. Nor are the above adoptions the end of Shelley's influence in *Pauline*, for while pretending to regret his worship of Shelley and to renew his sympathy for a religion in which sin, lust and pride are punishable, Browning secretly carries the Shelleyan art of reversal to a new level of sacrilegious daring:

<pre>
                I am *knit* round   (846)
As with a *charm* by sin and lust and pride,   (Christian pretension)
Yet though my wandering dreams have seen all shapes
Of strange delight, oft have *I stood by thee* — (Mab 7.174; Prometheus)
Have I been keeping lonely *watch* with thee   (Panthea, PU 1.821)
In the damp *night* by weeping Olivet,   (Panthea, PU 1.822)
Or leaning on thy bosom, proudly less,   (proudlessly)
Or dying with thee on the *lonely* cross,
Or witnessing thine *outburst* from the tomb. ("uprise," PU 2.5.22, 28)
</pre>

"Watch" is the word reportedly used by Jesus Christ at Gethsemane, but "weeping" is unrecorded. Brash and risky yet carefully modulated, Browning's analogy truly out-distances Shelley's in subverting the Crucifixion. "Watch," "night" and "lonely cross" are as clever as "proudly less" and "outburst" are gratuitous. But there were three crosses at Calvary, no witness at the Resurrection, and both events occurred in the daytime. All of the descriptive and informative words are surreptitiously intended to invoke and honor Panthea's watch with Prometheus:

Hast thou forgotten *one who watches* thee   (PU 1.821)
The cold dark *night*, and never sleeps but when
The shadow of thy spirit falls on her?

Nailed to this wall of eagle-baffling mountain,   (PU 1.20)
Black, wintry, dead, unmeasured; . . .
The crawling glaciers pierce me with the *spears*   (PU 1.31)
Of their moon-freezing crystals; . . .
Heaven's wingéd hound, polluting from *thy lips*   (Jupiter's; PU 1.34)
His beak in poison not his own.

The nailing of Jesus Christ to the cross, the offering of vinegar to quench his thirst and the spearing of his side to confirm death — all are adapted by Shelley to depict Prometheus in a cruciform posture and readapted by Browning with falsely devout hints of sweat as drops of blood at Gethsemane, of mutual love between Jesus and John at the Last Supper, and of the appearance of Mary Magdelene at the tomb. Perhaps the more skillful Visions of Prometheus disguised as Jesus Christ in *Christmas-Eve* and of Shelley's Jupiter disguised as God Almighty in *Easter-Day* will seem less startling only because the youthful Browning selected Shelley's climactic sacrilege to Christianity to introduce his vow of lifelong allegiance to Prometheus:

A mortal, sin's familiar friend, *doth here*   (Robert Browning)
Avow that he will give all earth's reward   (856)
But to *believe* and humbly *teach the faith*   (in Prometheus)
In suffering and poverty and shame,
Only believing he is not *unloved*.

Double-edged, "unloved" by Jehovah, loved by Prometheus, is as conspicuous as Browning could place it, for it is most characteristic of him to change paragraph at emphatic enunciation, and just as characteristic of him to revert to unfinished thought once he has distracted attention. So Browning first pretends that the "avowal" pertains to Pauline by reference to a "dedication" of his poem (870), before suddenly deifying her "a Pauline from heights above" (900) to whom he repeats, "I stained myself / But to behold thee purer by my side, / To show thou art my breath, my life, a last / Resource [Imagination]" (905-8). Now "Love's slave," looking no farther than his liege Prometheus commands (949), Browning intends to live with her where Nature lies all wild to them though all bare to the stinted and deformed about them (950-7; "fly with me," 731, Epipsy 388). "Feeling God [Prometheus] loves us, and that all which errs / Is but a dream which death will dissipate" (978-9), the poet wonders what need there is for longer exile. And when exiled no longer, whether from Prometheus or England as it was with Shelley, Browning will then look on

```
The works of my past weakness, as one views              (983)
Some scene where danger met him long before.
Ah that such pleasant life should be but dreamed!       (up to now)

But whate'er come of it, and though it fade,         (R.B.'s avowal)
And though ere the cold morning all be gone, . . .
And I the first deny, decry, despise,                    (991)
With this avowal, these intents so fair, —
Still be it all my own, this moment's pride!
No less I make an end in perfect joy. . . .
For this song shall remain to tell forever      (Pauline; 1004)
That when I lost all hope of such a change,   (cf., 976, PU 3.4.54-204)
Suddenly beauty rose on me again.                     (Shelleyan)
No less I make an end in perfect joy. . . .         (refrain, 994)

Sun-treader, I believe in God and truth       (Prometheus; 1020)
And love; and as one just escaped from death      (in Christianity)
Would bind himself in bands of friends to feel
He lives indeed, so, I would lean on thee!               (Shelley)
Thou must be ever with me, most in gloom          (Will, Demand)
If such must come, but chiefly when I die,      (D's law of Necessity)
For I seem, [on] dying, as one going in the dark
```

To fight a *giant:* but live *thou* forever,   (Jehovah; Shelley)
And be to all what thou hast been to me!
All in whom this wakes pleasant thoughts of me   (typical intrusion)
Know my last state is happy, free from doubt
Or touch of fear. Love me and wish me well.

Browning's parallelisms effectively disguise the everlasting bond he has made to the supposedly disenfranchised Shelley. Christians and pagans are both known to band together in likemindedness, but unlike Browning who has escaped a living death in Christianity and now wishes to feel "he lives indeed," the true Christian is said to forget himself, to live for Christ and to believe that to die to the world is gain (Ph'p 1.21). "Know ye not," St. Paul reminds Christ's followers, "that ... ye are not your own? For ye are bought with a price" (1 Cor 6.19). When Browning speaks of GOD, Truth and Love, carefully excluding Beauty which wrought his sudden change, he implies the Christian Jehovah but indicates the Prometheus of Shelley. Five times Browning calls upon the Sun-treader, not the unmentioned Jesus Christ implied in "lean on thee," and the most ardent call is for Shelley's presence after Browning's death, the time at which the Christian's fight is ended. Clearly Demogorgon's promise to grant all things one darest demand is invoked in *"Thou must be ever with me"* and confidently rendered a fait accompli in Browning's happy state which is free from doubt or touch of fear. It was no pampered Will, critical thought to the contrary, which thirty-one years later renamed the Giant he and Shelley were to fight after death "the Arch Fear in a visible form" and fifty-six years later cried, "Speed, — *fight on*, fare ever / There as here!"

PARACELSUS
1835

In *Sordello*, which brackets *Paracelsus* in composition, the thematic emphasis only seems to fall on Strength (36) and Weakness (6) as the words are normally construed. For an apparent semantic change in Browning's thought is made clearer by an explanation of how Sordello learns "to live in weakness as in strength" (2.280). By means of "a magical equipment, strength, / Grace, wisdom" (2.361-3) Sordello simply "willed" into being his former dreams of world mastery. "The seal was set" and never again was he to be "one of the many" with "hopes and cares / And interests nowise distinct from theirs." Never again was he to "square his course / By any known example [common law, 2.374]":

<pre>
            abiding *free* meantime, uncramped   (2.391)
By any *partial organ*, never stamped   (God's organ, Para 1.295)
Strong, and to *strength* turning all energies — . . .
That is, he loves not, nor possesses *One*   (2.395)
Idea that, star-like over, lures him on   (Jehovah)
To its exclusive purpose. . . .
            whereas *flesh* leaves *soul free* to range   (2.402)
Remains itself a blank, cast into shade,
Encumbers little, if it cannot aid.   (R of Islam 3549)
So, range, *free soul! who, by self-consciousness*,   (Shelleyan)
The last drop of all beauty doth express — . . .
            while for the *world*, that can dispense   (Christian)
Wonder on men who, themselves, wonder — make   (2.409)
A shift *to love at second-hand*, and take   (through Christ)
For idols those who do but idolize   (Jehovah)
Themselves — the *world* that counts men strong or wise,   (secular)
Who, themselves, court *strength, wisdom,* — it shall bow
Surely in unexampled worship now,
Discerning me! —
            (Dear *monarch*, I beseech,   (Jehovah, PU 1.1, 3.1.69)
Notice how lamentably wide a breach
Is here: *discovering* this, discover too   (repeated, Para 1.775-6)
What our *poor world* has possibly to do
With *it!* As pigmy natures as you please —   (the breach)
So much the better for you; take your ease,
</pre>

Look on, and laugh; *style yourself God alone;*
Strangle some day with a cross olive-stone! . . .

             no *machine*   (pain & pleasure, reward & punishment)
To exercise *my utmost will* is mine: (2.427)
Be mine *mere consciousness!* . . .   (extreme awareness of being)
             would live content,   (2.445)
Obstructed else, with *mere verse* for vent.   (mere singer)
Nor should, for instance, *strength* an outlet seek
And, striving, be admired: . . .
Such a *strength*, such a *weakness*, added then   (2.525)
A touch or *two*, and turned them into *men*.   (of Will; not pigmies)

No more paganistic in tone and word than many other speakers in Browning's poetry, Sordello foils the poet's design by not truly aspiring to godlike stature. He does not learn to live in Weakness as projected, for after long dreamy rationalizing he admittedly desires only worldly power and thus fails to comprehend the Strength which may be aroused by the weak yet willful soul or spirit. Like Browning's Paracelsus, Sordello worships self-consciousness and, unencumbered by the flesh, believes that men shall love in him the love that leads their "souls to *power's* perfection" (2.439-40). For each of these heroes, as for Pauline's lover, the "seal was set" (Adonais 453); neither was to be "one of the many" and neither was to be drawn off his free course of aspiring (PU 3.1.17) by an exclusive or single purpose, human or divine. Both Sordello and Paracelsus therefore accept their Genius as a birthright (PU 2.4.39-99), even though they fall short of the Shelleyan obligation of expending it for mankind. With identical metaphysical and theological beliefs Sordello and Paracelsus would serve equally well as prototype in Browning's poetry for the attainment of power (Shelley's Life — totality, Light — wisdom, Love — supremacy). But in *Paracelsus*, where the hero aspires to his limit, the poet's contrast of Weakness with Strength approaches full circle and more immediately delineates the consistency of Browning's disagreement with St. Paul and opposition to Jehovah. Or as Sordello theorizes, the freedom of the soul is not to be hindered by the restrictions of gods who only idolize themselves; nor is the individual ever to move out of "infancy" (3.983) as long as he mistakenly places his trust in an unknown force thought to be stronger than himself.

Obviously the dramatic extravagances of *Paracelsus* preclude its being utilized as an unembellished demonstration of Browning's personal thought, but specific points of view and specific diction, when shown to conflict directly with St. Paul's formulations and diction, are helpful in determining the regularity with which Browning felt compelled to enunciate an opposing conviction. Twenty-eight times in *Paracelsus* Browning uses the word Strength, fifteen times the word Weakness, with four usages coming together. And though he may deliberately obscure the meaning or sometimes seem to follow St. Paul's line, his poetic use of and allusion to the juxtaposed words and thoughts of 2 Corinthians in particular reveal that Browning's Paracelsus, not the historical one, is vastly unhappy with St. Paul's harping on the insufficiency of man, the absolute sufficiency of Jehovah. The most memorable of Paracelsus' injunctions is representative:

Therefore, *set free the soul* alike in all,   (1.775)
Discovering the true laws by which the flesh   (cf., Sordello 2.357)
Accloys the spirit! We may not be *doomed*   (fated)
To cope with seraphs, but at least the rest
Shall cope with us. Make no more giants, *God,*   ("demand"; Jehovah)
But elevate the race *at once!* We ask
To put forth just *our strength, our human strength,*   (Mont B 37)
All starting *fairly*, all equipped alike,
Gifted alike, all eagle-eyed, true-hearted —
See if we cannot *beat* thine angels yet!

Because Browning's earlier injunction to strangle on a cross olive-stone could not very well be intended for Sordello his main character, it was suggested that Jehovah becomes the only acceptable alternative. Now, with the poet's incautious repetition of "discovering" and essentially the same thought, Paracelsus' speech adds stronger credence to the reading, "Dear *m*onarch [Jehovah]" (Sord 2.415), "*M*onarch of the World [Sordello]" (Sord 2.355). Sordello talks about the lamentably wide breach between Christian pigmies and wise men of the secular world; Paracelsus talks about the "true" laws by which the flesh accloys the spirit. And both are hammering home the unjust and unequal nature of Jehovah's laws. Already possessed, he thinks, of the talents (Genius) he commands Jehovah to bestow upon all other men at once, Paracelsus prides himself on having overcome the hindrances of a deceptively imposed flesh with which a fearful and suspicious Jehovah unfairly impedes man's spirit and natural progress. Having found Sordello's way of pushing the flesh aside, leaving it a blank or cast into shade, Paracelsus clearly means by "human strength" the potential of man's spirit or soul:

Truth is *within* ourselves; it takes no rise   (the Mind; 1.726)
From *outward things*, whate'er you may believe.   (self-awareness)
There is an *inmost* centre in us all,   (Gisb 169, PU 2.1.119)
Where truth abides in fulness; and around,
Wall upon wall, the *gross flesh* hems it in,   ("wronged body," 3.689)
This *perfect, clear perception* — which is truth.   (Shelleyan)
A baffling and perverting carnal mesh   (imposed by Jehovah)
Binds it, and *makes all error:* and to know   (Shelleyan)
Rather consists in *opening out* a way   (from the Mind)
Whence the imprisoned *splendor* may escape,   (truth)
Than in *effecting entry for a light*   (2 Cor 4.6-7)
Supposed to be without.

Although the last two quotations are a mixture of pagan and Christian innuendoes, it does not take long to decide, or to show, that St. Paul is responsible for much of the adverse thought and diction which Browning allots to Paracelsus. The pivotal passage is 2 Corinthians 12.8-11 (also see Galatians 6.3):

For this thing ["a thorn in the flesh" — Verse 7] I besought the Lord thrice, that it might depart from me.

And he [the Lord] said unto me, *My grace is sufficient for thee: for my strength is made perfect in weakness* [Red Letter Edition]. Most gladly therefore will I rather *glory* in my infirmities, that the *power* of Christ may rest upon me.

Therefore I take *pleasure* in infirmities, in reproaches, in necessities, in persecutions, in distresses for Christ's sake: for when I am *weak*, then I am *strong*.

I am become a fool in *glorying;* ye have compelled me: for I ought to have been commended of you: for in nothing am I behind the very chiefest apostle, though I be nothing.

While St. Paul considers himself "nothing" before Jehovah, Paracelsus considers himself everything, even receptacle of truth in its fullness. While St. Paul admits to personal insufficiency and thus dependence upon Jehovah's grace, Paracelsus claims self-sufficiency and thus rejects dependence upon "outward things." While St. Paul waits patiently for and counts on the "light / Supposed to be without," Paracelsus embodies the light, assured as he is by an inmost centre of perfect truth. While St. Paul knows only "Christ, and him crucified" (1 Cor 2.2), Paracelsus understands all wisdom and ultimately would use it, provided man can be made cognizant of the imprisonment of his soul by the flesh, for the elevation of mankind to godlike stature. When Browning permits Paracelsus to denigrate "a light / Supposed to be without," he could be thinking of numerous Pauline lines, for St. Paul often writes that "God . . . hath shined in our hearts" (2 Cor 4.6-7) and explains that this treasure is in earthen vessels so that "the excellency of the *power* may be of God." Only superficially then do Paracelsus and St. Paul agree even on the Weakness and Strength of the flesh and its tendency to mislead or inhibit the soul, for while Paracelsus sees the flesh as "a baffling and perverting carnal mesh" which has been imposed from without, St. Paul sees it as a gift of Jehovah, the temple of the spirit, and no more culpable than the soul when the soul is led astray. In different words, St. Paul speaks of both physical and spiritual sins (2 Cor 7.1); Paracelsus deems the spirit beyond sin or error (1.733) as a true Shelleyan must.

In a second quotation, for which there are also clearer Paracelsian glosses, Paracelsus insists even more firmly upon his self-sufficiency and personal independence, his supernatural wisdom (understanding), and his proximity to personal divinity. Here, because of the scrambled pronouns, only a knowledge of Shelley's assigned characteristics tells whether Jehovah or Prometheus is being rebuffed or invoked:

God! Thou art *mind!* Unto the *master-mind*   (Peter Bell 4.9.5; 2.229)
Mind should be precious. Spare my mind alone! . . .
Crush not my mind, dear God, though I be crushed!   (Q Mab 4.192,

Hold me before the frequence of thy seraphs   7.203; 2.242)
And say — "I *crushed* him, lest he should disturb   (Lam 1.15)
My law. Men must not know their *strength*: behold   (potential)
Weak and alone, how he had raised himself!"

But if delusions trouble me, and *thou*,   (Jehovah)
Not seldom felt with rapture in thy help (machine: *helps* & hindrances)
Throughout my toils and wanderings, dost intend
To work man's welfare through my *weak* endeavor,
To crown my *mortal* forehead with a beam   (saint, martyr)
From thine own blinding crown, to *smile*, and guide   (PU 1.260)
This puny hand and let the work so wrought
Be styled my work, — *hear me! I covet not*   (1 Cor 12.31)
An influx of new power, an angel's soul: (Christ's; Adonais 153)
It were no marvel then — but I have reached   (2 Cor 11.14)
Thus far, *a man;* let me conclude, *a man!*   (Job, 91 times)
Give but one hour of my first *energy*   (grant; Will)
Of that *invincible faith*, but only one!   (in self)
That I may cover with an *eagle*-glance   (Adonais 147)
The truths I have and spy some certain way   (self-supremacy)
To mould them, and completing them, *possess!*   (godhood)

Since much is to be shown of Browning's mastery of the
Scriptures and his tenacious memory, which gives ample
evidence of being photographic, it may suffice now to point
out that the likely choice of "crush" from "The Lord hath
... called an assembly against me *to crush* my young men"
is not at all farfetched. Browning's sympathy for talented
"young men" makes it the most appropriate scriptural quotation. As he knew, the very short Book of Lamentations
contains one of the most persuasively written passages in the
Scriptures on Jehovah's Mercy, as limited in Browning's mind
as "that brave *curry* of his Grace" (E-Day 339). As he knew,
"*covet* earnestly the best gifts" immediately precedes St.
Paul's famous chapter on Faith, Hope, Charity. And the near-
ness of "angel's soul" to "no marvel" does not easily exempt
it from alliance with "no marvel; for Satan himself is transformed into an *angel* of light," scriptural words Browning
could never forgive nor forget. An unrelated but exemplary
illustration of Browning's broad and diverse method of lifting
scriptural words occurs in "The Bishop Orders His Tomb."
The Book of Ecclesiastes provides the setting for instant

understanding by the reader, Job 7 provides inspiration and probable format for the poet however, and yet Genesis 47.9 provides the substance of the perfect line "Evil and brief hath been my pilgrimage." Jacob, the father of Joseph, says to Pharoah, "The days of . . . my pilgrimage are . . . few and evil."

Browning simply could not believe in a God of both Justice and Mercy — to him law and love are eternally irreconcilable — and for a God "to crush" young men because of a ruler's disobedience was beyond his conception. Such intense opposition, if anything, may explain why Browning reveals no appreciation of St. Paul's exaltation of Love, elects instead Shelley's exaltation and ineffable function of Love. But the point here is that Paracelsus refuses help from Jehovah if it is to be assessed as an indebtedness or cooperative effort and, in asking Prometheus for one hour of his youthful energy, turns his back on an influx of Jehovah's strength daily coveted by Old and New Testament characters. By asking Prometheus not to crush his "mind," though Jehovah crush his body, Paracelsus has cause as substantial as Shelley's confidence in Mind, for to Paracelsus as to Browning's Pope Innocent mind is not matter and thus not subject to being crushed by Jehovah. Only Jehovah would hold Paracelsus before his seraphs and say that his body was crushed lest he disturb "my law." Prometheus abjures all implication of law and constantly encourages his "beloved race" (PU 1.386) of men to strive, lovingly, for the uttermost attainments. Once in appraising his spent body Paracelsus says that "mind" is nothing but disease (4.279). But in less excitable moments he always associates mind with soul, in whose essence, whose Myself, is a fierce energy eternally imparted as a Right, a Seal, an Earnest (all in St. Paul and Shelley), in which is lodged an unshakable trust in Self and in other talented individuals to a lesser degree. Unlike St. Paul, Paracelsus will not, can not, tolerate an external strength made perfect in his weakness. His birthright (Wisdom, PU 2.4.39) vouchsafes Will and Power, and incites a self-sufficiency which is here noticeably vexed by suspected intrusion of a jealous and preemptive

Jehovah. Gifted with the same talents Browning claims for himself in *Pauline*, Paracelsus takes inordinate delight in his self-consciousness, his sense of self-supremacy and his unfailing mind. He must therefore dissipate his restless energy in an unearthly cause. Doubtlessly Prometheus is saddened by Paracelsus' overweening conceit and disregard of love, but it is only Jehovah who fears that his plan and law might be endangered by a new aspirant. And well he might fear, since Paracelsus is "above [other men] like a god" (4.294) and should have taken his natural station over them, "owning all the glory was a man's! / — And in my elevation man's would be" (4.300-1).

When angry Paracelsus is prone to command the deity: "Give but one hour," "make no more giants, God"; to address the deity: "you" or "your" (5.134-56) or to say "thou" with a small t. When complaining of man's ill treatment by the deity, he prefers to use "my lord" with a small l (4.596) or to apply to mankind "God cursed" (4.144) or an unfavorable "fate." When imploring or undecided about God's care and guidance, he ingratiatingly says "dear God" (5.257). And when aspiring he grows more formal and resorts to "God," "O Thou" or "my God." Whatever the address, however, it is either joyous or petulant, never calm and conciliatory, and as likely as not to be pantheistic unless "praise" or "glory" is the theme. Then the recipient of his protest is always the Judeo-Christian Jehovah, who only among the deities or spirits invoked by Browning's Paracelsus demands or expects unmerited glorification and praise. Yet these are minor irreverences when compared with the possible blasphemies of the next quotation:

Hell-spawn! I am *glad*, most *glad*, that thus I fail!   (5.134)
Your cunning has o'ershot its aim. One year,   (Jehovah's)
One month, *perhaps*, and I had served your turn!   (become a convert)
You should have curbed your spite awhile. But now   (Jehovah)
Who will believe 't was *you* that held me back?   (Jehovah)
Listen: there's shame and *hissing* and contempt,   (Job 27.23)
And none but *laughs* who names me, none but spits   (Job 12.4, 30.10)
Measureless scorn upon me, me alone,
The quack, the cheat, the liar, — all on me!   (graphic)

And thus *your famous plan to sink mankind*   (Jehovah's)
In silence and despair, by teaching them
One of their race had probed the *inmost* truth,   (Gisb 169, PU 2.1.119)
Had done all man could do, yet failed no less —
Your wise plan proves abortive. Man despair?   (Jehovah's)
Ha, ha! why, they are hooting the empiric, . . .   (Job & Shelley)
So pick and choose among them all, *accursed*! (4.144, Gal 1.8-9; 5.153)
Try now, persuade some other *to slave* for you,   (*Pauline* 412)
To ruin body and soul to work *your* ends!   (Jehovah's)
No, no; I am the first and last, *I think.*   (graphic)

The unsuspecting reader would find textual reasons for insisting that these lines, rather than being addressed to Jehovah, are addressed to the "fiends" of the opening line (5.129). But internal allusions and a ready gloss make it clear that Paracelsus is speaking directly to Jehovah of his unwise plan, his unfair law and his unloving conduct, again through utilization of familiar diction from St. Paul, probably intensified by Shelley's earlier use:

I am of different mould.   (4.595)
I would have *soothed* my lord, and *slaved* for him   (Shelleyan)
And done his service past my narrow *bond*   (Col 3.14)
And thus I get *reward* for my pains!   (1 Cor 9.17)
Beside, 't is vain to talk of *forwarding*   (2 Cor 8.8-10)
God's glory otherwise; this is alone   (Jehovah's)
The sphere of its *increase*, as far as men   (Col 2.18-23)
Increase it; why, then, look beyond this *sphere*?   (Shelleyan)
We are *his* glory; and if we be glorious,   (Jehovah's)
Is not *the thing* achieved?   (Jehovah's glory)

Beseech, care(s), covet, crown, dependency, despair, earnest(ly), earthen vessels, excellency, fear(s), flesh, forward(ing), free(ly), fruit, gift(s), glad, glory, good, grace, hinder(ed, ing), hope(s), increase, joy, labor(ing), law (example), light, Lord (lord), love, mercy, minister(ed, ing), perfect, pleasure, reward, right, seal, serve (service), servant(s), shame, soul (spirit), stand, strive, strong, sufficiency, thing(s), treasure, vain, weak and will are thematic words from 1 and 2 Corinthians so closely interwoven by Browning and so obviously in strife with St. Paul's directives on service to Jehovah that their choice cannot be any less deliberate than Shelley's. Nor do "Ha, ha" and "laugh," which are from Job, perhaps through Shelley, appear any less sardonic than in Shelley. But it is the gloss "slaved for him" (PU 1.606) which identifies Jehovah as the object of Paracelsus' anger, and though he here avoids answering Festus' question on "who are accursed," Paracelsus earlier identified the object of the curse too: "I would lay bare to you the *human heart / Which God cursed* long ago, and devils make since / Their pet nest and their never-tiring home" (4.143-5). Placed immediately after the incomparable lines " 'T is an old tale: Jove strikes the Titans down, / Not when they set about their mountain-piling / But when another rock would crown the work," Paracelsus' failure is even more directly attributable to a spiteful Jehovah. However Browning juggles and obscures the meaning, in the end Paracelsus always comes out forthrightly and decidedly "of a different mould": "I must know! / Would God translate me to his throne, believe / That I should only listen to his word / To further my own aim" (3.706-9). Thus Browning manages for Paracelsus to address two GODs in one, one of whom he is only disappointed in if his aspiring is not going well, one he contemns for spitefully holding him back.

Where more satisfyingly than in Job could Browning or Shelley have found opposition to "the insufficiency of a man" and justification of a man's righteousness or at least desire to stand equally with God to declare displeasure with earthly justice? For Job repeatedly talks about strength, weakness, power, wisdom, knowledge, righteousness and justice in chapters 3, 4, 6, 9, 23, 28 and 42. Like Job in the development of his thought, Paracelsus talks directly to God and would have the Almighty answer him. But here the analogy falls apart because Paracelsus is not suddenly in-timidated into confessing, "I uttered that I understood not, *things* too wonderful for me, which I knew not. . . . Where-fore I abhor *myself*" (42.3-6). Continuing instead to protest the purity of his thoughts and actions and the unjust severity of his fate, Paracelsus rests his defense in the subjectivism of his nature, the supremacy of his Myself and the unfailing quality of his mind which shall eventually displace all barriers, including Jehovah, between him and Prometheus. "Mind" thus becomes the ultimate concern of Paracelsus who was conceived in a Shelleyan world of thought which is eternalized in the One Mind, Prometheus. If the only true reality is what the mind tells one, the move from solipsis to spirit is not inconceivable. Perhaps this assumed affinity explains why Paracelsus acts as if spirit is all and as if he is already spirit. Whether "God! Thou art mind!" is a recognition of Shelley's "immanent intellect" is left a moot question, since Browning would rather see Paracelsus concentrate on and thwart Jehovah who blocks passage to communion with the benevolent Prometheus than engage in philosophical speculation. But it seems clear that Browning saw English empiricism as the underlying principle of Shelley's idealism and emphasis on experience. Oddly one of the few historically accurate traits of Browning's Paracelsus is struck in "Ha, ha! why, they are hooting the *empiric*" (5.148).

What however of the many references to God elsewhere in the five cantos of *Paracelsus*? Because Paracelsus is falsely evasive with his friends their last night together, Festus pointedly explains that he does not wish to sorrow later over his friend's undoing through "uncertain words / Erringly apprehended, *a new creed* / Ill understood" (1.204-6) which may beget rash trust in Paracelsus. Not to be outflanked, Paracelsus replies, "Choose your side, / Hold or renounce." But his evasiveness is again checked by the reminder that he had "prepared to task to the uttermost / [His] *strength*, in furtherance of a certain aim . . .

the secret of the world,	(cf., E-Day 764)
Of man, and man's true purpose, path and fate.	(1.277)

— That you, not nursing as a mere vague dream
This purpose, with the sages of the past,
Have struck upon a way to this, if all
Your trust be true, which following, heart and soul,

You, if a man may, dare aspire to KNOW:	(R.B.'s emphasis)

And that this aim shall differ from a host
Of aims alike in character and kind,
Mostly in this, — that *in itself alone*

Shall its reward be, not an alien end	(wisdom its own reward)

Blending therewith; *no hope nor fear nor joy*   (Q Mab 6.212-9;
Nor woe, to elsewhere move you, but this pure   Revolt of Islam 8.5)
Devotion to sustain you or betray: (to knowledge)
Thus you aspire.

To which Paracelsus rather peevishly and again evasively responds:

You shall not state it thus: (1.290)
I should not differ from the *dreamy crew*   ("sages" below)
You speak of. I profess no other share
In the selection of *my lot*, than this   (seal, mission)
My *ready answer* to the will of God   ("sweet desires," PU 2.2.56)
Who summons me to be his *organ*. All   (Q Mab 1.143-55, Sord 2.392)
Whose *innate strength* supports them shall succeed(physical "machine")
No better than the sages.

Paracelsus may hoodwink the tender and simple Michal but Festus is privy to the whole aspiration. He knows that by allusion to "innate [human] strength" Paracelsus is truly talking about Weakness, a spiritual potential ("sempiternal heritage") which in Paracelsus has already rejected the strength Jehovah offers through Christ. Paracelsus' ready answer, like Sordello's, is thus confirmation of a positive refusal to become a "partial organ" of Jehovah's and of a "sweet surrender" to Necessity. In fact, Paracelsus sounds almost as if he would take over the operation of Necessity. Festus had heard the same double talk before:

the sovereign proof   (1.186)
That we devote ourselves to God, is seen
In living just as though no God there were;
A life which, prompted by the *sad and blind*   (unquestioning faith)
Folly of man, Festus abhors the most;
But which these tenets sanctify at once,
Though to *less subtle wits* it seems the same,
Consider it how they may.

Reject those glorious visions of *God's* love   (imperative; Jehovah's)
And man's *design; laugh* that God should send(future glory; imperative)
Vast longings to direct us; *say* how soon   (PU 2.4.55-7; imperative)
Power satiates these, or lust, or gold; *I know*
The *world's* cry well, and how to answer it.   (Christian)
But this ambiguous warfare . . .   (double entente)

Knowing the true "aim" (1.298) to which Paracelsus had

been provoked, the less daring Festus warns his professed disciple (1.154-9) not to arouse Jehovah's anger needlessly with perfect tribute, since Jehovah cares not who feeds his altars as long as they are fed. Then with a bit of double talk of his own Festus, who frankly assumes Jehovah's indifference, *supposes:*

that *God* selected you . . .	(Prometheus; 1.311)
I cannot think you dare annex to such	(1.314)
Selection aught beyond a *steadfast will,*	(PU 3.4.199, 4.406)
And intense *hope;* nor let your *gifts* create	(PU 4.570; PU 2.3.6)
Scorn or neglect of ordinary means	
Conducive to success, *make destiny*	
Dispense with man's endeavor.	("dispense," Hom Merc 728)

To which Festus then dares Paracelsus give a forthright answer:

No, I have naught to fear! Who will may know	(1.328)
The secret'st *workings* of my soul. *What though*	(Hellas 778)
It be so? — if indeed the strong desire	(PU 2.2.41-63)
Eclipse the aim in me? if splendor break	(radiance, PU 1.693,
Upon the outset of my path alone,	Epipsy 223)
And duskest shade succeed? What fairer *seal*	(St. Paul & Shelley)
Shall I require to my authentic mission	("great commission," 1.141-62)
Than this *fierce energy?* . . .	(Will)
How know I else such glorious fate my own,	(1.339)
That works within me? Is it for *human* will	(double talk)
To institute *such impulses?* — still less,	(R of Islam 677)
To disregard their *promptings!* . . .	(R & B 10.1067-8)
Be sure that *God*	(Jehovah; 1.345)
Ne'er dooms to waste the strength he *deigns* impart! . . .	(PU 1.18)
Be sure they sleep not whom *God* needs! *Nor fear*	(Jehovah; 1.352)
Their holding light his charge, when every hour	
That finds that charge delayed, is a new death.	(vindictive death)
This for the faith in which *I trust.*	(graphic)

Clearly Paracelsus is not speaking about the God of St. Paul who is man's sufficiency or about the God of Milton who needs least of all frenetic activity. Nor does Paracelsus' admission that he is about to dispense with human, take on divine, endeavor conform to recommended service of Jehovah. The implications of "deigns" and "needs" conform to Festus' indifferent God but not to the Jehovah who spins for the lilies of the field. And the "new death" "every hour" is as incompatible with "My grace is sufficient: my strength is made perfect in weakness" as it is with the unshakable faith of the historical Paracelsus. Thus Browning's Paracelsus has more than average difficulty with his double entente, but he is saying that a totally selfish Jehovah brooks no delay in service by his charges as emphatically as he advises all *to reject* the false visions of Jehovah's love, *to laugh* that Jehovah deceives his slaves with vast longings, and *to proclaim* how soon Jehovah's unjust power overwhelms man.

Festus, who plays devil's advocate to Paracelsus as deftly as Browning switches from pagan to Christian persuasiveness, is not allowed to forget the instigative part he has played in Paracelsus' aspiring. So it is important to remember that when Festus momentarily asks Jehovah to "save" (5.67) the dying Paracelsus, his appeal is contingent upon:

> Reward *him* or I waive   (Paracelsus; 5.410)
> Reward! If thou canst find no place for him,
> He shall be king elsewhere, and I will be
> His *slave* forever. There are two of us.

> I am for noble Aureole, *God!*   (Jehovah; 5.407)
> I am upon his side, *come weal or woe.*
> His portion shall be mine.

Festus had heard the strange tale of Prometheus' visitation with no more alarm than "I will divest all fear" (1.608), and he was to speak the worshipful praise of Paracelsus (3.826-67) which is a clear-cut revision of Browning's worshipful praise of Shelley in *Pauline* (151-259). The tale began with Paracelsus loathing his weakness (Epipsy 232) while feeling that a mighty power was taking shape within him. One night as he sat "revolving [the power, Epipsy 232] and more," a still voice (low voice, Sord 5.80) from without said, "Seest thou not, / Desponding child, whence spring defeat and loss? / Even from thy strength" (1.513-5). "Waste not thy gifts [Genius] / In profitless waiting for the gods' descent, / But have some idol of thine own to dress / With their array. Know not for Knowledge's sake, / But to become a star to men forever." Whereupon Paracelsus smiled not, being well aware of who stood by him and asked if he would adventure for his sake and man's, apart from any promise of reward (Q Mab 2.65). "Be happy, my good soldier; I am by thee, / Be sure, even to the end" (1.544-5). Thus was Paracelsus "endued / With comprehension and a *steadfast will*" and vouchsafed Prometheus' own with a seal (Hellas 703, PU 4.576) which changed the whole world. So when quailing at the mighty range of secret truths which yearn for birth, Paracelsus hastens to contemplate undazzled some one truth as it expands from speck to star. He must go to prove his soul, unless perchance Jehovah sends his hail or blinding fireballs, sleet or stifling snow; even then he will arrive in Prometheus' own good time.

Enough paganism is obvious in the account of Paracelsus' commission to forestall all but the briefest comments, but it may not be presumptuous to point out that Jesus did not speak to his followers as either soldiers or *good* men. Nor did he endue them with a steadfast will of their own, send them out in search of a Star or promise to be with them to the end of less than the world which Prometheus is ever to favor. And if Jesus was familiar with the traditional pagan belief that Jupiter's eagle was unblinded by the dazzling light of the sun (or lightning), he never recommended "blinkers" as a safeguard against Jehovah's false splendor, an habitual Browning way of saying that the steadfast will need not be overawed by threat of Jehovah (PU 3.2.11-7). As scriptural diction is the shortest route to proof of Browning's and Shelley's reversals and appropriations of Christian theology, so Shelleyan diction is the shortest route to proof of Browning's unbelievable dependence upon Shelley's every thought. Avow, beams, calm, champion, chance, change(d), check(ed), circle, clasp, clog(ged), contagion, dare, darkling, dazzling, death, decay (ing), delight, desire, dim, entangling, fear, fierce, films, flit, forms, foul, free, friend, fruit(less), gaze(d), girt, hinder(ed), hollow, hope, joy, lair, life, light, manifold, marvels, melodies, myself, naught, nursling, ought, pant(ing), pent, phantoms, plague, point(s), power, pure, quiet, ruin(ed), sage, sea-shells, serene, service, shadow, show(s), shrine, slave(s), smooth(ed), snake(s), soothings, sorrow, spasm(s), spear, speckle, sphere, star, spring(s), strange, strangling, tincture, truth, vapors, wanderings, wells, whelming, wither(s), wink, wrench and writhing are only the commonest of Shelley's "non-scriptural" favorites which become thematic words in Browning with *Paracelsus*, if not earlier with *Pauline* and *Sordello*. Normally they may be expected to contribute to the joyous aspects of Browning's Prometheanism. But Browning, no more than Shelley, was ever able to enthuse over the joys of a new Promethean day without afterthoughts of the length of Jehovah's tyrannical reign.

In one way Browning had an advantage over Shelley in that the latter poet first stripped the Scriptures of all the words which would conform to his pagan theology, thus simplifying Browning's search. But in another way Browning had less advantage than Shelley since he had to conceal his opposition to disquieting Christian beliefs and practices from which Shelley gained relief in open and devastating parody, burlesque and denunciation. Only an indefatigable Will to memorize and systematically file thousands of references can account for the breadth and repetition of information Browning introduces into his poetry from Shelley and the Scriptures; careful reading and excellent memory are simply insufficient explanation. His remarkable applications, whether from the Scriptures or Shelley, are too precise, too subtle and too varied to be explained before credit is given to endless hours with Shelley's poetry and the Scriptures, including concordance and commentaries. The clusters of religion-oriented words and the applications of individual words which Browning constantly uses are nowhere else as prevalent or as readily identifiable as in St. Paul's epistles, Job, Psalms and the Prophets, the same Books Shelley systematically perused (Oxford Shelley pp. 156, 551). For Browning many of the scriptural words and doctrines could have been picked up at York Chapel, from his mother's conversation or from the famous Westminster Hymnal to which the poet jestingly refers in "Easter-Day." But whatever the way, Browning's promise to become a slave to Shelley and his Prometheus was not idly made. From the initial industry grew such an ingrained practice that whenever Browning thinks of Power, Strength, Weakness, his mind automatically casts up corresponding clusters of scriptural words or phrases as quickly as it casts up words from Shelley. His compulsive mastery of the language of the Scriptures and Christian apologetics was thus so nearly complete that probably not even he knew the control it exercised over his expression.

Whatever the degree or quality of human weakness espoused by Paracelsus, its misuse is not man's but Jehovah's fault, originating in his restraint which imposes discouragement and inactivity on the spirit of most human beings, worldly ambition on the spiritually talented few and physical deterioration too soon on Paracelsus' fierce spiritual energy. In Paracelsus' case, however, as in those of Sordello and Pauline's lover, Weakness is preferable to Strength, since the weakness of all three is evolvable into strength by a unique "tendency to God":

Imperfect qualities throughout creation,   (5.688)
Suggesting some one creature yet to make,
Some *point* where all those scattered *rays* should meet   (PU 3.3.41-53)
Convergent in the faculties of *man*.   (Q Mab 6.101-2; PU 1.657-62)
Power — neither put forth blindly, nor controlled
*Calm*ly by perfect knowledge; to be used   (Alastor 643)
At risk, inspired or *checked* by hope and fear: (PU 1.125-7)
Knowledge — not intuition, but the slow   (PU 1.542-5)
Uncertain *fruit* of an enhancing toil   (PU 3.3.140)
Strengthened by love: love — not *serenely* pure,   (PU 4.354; 3.3.133)
But strong from weakness, . . .
For these things tend still upward, *progress is*   (PU 4.332-423)
The law of life, man is not Man as yet. . . .   (PU 4.382-423)
But when full roused, each giant-limb awake, . . .   (5.762)
He shall start up and stand on *his own earth,* . . .   (5.764)
What he achieves shall be set down *to him.*   (5.767)
When all the race is perfected alike
As man, that is; all tended to mankind,
And, man produced, all has its end thus far:
But in *completed* man begins anew
A tendency *to God.*   (to divinity)

By writing discerningly on evolutionary theory while ex-

ploiting two key passages from Shelley, Browning successfully conceals his dependence upon both THE EARTH's
restored cave (PU 3.3.124-47), where maddening vapors have
been changed to benevolent vapors by Jupiter's fall, and
Shelley's climactic eulogy: "Man ... a chain of linkéd
thought, / Of *love and might* to be divided not, / Compelling
the elements with adamantine stress." Sufficiently compelling that "the abyss shouts from her depth laid bare, / Heaven,
hast thou secrets? Man unveils me; I have none." Despite his
vicissitudes Paracelsus may count on the replacement of
Jupiter's (Jehovah's) hatred (PU 4.349) by Prometheus' love
(PU 4.410, 557-61) in the new day to rise. Progress, which
Paracelsus calls the law of life, springs from the power,
knowledge and love of man as Shelley's perfectability springs
from the freedom, power and love of the Mind. So Paracelsus
argues informatively with Shelley that man's completion is
inevitable, since his perfection is neither a gift from Jehovah
nor by a light from without but a gradual discovery of the
truth within himself.

As for a tendency to God, Paracelsus knows that talented
men begin to pass their nature's bound, finding new hopes
and cares to supplant their former joys and griefs. They grow
too great for narrow creeds of right and wrong, which fade
before the unmeasured thirst for good. Thus they live
serenely at peace amid the half-formed creatures round about
"who should be saved by them and joined with them":

Such was my task, and I was *born* to it —	(birthright, seal; 5.786)
Free, as I said but now, from much that *chains*	(Q Mab 5.131)
Spirits, high-dowered but limited and vexed	
By a *divided and delusive aim*,	(joys & griefs)
A *shadow* mocking a reality	(Jehovah, Col 2.17, Heb 8.5, 10.1)
Whose truth avails not wholly to disperse	
The flitting *mimic* called up by itself	(Jehovah; PU 3.4.191)
And so remains *perplexed* and nigh put out	(2 Cor 4.8)
By its fantastic fellow's *wavering* gleam.	(Pauline 1018)
I, from the first, was never cheated thus;	(graphic)
I never *fashioned* out a fancied *good*	(for Jehovah)
Distinct from man's; a service to be done,	("finding they are one,"
A glory to be ministered unto	1.790; St. Paul)
With *powers* put forth at man's expense, withdrawn	(Jehovah's)

From *laboring* in his behalf; a strength   (St. Paul)
Denied that might avail *him*. I cared not   (Man)
Lest *his* success ran counter to success   (Man's)
Elsewhere: For God is glorified in man.   (Jehovah's)
And to man's glory vowed I soul and limb. . . .   (*Pauline* 425)
              I saw no cause why man   (5.815)
Should not stand *all-sufficient* even now.

Too many parallels in diction with reversal in thought exist between this quotation and St. Paul's epistles for each to be noted, but the poetic Paracelsus, like his creator, seems infuriated by St. Paul's attack on belief in elemental spirits in Colossians 2. "A *shadow* [Jehovah] mocking a reality" was probably inspired therefore by the most fervent of St. Paul's warnings against beguilement by philosophy and human speculation, that is, against pagan mystery cults. Let no man judge you in meat or drink, or in respect to holidays, new moons or the sabbath, St. Paul writes, for these "are a *shadow* of things to come; . . . the body is of Christ," "in whom are hid all the treasures of wisdom and knowledge." But since Paracelsus is adamantly opposed to laws of any kind, especially laws of Jehovah, Browning could easily have favored Hebrews 8.5 in which priests "serve unto the example and *shadow* of heavenly things" or 10.1 in which "the *law* having a *shadow* of good things to come, and not the very image" cannot make man perfect. Non-scriptural and confirmed in *La Saisiaz* (153), "flitting mimic [Jehovah]" is simply another way of saying shadow. And as shadow and mimic reinforce each other in belittlement of Jehovah, "fashioned out a fancied good [for Jehovah]" desecrates such passages as Job 10.8, 31.15; 1 Corinthians 7.31; and Philippians 2.8, 3.21, the last of which runs "Who shall change our vile body, that it may be *fashioned* like unto [Christ's] glorious body."

Paracelsus spurns all efforts at and results from Glory, Service, Ministration and Sufficiency which are not directly beneficial to man's advancement and glory, and for the third time reasserts it is enough that "God is glorified in man." For St. Paul the same cluster of words is substantive to 2 Corinthians as well as consonant with all the epistles, and that substance is dedicated to Jehovah and his divine purpose. Browning may have been thinking of 2 Corinthians 9.12-3 where all four thoughts are clustered, but "he that glorieth, let him *glory* in the Lord" (10.17) and "who also hath made us able *ministers* of the new testament" (3.6) would have been more than enough to set Paracelsus off. Twenty-two times in 2 Corinthians St. Paul employs the word Minister or a variant to fashion out a Good for a beneficient Jehovah, who according to the opposite-thinking Paracelsus uncaringly preempts power and strength rightfully due to man. How then could Browning's Paracelsus be expected to countenance with less than contempt St. Paul's "Not that we are sufficient of ourselves ... but our sufficiency is of God" (2 Cor 3.5) or Christ's "My grace is sufficient for thee" of the pivotal Corinthians quotation?

Poetic confrontation so spirited, when the historical Paracelsus was an individual whom not even the Reformation could dislodge from the Roman Catholic Church, is inescapably indicative of deep-seated disapproval of Jehovah in Browning's nature. In saying that he "saw no cause why man / Should not stand all-sufficient now" Paracelsus repeats his insistence upon self-sufficiency for the fourth time, that is, whenever will, power, love, knowledge, wisdom, strength and weakness are activated. Almost as if in defiance of St. Paul's warning against meddling with, as if in competition with St. Paul's success in understanding, "the *mystery* of God," Paracelsus departs not to possess the world but to possess a Star (1.66)! What else, if further proof were missing, can Star signify than still greater divinity than he already possesses, when Paracelsus' "aim's extent" is "to comprehend the works of God, / *And God himself*, and all God's intercourse / With the human *mind*" (1.533-5)? That Browning's Paracelsus berates a divine power for frustrating man's upward climb, one in which heaven and earth are at stake (1.98); that Spirits, perhaps Jehovah among them, initially encourage Paracelsus to shun material and seek spiritual power (3.794); that Paracelsus persists in believing that his birth-

right, seal and fierce energy assure him full access to knowledge and power (3.679-719); that Shelleyan Love (Aprile's),
superior to power, knowledge and truth, is recognized in
theory if not in practice by Paracelsus; that Paracelsus' aspiring is not different from that of Jehovah's Christians, except
that theirs is a hopeless dream (1.795); and that his subtle
warfare for Prometheus will sooner or later take effect, in
spite of the Christian obtuseness (3.880-948) — all these
beliefs and arguments seem deliberately marshalled against a
primary scriptural promise which culminates in "My grace is
sufficient for thee: my strength is made perfect in weakness."

Few if any other secular poets have employed prayer as
often as Browning, and the talent exhibits sharp refinement
in *Paracelsus* where convincing-like prayers are much less
forced and naive than in the oft-quoted and suspicious lines
of *Pauline*. Paracelsus is inclined to begin:

If thou shalt please, dear *God*, if thou shalt please! (Prometheus; 5.258)
We are so *weak*, we know our motives least   (double talk)
In their confused beginning. If at first
I sought . . . but wherefore bare my heart to thee   (R.B.'s ellipsis)
I know *thy* mercy; and already thoughts   (Prometheus')
Flock fast about my soul to comfort it,   (Ode W Wind 11, 63)
And intimate I cannot *wholly* fail,   (not even Guido wholly fails)
For love and praise would clasp me willingly   (double entente)
Could I resolve to seek them. Thou art *good*,   ("good," PU 1.143, 360)
And I should be content. Yet — yet first *show*   ("shew," Job 10.1)
I have done wrong in daring! Rather give   (ameliorative)
The supernatural consciousness of strength
Which fed my youth. Only one hour of that
With *thee* to help — O what should *bar* me then!   (Prometheus; from
                                            wisdom & divinity, PU 2.3.59)

Lost, lost! Thus things are ordered here! *God's* creatures,
And yet *he* takes no pride in us! — none, none!   (must be Jehovah)
Truly there needs *another life to come!* (yet unevolved in "new creed")
If this be all — (I must tell Festus that)
And other life await us not — for one,
I say 't is a poor cheat, a stupid bungle,
A wretched failure. I, for one, protest
Against it, and I hurl it back with scorn.   (graphic)

Like Browning's Johannes Agricola of the same vintage, Paracelsus does not hesitate to proclaim his intimacy with

Prometheus under the guise of GOD. Nor does Paracelsus require Browning's pretentious quoting from Defoe's *Dictionary of All Religions* to help camouflage a most compact Promethean confessional by Agricola under a supposed parody of Antinomianism as he moves without pause from prayer to Prometheus (GOD) to protest against Jehovah (GOD). Prometheus, who fed Paracelsus' youth with supernatural consciousness of strength, would encircle him even now with love and praise, were Paracelsus not so overly zealous to KNOW, thus neglectful of the more essential traits of Love and Beauty which inspire self-sacrifice. Because Jehovah, who created Paracelsus, takes no pride in his creatures, an alternative for this wretched life was unprovided. Therefore if he cannot have his "great approval" (5.244) here and now — a continuing thought which takes precedence over the expressed desire to know whether as a perfect human being he would be permitted to live on earth or be translated to heaven — Paracelsus wants a second life. And if he cannot have it, he scornfully hurls the first life back to Jehovah. It sounds very much like the youthful Shelley, whose influence may be spotted visually not far from the opening of Paracelsus' prayer: "Cruel! I seek her [Michal, sweet human love] now — I kneel — I shriek — / I clasp her vesture" (5.213-4).

When Paracelsus calls Festus to Colmar to tell him that he has been cast off by the University and will once more aspire (4.48), Festus is transported with joy. "But your plans, your plans! / I have yet to learn your purpose, Aureole!" (4.155-6). Then shocked by Paracelsus' strange indifference and unexpected acceptance of normal means of striving, Festus rebukes his friend, "Your aims? the aims? — to know? and where is found / The early trust . . ." (4.181-2). Filling in the ellipsis Paracelsus explains, "Nay, not so fast; I say, the aims — not the old means." The old means had made him a laughingstock and, in spite of their unparalleled beauty, were dreams which should be permitted to vanish. This time Paracelsus seeks *to know and to enjoy* (4.240); his *soul* can then *die* and not be taunted with "What was gained?" He will fight the battle out though a little spent (4.269), for he can "turn even *weakness* to account." Warned however by Festus that the delights he places above his nobler aims will never satisfy him, Paracelsus admits that his design to storm the citadel of Spirituality was doomed to failure but insists that his "fluttering pulse" gives proof that GOD still means good to him and will make his cause his own (4.401). Therefore he now rejects the remorseless care "which *clogged* [PU 3.4.202] a spirit born to soar so free" and resolves that his *dim chamber* (Alastor 632) shall become a tent, that is, a waiting place. Festus understands and adds, "It seems, then, you expect to reap / No *unreal* joy from this your present course, / But rather . . ." (4.413-5). Again filling in the ellipsis, Paracelsus agrees that he aspires for "Death! To die! I owe that much / To what, at least, I was."

Read rapidly the above scene might not tax the reader's credulity, but it is clearly evident that Festus is again playing the foil to Paracelsus, this time in a complete reversal of the caution and daring displayed in the first aspiring. Then, Festus advised moderation, not rashness; now, he interposes, "You have never mused and said, 'I had a noble purpose, and the strength / To compass it; but I have stopped half-way?'" Whereupon Paracelsus recounts "the sad rhyme of the men who proudly *clung* [R of Islam 2.21, 11.8] / To their first fault, and *withered* [R of Islam, ded, 6.8] in their pride" (4.526-7). Even more emotionally distraught, Festus cries out, "Come back then, Aureole; as you fear God, come! / This is *foul sin* [Eug Hills 192]; come back!" But of course Browning's plan is so to confuse the reader with talk about penance due in Christianity, when penance is unheard of in Prometheanism, that he will be distracted from Festus' plea to come back to wholehearted service of Prometheus. For both men know that the true Promethean looks upon Death as the ultimate human attainment and the point of reunion with Prometheus at which further "clogging" by the flesh is impossible. To Paracelsus and Festus the last aspiration is the noblest, as is Childe Roland's plunge into the grotesque land of the Dark Tower:

Yet acquiescingly   (15)

I did turn as he *pointed:* neither pride   (Shelleyan)
Nor hope *rekindling* at the end descried,   (Shelleyan)
  So much as *gladness* that some end might be.

For, what with my whole world-wide *wandering,*
  What with my search drawn out thro' years, my hope
  Dwindled into a *ghost* not fit to *cope*
With that obstreperous joy success would bring,
I hardly tried now to rebuke the *spring*
  My heart made, finding failure in its *scope.*

Very much in conformity with Shelley's metaphysics, including an excessive number of Shelley's favorite words, Browning plays out the whole scene for Paracelsus and Roland in THE EARTH's promise that Death is a mere veil between the existence man is forced to endure in the flesh and a true Life beyond (PU 3.3.110-24). So when he wishes to detract attention from the joyousness of Paracelsus' imminent attainment — the only other attainment in *Paracelsus* being the death of Aprile — Browning belatedly allows Festus to announce Michal's death and inserts Paracelsus' stuporous response: "I think the soul can never / Taste death" (4.678-9). Yet the obvious joy in Aprile's death and the anticipation of Paracelsus' death cannot be disguised any more than the insinuation that Paracelsus and Aprile are representative of Browning and Shelley and their lasting bond of brotherhood. In and out of his stupor as quickly as he forgets about Michal, Paracelsus exclaims, "Away, away! / Have your *will,* rabble! While we fight the prize [Q Mab 9.1-11] , / Troop you [Christian bigots] in safety to the snug backseats / And leave a clear arena for the brave / About to perish for your sport! — *Behold!*" That is, *behold* my brave passage through Death into Life. For it is Demogorgon who answers "Behold!" when Asia, knowing only that "Prometheus shall arise / Henceforth *the sun* of this rejoicing world," asks when the destined hour of the Golden Age will arrive (PU 2.4. 126-9). Not one of the poet's more subtle moves, Browning must have felt secure in Shelley's exploitation of St. John's Revelation to the extent that exultation in death scarcely

differs between extreme Christian and Promethean. No doubt
this verbal similarity also explains the frankness Browning
dares to display in Paracelsus' conclusion on what is truly
significant in this life:

<pre>
                  — *myself*   (self-consciousness; 5.495)
A careless looker-on and nothing more,
Indifferent and amused, but nothing more.
And this is *death:* I understand it all.
New being waits me; *new perceptions* must   (Shelleyan)
Be born in me before I plunge therein;
Which last is Death's affair; and while I speak,
Minute by minute *he* is filling me   (Prometheus)
With *power;* and while my foot is on the threshold
Of boundless life — the doors unopened yet,
I turn *new knowledge* upon old events,   (cf., 1.372-80)
And the effect is . . . but I must not tell: (R.B.'s ellipsis)
It is *not lawful. . . .*   (2 Cor 12.4)

                  What's *life* to me?   (on earth; 5.512)
Where'er I *look* is fire, where'er I listen   (now that all's spirit)
Music, and where I tend *bliss* evermore.   (Q Mab 9.213-7)
Yet how can I refrain? 'T is a refined
Delight to view those *chances,* — one last view.   (PU 2.2.92, 2.4.119)
I am so near the *perils I escape,*   (Jehovah's sorrows & pains)
That I must play with them and turn them over,
To *feel* how fully they are past and gone.
Still, it is like, some further cause exists
For this peculiar mood — *some hidden purpose;* . . .   (R of Islam 7.28)

Ha, the *purpose:* the true purpose: that is it!   (5.540)
How could I fail to apprehend! You here,
I thus! *But no more trifling:* I see all,   (Calderon 1.175)
I know all: *my last mission* shall be done   (to oppose Jehovah)
If strength suffice. *No trifling!* Stay; this posture
Hardly befits one thus about to speak:
I will arise.
</pre>

As Paracelsus wilfully rises from his deathbed to reiterate
his opposition to Jehovah's purpose of making man "for
weakness, and should wait / In patient ignorance, till God
appoint" (5.538-9), so Paracelsus will rise from death to Life
with God's lamp [Prometheus' lamp] pressed close to his
breast, that is, with the emblem of Prometheus' followers
(PU 3.3.170; Q Mab ded. 13). He joyously bids the walls be

consecrate, the wretched cell become a shrine, and to Festus' question on his happiest moment Paracelsus evinces no doubt in replying, "When but the time I *vowed myself* to man ['s freedom]" (5.597). As at first he was the One who should animate the race so long weighed down and forgotten with new hopes, new light and new revealings (1.369-80), so now he is the one with new being, new perceptions and new knowledge to validate his great commission:

```
Doubtless a searching and impetuous soul              (5.601)
Might learn from its own motions that some task
Like this awaited it about the world;
Might seek some where in this blank life of ours
For fit delights to stay its longings vast;      (Q  Mab 5.137-9)
And, grappling Nature, so prevail on her
To fill the creature full she dared thus frame
Hungry for joy; and, bravely tyrannous,      (Q Mab 9.146, 189)
Grow in demand, still craving more and more,
And make each joy conceded prove a pledge
Of other joy to follow — bating naught
Of its desires, still seizing fresh pretence
To turn the knowledge and the rapture wrung
As an extreme, last boon, from destiny,
Into occasion for new covetings,          (R of Islam 2095, satiety)
New strifes, new triumphs: . . .                   (Progress)
But this was born in me; I was made so; . . .          (5.621)
              — not to idly gaze, but cast          (5.633)
Light on a darkling race; . . .
I stood at first where all aspire at last          (5.635)
To stand: the secret of the world was mine.      (R of Islam 1.35)
```

And this was Paracelsus, as he passed into Promethean bliss "hand in hand with you, Aprile!" Browning was especially careful to disguise the animadversions of ancient Celsus for Christianity in the emotionalism of Paracelsus. But Browning (or Shelley) never forgot this Man of the World whose *True Word* anticipates the classic objections to Jesus Christ: divine dignity vs. the absurdity of Incarnation of God; intellectual integrity (elect soul) vs. ignorance; enlightened Mystery masters vs. hell-threatening Christians; purified monotheism with regional gods and demons vs. Jehovah's "chosen

people"; education and purity from the cradle vs. divisive
appeals to the incurable vulgar, barbaric masses; Empire vs.
illicit collegium.

CHRISTMAS-EVE AND EASTER-DAY
1850

Paracelsus was composed between the earliest and latest composition of *Sordello; Christmas-Eve and Easter-Day* was composed between the completed *Sordello* and fragment "Saul" and the completed "Saul." And it is now obvious that the painstaking speculation on Browning's most enigmatic popular poem would have been more rewarding if it had been directed at why he composed in this manner. Scarcely two interpreters agree on the meaning of either "Christmas-Eve" or "Easter-Day," but individuals who suspect Browning's loyalty to Christianity are most likely to depend upon arguments supplied by these two poems in one. Those who accept Browning essentially as a Christian are still less than sure of the intent of the vacillations in "Christmas-Eve," but they are usually willing to take the narrator's apparent choice as the form of worship Browning personally preferred. Yet, even though the narrator would give the impression of speaking objectively about the simplicity and earnestness of the Nonconformists, the intelligent love of the Roman Catholics and the search for truth of the rationalist, it only seems, because it should, that the narrator's (Browning's) sympathy falls on one of these forms. For the narrator quite frankly states and restates a preference for worship outside all forms of organized religion:

With this sky of thine, that I now walk under,	(C-Eve 370)
And *glory* in thee for, as I gaze	(*for* sky)
Thus, thus! Oh, let men keep their ways	(PU 1.105, Sord 2.424)
Of seeking thee in a *narrow shrine* —	(church or place of worship)
Be this my way [under Nature's sky]! And this *is* mine!	(graphic)

Free of admitted levity (1346) if not of the doggerel and flippancy with which the poem has often been charged, this passage is spoken by a narrator identified by many critics as the poet himself. If Browning is then speaking through a mask, means should not lie far away in the progression of his poetic thought to reconfirm the avowal in *Pauline* of resorting to "wit, mockery, light-heartedness" in his warfare with Jehovah. Probably the most direct means is in the four-times refurbished *Sordello* (1840), the third narrative part of which (or at least the digression therein) is definitely Browning's own commentary. For here the poet addresses a eulogy to Walter Savage Landor, whose acquaintance he made (1836) after the publication of *Paracelsus* (1835), whose sonnet favorably comparing Browning with Chaucer appeared in 1846, and whose pagan attitude gives broader perspective to the thought:

So, to *our business now,* — the *fate* of such	(Sord 3.975)
As find *our common nature* — overmuch	("business," Cenci 2.2.57,
Despised because restricted and unfit	Gisb 163, 249, Islam 3796,
	Hellas 908)
To bear the *burthen they impose on it* —	(religious restrictions)
Cling when they would discard it; craving *strength* [instead	
of employing *weakness*]	
To leap from the allotted world, at length	("cling, leap," Shelleyan)
They do leap, — *flounder* without a term,	
Each a *god's germ, doomed* to remain a germ	(Q Mab 5.147; fated)
In unexpanded *infancy,* unless . . .	(PU 2.5.102; R.B.'s ellipsis)
But that's the story — dull enough, confess!	("unexpanded," Deject 6)

The "business" about which Browning here speaks without a mask is the hopeless fate of individuals who impose upon their restricted and unfit nature the burdensome worship of Jehovah with expectation of future reward. Moreover, this business follows indistinguishably close on earlier business of pitying "warped souls and bodies" (3.781), "Love triumphed o'er / And sad" (3.903-4); of denouncing "Evil, the *scheme* by which, thro' *Ignorance,* / Good labors to exist" (3.803-4); and of advising "Attack / The *use and purpose* of such sights" (3.916-7), *gain* "The water of life" (3.811). That is, the water of Meribah "where the children of Israel *strove* with the Lord" (Nu 22.13), the water Moses disobediently smote (3.826) from the desert rock and thereby forfeited the Promised Land. "Meribah!" Browning exclaims; "then quaffing at the fount *my courage gained,* / Recall — *not that*

I prompt ye — who explained . . ." (R.B.'s ellipsis; 3.830-2). Remindful of "let me strive / To find [our best way of worship] , and when found, *contrive* / My fellows also take their share! / This constitutes my earthly care" (C-Eve 1171-4), the proselytical zeal of Browning's avowal is reinforced by a self-imposed courage which is fundamental to Shelleyan strategy.

Then, seemingly as abrupt and disjointed as before but really in keeping with the developing prompting, Browning turns to the *withholder* of the water, Jehovah, who only pretends to be constructing an "engine" or orderly earth, since its sole workable wheels (PU 1.141) are a tantalizing alternation of joy and sorrow, reward and punishment: "We watch construct, / In short, an *engine:* . . . and, while you turn upon your heel, / Pray that I be not busy slitting steel / Or shredding brass, *camped on some virgin shore / Under a cluster of fresh stars*, before / I name a tithe o' the wheels [PU 4.214, 274] I trust to do!" (3.840-61). Taking "wheels" from Shelley who took them from Ezekiel 1 and 10, Browning is also thinking of Shelley's isles and stars and Prometheus' fire which made steel and brass possible. Henceforth, as earlier in *Paracelsus* and *Sordello*, engine or machine will consistently symbolize Jehovah's unjust and tricky plan, eventually becoming "machinery of sin and sorrow" in *The Ring and the Book* ("enginery," Gisb 107: Aristoph 76, Avison 154). So the uniformity and persistency of Browning's poetic thought between *Paracelsus* and "Christmas-Eve" involve more than just a proper place of worship, if that were ever his design. Indeed the fundamental thought of his poetry — Jehovah's injustice, parsimony, insecurity and spitefulness — is so rapidly becoming routine that only the cumulative variations seem noteworthy, as a miserly Jehovah who withholds the water of life and a Setebos-like God who spitefully jostles men between joy and sorrow is merged into the famous Landor eulogy:

<pre>
          Meanwhile where's the hurt   (3.927)
Of keeping the *Makers*-see on the alert,   (Job, Psalms & Shelley)
</pre>

At *whose defection* mortals starve aghast
As though heaven's bounteous windows were slammed fast
Incontinent?

And as if to assure Landor that the courage needed for such a vigilance is not lacking in Browning's plan, a pagan hierarchy is invoked. No less determined than Hercules who, with the aid of the demigod, slew the hundred would-be slayers in Egypt (3.939), Browning will seize the chance of thwarting whatever the Makers-see devises. To placate any who may have been offended unavoidably by his daring, however, Browning tells his "gentle audience" that he means no "affront" to them or danger to their brow-worn "chaplet" (Q Mab 9.116).

Thus *Christmas-Eve and Easter-Day* may be Browning's most pertinacious effort to pit the Mind against Faith, his most determined attack on the simple ones who renounce the *World* of Prometheus for such an impossible fabrication as Jehovah's heaven. Though never neglectful of the power of the obvious to mislead or to lull into indifference, Browning is here especially adept at balancing countless familiar scriptural references, all of which are scoffed at, with parallel Shelleyan adoptions which confirm his disbelief in the slavish promises of Christ. For example, the poet's "revulsion" to Christian "hopes and fears" is balanced with Shelley's "as the star of Death / And Birth is worshipped by those sisters wild / Called Hope and Fear — upon the heart are piled / Their offerings, — of this sacrifice divine / A *World* shall be the altar." And its adoption is verified in the context, for it is here that Browning found the essence of Shelley's philosophical idealism and his own opportunity to declare for a Promethean World. But the more interesting fact is Browning's fear of detection, as witnessed by his deceitful change of *repulsion* (Epipsy 371) to *revulsion* (E-Day 293). So it may be seen that when Browning exploits the most obvious scriptural allusions or the crudest humor he is also scheming at a higher intellectual level. Otherwise the context of "condiment" (E-Day 337) is an insult to the Mind. And this is disproved by the contextual light of lines 1642-48 of *Fifine at the Fair.*

"Christmas-Eve"

Given the cumulative expression of disagreement with St. Paul and disapproval of Jehovah in Browning's early poetry, it seems pointless to enter a debate over whether the poet forthrightly resolves to speak in his own voice in "Christmas-Eve" or continues to employ an imaginary narrator. The only convincing argument against making the voice Browning's is that the narrator is considered too conceited and hypocritical to be Browning himself. But with the secrecy of his purpose suspected or known, this judgment would ignore the significance of Browning's self-awareness and the avowed intent of being witty, mocking and lighthearted in self-defense. The mask or something like it Browning surely continues to impose though more loosely, especially in the so-called religious poetry, and unconvinced individuals will have to decide how willing they are to contend with quotes within quotes within quotes, thoughts within thoughts within thoughts. But that Browning strove, with a purpose, to conceal or confuse through indirectness of thought as well as through excessive use of dashes, parentheses, colons and exclamation or question marks is not a mystery. That he deliberately obscured some matters to give the impression of objectivity and to gain an unknown end is not so well known but hardly new. The newness is that without Jehovah as permanent adversary, the obscurity and prolixity intermingled with Browning's oft-lucid verse virtually disappears. Hence in the ongoing essay, even though the epithet will be used to honor the debate, "narrator" symbolizes little more than "mask" until it becomes fruitless to continue the charade. A congenital polemicist who did not hold the intellect of his Christian fellow men in high esteem, Browning records too consistently and too prevalently strife with Jehovah and scriptural thought to be exonerated on artistic and dramatic grounds. His deceptions, as evidenced by increasing irritation and animosity, lend stronger and stronger credence to the reality of a lifetime opposition, not to Christianity which Browning openly discounted but to Jehovah's being God the Father Almighty.

As the heart of "Easter-Day" lies paradoxically in the scene of the Last Judgment rather than in Christ's resurrection, so the heart of "Christmas-Eve" lies paradoxically in the narrator's comments on the speech of a rationalistic professor rather than in Christ's birth. "Christmas-Eve," which is neither so frankly candid nor so readily explicated as the Landor lines quoted from *Sordello*, embodies other obstacles which have long seemed insuperable to clear understanding and objective appraisal. For example, the poem is entrenched in many minds as a reconfirmation of Browning's Christian faith in the midst of a doctrinal upheaval caused by the Higher Criticism, and it is most unlikely to be abandoned soon because of its Christian setting and calculated celebration. Yet for all its implied and real difficulty, including a negative response to Christianity which persistent critics impute to the poem, "Christmas-Eve" remains crucial in the unravelling of Browning's poetic thought and of his personal thought too if the poem confirms in unaltered language and unaltered thought the attitudes toward Jehovah of his earlier poetry. Fortunately the narration of the poem is enlightened by a more visible and intelligible alter ego to the narrator than is that of *Paracelsus* and *Sordello*. It would have been unconvincing to deny full dramatic license to Paracelsus and Sordello before showing that their thought on God is exactly the same; and it would be unconvincing to deny dramatic license to the professor of Göttingen before showing that the narrator's comments on his thought are exactly the same as Paracelsus' and Sordello's. The Professor is the only vocal proponent in "Christmas-Eve" and rationalism is the only subject with its own private advocate. Since Catholicism and Protestantism must depend for their representation upon the wishes of the narrator alone, the favored treatment of rationalism invites closer attention. And in that "Christmas-Eve" also marks a decided advance in Browning's technique at manipulation — wrong speaker for right speech, right speaker for wrong speech (God's special pleading against himself), extraneous additions and distracting observations, incoherent single-line sentences, punctuation distortions, and subtle and graphic authorial intrusions — the single most effective of the duplicities should be pointed out first. Tucked in at the very end of "Christmas-Eve," after a ubiquitous dash, is the narrator's final adjudication, and it seems to say unequivocally that he chooses the Dissenting group of Christians with whom to worship. Yet the well-positioned "I choose here" (1341), which has accordingly attracted wide attention, may refer not to what is stated below — Nonconformist worship — but to what is stated above, "May Christ [Prometheus] do for [the rationalist] what no mere man shall, / And *stand confessed as the God of salvation!* . . . I praise the heart and pity the head of him, / And refer *myself* to THEE [Prometheus] instead of him [Jehovah], / Who head and heart alike discernest." For just forty lines earlier the narrator says:

I then, *in* ignorance and weakness,	(in the midst of; 1301)
Taking God's help, have attained to think	(as do Paracelsus & Sordello)
My heart does best to receive in *meekness*	(PU 2.3.94)
That mode of worship, as most to *his* mind,	(Prometheus)
Where earthly *aids* being cast behind,	(churches)
His *All in All* appears serene	(double entente)
With the *thinnest veil* between	(no intermediary)
Letting the mystic lamps, *the seven*,	(Rev 4.5)
The motions of his *spirit*	(Jehovah's)
Pass, as they *list*, to earth from heaven.	

Unfeigned Nature-worship, the narrator's confession would disguise the rejection of Jehovah in a double entente. As the passage fails to reveal a respectful attitude toward the Christian God, so do the lines which are intended to convey "ignorance and weakness" in the Christian sense actually convey the ignorance and weakness of his Christian countrymen. When Browning permits the narrator's heart to divine what most pleases God's mind, he is no less cynical of the import that when he adds as superscription to "Caliban upon Setebos" "Thou thoughtest that I was altogether such a one as thyself" (Ps 50.21). By a reader like Landor, Browning expected the flippancy of "His All in All" (Nature) to be enjoyed along with the humorous splintering of Jehovah's unity into seven "listing" spirits. One of his four emphatic confessions of pantheistic faith, these lines exclude the narrator from organized Christian worship and seriously challenge his sincerity toward Jehovah whom, like Paracelsus, he is nonetheless always willing to thank for providing him Nature.

Only ostensibly is Browning's narrator in greater disagreement with the rationalistic professor than with the vulgar Protestant or presumptuous Catholic worshipers. He takes the normal Christian umbrage at learning's conceit, scolding the university wit who would find in Christ "A Man! — a right true man" and then merely praise a not uncommon intellect (914) and morality (1030), instead of suspecting that Christ "was also one with the creator" (925) as are all men according to Shelley:

<table>
<tr><td>Make that Creator which was creature?</td><td>(Saul 268, Pillar 132,</td></tr>
<tr><td>Multiply gifts upon man's head,</td><td>Fust 281; 1005)</td></tr>
<tr><td>And what, when all's done, shall be said</td><td></td></tr>
<tr><td>But — the more gifted he, I ween.</td><td>(Devil 29.3)</td></tr>
<tr><td>   That one's made Christ, this other, Pilate,</td><td></td></tr>
<tr><td>And this might be all that has been, —</td><td></td></tr>
<tr><td>   So what is there to frown or smile at?</td><td></td></tr>
<tr><td>What is left for us, save, in growth</td><td>(from Jehovah)</td></tr>
<tr><td>Of soul, to rise up, far past both</td><td>(Christ & Pilate)</td></tr>
<tr><td>From the gift looking to the giver,</td><td></td></tr>
<tr><td>And from the cistern to the river,</td><td></td></tr>
<tr><td>And from the finite to infinity</td><td></td></tr>
<tr><td>And from man's dust to God's infinity?</td><td>("Man, one harmonious soul</td></tr>
</table>

of many a soul, / Whose nature is its own divine control, / *Where all things flow to all, as rivers to the sea,"* PU 4.400-2; even Shelley's pattern of indentation is emulated by Browning.)

As Paracelsus earlier says of the act of aspiring, "See if we cannot beat thine angels yet" (1.784), Browning's narrator now says of the spiritually adept, they may rise far above Christ. Nor is the Gift to be attributed to the Strength of the Giver, as St. Paul repeatedly urges, but to the Weakness (spiritual potential) of the adept, now rightfully, solely possessed and capable of unlimited "growth / Of soul" when fully vitalized and free from hindrance. For Paracelsus and the narrator the process of attainment comes out the same:

one believes that "the truth in God's breast / Lies *trace for trace* upon ours impressed" (1018-9); the other believes that "there is an *inmost centre* in us all, / Where truth abides in fulness" (3.691-2). As innocent- and faithful-sounding as an anaphora by Christopher Smart, the concluding four lines on infinity repeat the belief of Paracelsus and David that they have the spiritual quality to become gods in their own right: Paracelsus, "Taking my natural station . . . / — And in my elevation man's would be" (4.299-301); David, "God's throne from man's grave" (Saul 198). The narrator's quarrel with the Göttingen professor then is not at all that divinity and sonship have been taken from Christ but that in the rationalistic approach divinity has been denied to man altogether. The rationalist's residuum is only:

<pre>
A Man! — a right true man, however,   (878)
Whose work was worthy a man's *endeavor:*   (Ode to Liberty 243)
Work, that gave *warrant* almost *sufficient*   (St. Paul's words)
    To his disciples, for *rather* believing
He was *just* omnipotent and omniscient,
    As it gives to us, for as frankly receiving
His word, their tradition, — which, though it meant
Something entirely different
From all that those who only *heard* it,   ("averred," Epipsy 126-7)
In their *simplicity* thought and averred it,   (2 Cor 1.12, 11.3)
Had yet a *meaning* quite as respectable: (divine nature)
For, among other *doctrines delectable,*   (levity)
Was *he* not surely the *first* to insist on   (Christ; irony)
    The natural sovereignty of our race?   ("sovereign sway," PU 4.411)
</pre>

Disguised as a praiseworthy quality in Christ's disciples, "simplicity" here as elsewhere in Browning's poetry designates ignorance, diminution of one's birthright and the poet's strongest annoyance with St. Paul: "For our rejoicing is this . . . that in simplicity and godly sincerity, not with fleshly *wisdom*"; "But I fear . . . so your *minds,* should be corrupted from the simplicity that is in Christ." One of the best examples of Browning's talent at interlarding nonsense with sense, this narration runs on to individuals other than Christ who also have possessed superior intellects as their accomplishments attest, individuals who also have devised moral systems of no less worth than Christ's. Yet in personal limitations they all, including Christ, fall short of the absolute truth which lies within each man's breast. So from John and Paul and Peter down to you and me if we become his followers, the narrator complains, we are then merely "sheep of a good man" (949) when we could be Christ's equal or superior:

The *goodness*, — how did *he* acquire it?   (Christ; 950)
Was it *self-gained*, did God *inspire* it?
Choose which; then tell me, on what ground
Should its possessor *dare* propound   (St. Paul & Shelley)
His claim to rise o'er us *an inch?*

Browning paces the deception with the increasing courage of the narrator. What reader would think to be diverted from the subject "goodness" by the little word "dare"? Yet Jesus' daring to be the Christ and man's daring to accept him as Christ is the inescapable theme of the New Testament. Again, who would be suspicious enough of Robert Browning, who had promised a gift book and sent it to London from Italy with the expectation that it would be published for the 1850 Easter celebration, to check with Romans 5.6-8?

For when we were yet without *strength*, in due time Christ died for the ungodly.

For scarcely for a righteous man will one die; yet peradventure for a good man some would even *dare to die.*

But God commendeth his love toward us, in that, while we were yet sinners, Christ died for us.

Unfearful of a doctrinal interruption, because of the "simplicity" of Christ's followers, Browning unobtrusively dispenses with the Professor to permit the narrator to ask: Does Christ's precept run "believe in good, / In justice, truth, now understood / *For the first time*" or "believe in *me*, / Who lived and died, yet *essentially* / Am the Lord of Life"? (1052). And if such heretical question be asked, can Shelley's phraseology be far behind: "He [Prometheus] who taught men to vanquish whatsoever / Can be between the cradle and the grave / Crowned him the *King of Life*. Oh, vain endeavor! / If on his own *high will*, a willing slave, / He has enthroned the oppression and the oppressor" (Ode to Liberty 241-3)? As Christ earlier was the "God of salvation," a phrase which reverses the Christian concept of Grace, so now Christ is *essentially Lord* (King) *of Life*, a euphemism which removes the need for the Christian redemption and substitutes "the wise, the mild, the lofty, and the just" (PU 1.605). The narrator's "He who trod / Very man and very God / This earth in *weakness*, shame and pain" (585-7) now flows pure Shelleyan idealism and smoothly coalesces with:

I would *praise* such a Christ, with *pride*	(not worship; 974)
And joy, that he, as none beside,	
Had taught us how to keep the *mind*	(Shelley's "One Mind")
God gave him, as God gave his *kind*,	(same rhyme, PU 4.93-94)
Freer than they from fleshly taint:	
I would call such a Christ our *Saint*,	
As I declare our Poet, him	(Exhortation 20)
Whose *insight* makes all others dim: . . .	(Mind)
No, freely I would *praise the man*, —	(997)
Nor one whit more, if he contended	("if" is a strange reversal)
That gift of his, from *God* descended	(double entente)
Ah friend, what gift of man's does not?	(R.B.'s masks are un-
	gracious only for what Jehovah does not give.)

One of the most confusing of Browning's many paradoxes has been the emphasis he simultaneously placed on the dignity of the Mind and on the untrustworthiness of the Mind. Here it may be seen that as he honors Shelley's One Mind he merely pretends to approve of Christ's mind since Christ regularly nullified independence of the mind in such replies as "Thou shalt love the Lord thy God with all thy heart, and with all thy soul, and with all thy mind. . . . Thou shalt love thy neighbor as thyself" (M't 22.37-9). Browning has so confused his readers with Fact (truth) and Fancy (faith) in a perpetual shuffling of position that two rational interpreters can reach opposite conclusions over lines and passages which are deceptively intended to accent both mental acumen and imaginative flight to the disadvantage of Fancy (faith). Too often readers have accepted Browning's false distrust of the Mind as geniune because, unlike Browning, they do not believe that absolute Fact (truth) is attainable by man. Yet the poet's stress here on the supremacy of Christ's mind and the simplicity (ignorance) of his followers conforms to a trend highlighted in Paracelsus' "Crush not my mind" and continuing unabated through Pope Innocent's "Mind is not matter, but *from above*" (R & B 10.1348). To Browning as to Shelley, Christ possessed the highest type of human mind, but this gift did not prevent Browning or Shelley from dismissing Christ as being without Will and therefore as being a slave to his Father (Hellas Note 8). "The wise, the mild, the lofty, and the just," Prometheus says to the image of Christ, "thy slaves [followers] hate for being like to thee" (PU 1.605-6). The difference between dying-to-fulfill-his-father's-will and keeping-the-mind-freer-than-other-human-beings-from-fleshly-taint places Browning squarely by Shelley's side.

Browning could as easily have been thinking of "For God hath not given us the spirit of fear, but of *power* and of *love*, and of a *sound mind*" (2 Ti 1.7), except that the God with whom the narrator duels is without love and overpowering in his might, characterized as a Giver of fear and sorrow rather than as a wellspring of hope and joy. As St. Paul and the other Apostles reasoned, Meekness, Compassion and Faith in his Father were the distinguishing earthly attributes of Christ, not Weakness, Shame and Pain as the narrator elaborates them above (587). It was this same Christ moreover whom St. Paul reported saying, "My *strength* is made perfect in [your] *weakness.*" It was also he "who for the *joy* that was set before him endured the cross, *despising the shame*" (Heb 12.2). Quite the opposite of Prometheus' "I would fain / Be what it is my destiny to be, / The savior and the *strength* of suffering man" (PU 1.815-7), a destiny which was to be fulfilled through the imposition of his Will and surrender to his fate rather than through submission to another's will. It is not a coincidence that the Professor's reference to "the natural sovereignty of man" (891) gives occasion for the poet's narrator to bid the lecturer adieu. Nor is it a coincidence, as the narrator judges that "those blue eyes had survived so much" (823), that to the hawk-nosed professor instantaneously "ran a shoot" (PU 3.3.89) of love from [the narrator's] heart" (815).

Bewildered readers of "Christmas-Eve" are not altogether at fault in naming the rationalistic approach Browning's own. So what devolves upon the true God and incapacitates Jehovah may have been inadvertently missed:

And thence *I* conclude that the *real* God-function   (narrator; 1040)
Is to furnish a motive and injunction
For practicing what *we know already*.

God's being relieved of all functions except motivation and injunction, the latter of which Pope Innocent calls "the monitory touch o' the tether" (R & B 10.801), it is encumbent upon the reader to determine at least why, and lines 263-374 seem to provide the answer. After a truly heartless attack on Mount Zion's parishioners, who are five times compared to dumb sheep, the narrator moderates his words long enough to say that these worshipers are no duller than the worshipers of many other modes. They all endeavor to make one believe with much the same effect. Each method is convincing to those already convinced "but scarcely to be swallowed without wincing / By the not-as-yet convinced" (271). All of which enables the narrator to describe for a third time his own pantheistic form of worship:

<pre>
            For me,   (271)
I have my own church equally,   (on departing Zion Chapel)
And in this church my faith sprang first!
    (I said, as I reached the rising ground,
And the wind began again, with a burst
    Of rain in my face, and a *glad rebound*
From the heart beneath, as if, *God* speeding me,   (Prometheus)
I entered his *church-door, nature* leading me)   (open spaces)
— In youth I looked to these very skies,
And probing their immensities,
I found God there, his visible power;
    Yet felt in my heart, amid all its sense   (Jehovah vs. Prometheus)
    Of the power, an equal evidence
That *his love*, there too, *was* the nobler dower.   (Prometheus')
For the *loving worm* within its *clod*   (Epipsy 128-9, Q Mab 4.96-7,
Were diviner than a *loveless god*   Adonais 319; Job)
Amid his *worlds, I will dare to say*.   (PU 1.2, 163, 205; Jn 10.16)
    You know what I mean: God's all, man's naught: (coherence
</pre>

But also, *God*, whose pleasure brought   vanishes; Jehovah)
Man into being, *stands away*   (without love)
  As it were a handbreadth off, to give
Room for the newly-made to live,
And look at him from a place apart   (unloving separation)
And use his gifts of brain and heart,
Given, indeed, but to keep forever.   (thematic)
Who speaks of man, then, *must not sever*
Man's very elements from man,   (not from Jehovah)
Saying, "But all is God's" — whose plan   (2 Cor 5.18)
Was to create man and then *leave him,*   (double entente)
Able, his own word saith, *to grieve him,*
But able to glorify him too,
As *a mere machine* could never do,   (Q Mab 1.155, Gisb 19f, 107)
That *prayed or praised*, all unaware
Of its fitness for aught but *praise and prayer,*   ("whom thou [Jupiter]
          / Requitest for *knee-worship, prayer, and praise,"* PU 1.5-6)
Made *perfect* as a thing of course.   (levity)
Man, therefore, stands on *his own stock*
Of love and power as a *pin-point rock:*   (thematic, Alastor 378)
And, looking to *God who ordained divorce*   (Jehovah)
Of the rock from his boundless continent,
Only excess by a million-fold   (Death Nap 27-37)
O'er the power God gave man in the mould.

With the faith in Nature which he has cherished since youth, the narrator continues to deprecate undesirable divine attributes such as those requiring prayer and praise, reward and punishment in an unfair display of power. Without the all-encompassing Love the narrator would have his God exhibit, that God would be less divine than a loving worm. Seeing that he may have spoken too frankly, if not that he had exposed Shelleyan influence, the narrator pretends to retract or ameliorate the observation on Love, but in so doing he reverses a subsequent stand on man's independence and expresses a disbelief in the Christian concept of "God's [being] all, man's [being] naught." For, now that he has set up opposing GODs, loving and unloving, the narrator is eager to get on with circumscribing Jehovah. Since Jehovah himself elected to orphan man, his true function is one of noninterference, a conclusion which negates the Christian belief in God's immanence as well as transcendence. So when Browning's narrator insists that a gift is a gift *forever*, that once man is created he becomes his own master with his own independent spirit, he directly denies St. Paul's "all things are of God" and comes perilously close to indorsing Shelley's Demogorgon or Caliban's Quiet.

As Browning presents it, the gift's permanence demands Jehovah's non-interference in human life after the "divorce" of man's pin-point rock from God's boundless continent. Later (Epi Dram Pers 75ff) Browning will perfect the imagery, thus eliminating a suggested original affinity and substituting an initial act of breaking the island of man from Jehovah's mainland out of spite and jealousy. Apparently the physical as well as the spiritual separation provided Browning proof of man's innate spiritual quality and of that quality's being only a millionth of God's in degree, not kind. But the main thrust, which echoes Browning's "only believing he is not unloved" in *Pauline*, is that man's independence results from a loveless act by Jehovah, willed out of hatred and lustful desire for unmerited praise and worship. Therefore to say, as all modes of Christian thought say, that "all is God's" is to deny man's spiritual significance and independence, leaving him a mere vassal capable only of automaton-like offerings of prayer and praise to Jehovah in order to avoid grief or to eke out happiness. The narrator of "Christmas-Eve" is new to Browning's gallery and more sophisticated than his forerunners, but his objections to a power-hungry God are repetitive and uniformly in keeping with the prevailing theme of Browning's poetry up to 1850. When his "soul brought all to a single test" (352, thematic), the narrator could not believe that "the Eternal First and Last," infinitely *powerful and wise*, would prove less *good* in bestowing whatever man requires. Nor could he have made plainer to a confidant, since "Eternal [PU 2.3.95] First and Last" does not appear in the Scriptures, that he was speaking of Demogorgon, not of an overbearing and injudicious Jehovah. Having been endlessly taught by Nature of "what love can do in the leaf or stone," he cannot imagine "*need* that [he], in turn / Should point

him [the true God] out defect unheeded, / And show that
God [Jehovah] had yet to learn / What the meanest human
creature needed,

— Not life, to wit, for a few short years,   (351)
Tracking his way through *doubts and fears*(PU 3.2.29; Jehovah's world)
While the *stupid earth* on which I stay   (double entente)
    Suffers no change, but passive adds
    Its myriad years to myriads,
Though I, *he gave it to*, decay [PU 4.550],   (Jehovah, the earth)
Seeing death come and choose about me,
And my dearest ones depart without me.   (graphic)

The narrator may have to "stay" on earth and be saddened
by the departure of loved ones whom his counterpart in
"Easter-Day" calls "masks and shows / Not living men and
women" (937-8), but his appeal for sympathy does not
moderate the response to a selfish and loveless God. With all
but the permanent gifts of the Christian Jehovah unacceptable, he turns to Nature's God, Prometheus, who will
"satiate" his every need and desire:

No: love which, on earth, amid all the shows of it,   (359)
Has ever been seen the *sole good* of life in it,
The love, ever growing there, spite of the strife in it,
Shall arise, *made perfect*, from death's repose of it. (PU 4.354-69, 410)
And I shall behold *thee, face to face*,   (Prometheus; Gen 32.30)
O God, and in thy *light* retrace   (PU 2.1.71, never applied to Jehovah)
How in all I loved here, still wast *thou*!   (Prometheus)
Whom *pressing* to, then, as I fain would now,   (Q Mab 6.236)
I shall find as able to satiate   (PU 2.1.38, 2.3.35, 4.471)
    The love, thy gift, as my spirit's wonder
Thou art able to quicken and sublimate.

The task of breaking through intermingled Shelleyan thought
and scriptural expression, scriptural thought and Shelleyan
expression, indicates why so many pagans and Christians have
been confused by "Christmas-Eve." But if one keeps an eye
on Shelley's "shows," "fain," "satiate," "sprung," "light"
and "thus — and thus," a less baffling explanation may be
found for the Vision which carries the narrator to Rome and
Göttingen and back to Zion Chapel. For the Vision which has
been thought to be of Christ is more likely a Vision of

Prometheus. The narrator makes clear his willingness to praise Christ as a superior man but not to worship him as "one whit more" or less divine than any other man. And in a contrast of loving and unloving GODs, which is preceded by one of Browning's most explicit statements on the absolute nature of Love, he emphatically (359) rejects a God of rewards and punishments who is grudgingly indisposed to satiate the slightest need of man, much less his every need. So whatever the "spectral creature" is in the Vision, it is not Jehovah or Christ, his enslaved Son. This spectral God is proffered eternal worship in "ecstatic acquiescence," far alike from "thriftless learning / And ignorance's undiscerning":

The black cloud-barricade was *riven*   (PU 1.100; 380)
Ruined beneath *her* feet, and driven   (PU 1.213; the moon's)
Deep in the West; while, bare and breathless,
   North and South and East lay ready
For a glorious thing, that, *dauntless, deathless,*   (Prom, Mab 7.89, 196)
   Sprang across them and stood steady.   (Ode Liberty 16, PU 1.214)
'T was a moon-rainbow, vast and perfect,
From heaven to heaven extending, perfect
As the *mother-moon's* self, full in face [a requirement]   (pagan)
It rose, distinctly at the base
With its seven proper colors corded,
Which still, *in the rising*, were compressed,
   Until at last they *coalesced,*   (Q Mab 6.42)
   And *supreme the spectral creature lorded* ("spectral," not scriptural)
In a triumph of *whitest white,* —   (PU 2.1.71; M't 17.2)
Above which intervened the night.
But above night too, like only the next,
   The second of a wondrous sequence,
   Reaching in rare and rarer frequence,
Till the heaven of heavens were circumflexed,
Another rainbow *rose*, a mightier,
Fainter, flushier, and flightier, —
Rapture dying along its *verge.*   (Shelleyan)
Oh, whose *foot* shall I see emerge,   (levity)
Whose, from the *straining topmost dark,*
On to the keystone of that arc?

Like Shelley who had used Christ's transfiguration as model for the staging of Prometheus' liberation, Browning uses the Transfiguration as model for his Vision but adds

spectacular double moon-rainbows. Like Shelley's Demogorgon, whose realm is placed in the direction opposite to the
Christian heaven, Browning's spectral creature *rises* from below rather than descends from above. Without suspicion of
such a turn of events, one might easily conclude that the
emerging "foot" is Christ's, but as the poet knew the *darkest*
("straining topmost") *night* is between the two rainbows and
the spectral creature already "lorded / In a triumph" over the
keystone of the *lower* rainbow. Moreover it was this first
rainbow — derived from "a glorious thing which, *dauntless*,
deathless, / Sprang* across them [North, South, East] and
stood ready" — that "*rose, distinctly at the base*" which
elicited the narrator's unstinted praise. And in imitation of
Shelley's Asia and Panthea who are fatefully drawn by the
famous "O, FOLLOW, FOLLOW!" to the Cave of Demogorgon, the narrator is now made to "follow" the spectral
creature, "sucked" along by the vacuum which an eddying
vesture creates:

With my senses settling fast and steadying	(496)
But my body caught up in the whirl and drift	("amplitude,"
	Hom Merc 628)
Of the *vesture's* amplitude, still *eddying*	(Hom Sun 18; PU 2.2.41)
On, just before me, still to be *followed*,	(PU 2.1.141)
As it carried me after with its motion:	
What shall I say? — as a path were *hollowed*	(Shelleyan)
And a man went *weltering* through the ocean,	(Eug Hills 18)
Sucked along in the flying wake	(PU 2.2.60)
Of the luminous water-*snake*.	(PU 3.4.119)

Almost gleefully Browning repeats the nine lines above
(772-80) for the narrator's second flight, that from Rome to
Göttingen, and he adds a third "follow" (516) which permits
the narrator to say that he is thus forever suffered to take his
own way without prayer and praise. Pagan terminology,
"mother-moon's," "spectral," "ecstatic" and "satiate" are
not only foreign to Christianity; they are also expressive of a
Shelleyan urge for satiety which St. John's apocalypse
sharply limits to "living fountains of water" for a perennially
thirsty desert folk in order that they might eternally praise
Jehovah for his love and mercy. So whatever Vision the nar-

rator "spreads" (488) himself before in a contradictory "terror" (430) and "ecstatic acquiescence" (416) while promising eternal worship, it simply cannot be Jesus Christ. The "terror" fits Prometheus no more appropriately than the "acquiescence" fits Christ. Nor does "the whole face turned upon me full" conform to the scriptural implications of man's seeing God's face and living any more than it does to Jehovah's "imaged vapor" in "Easter-Day." But this kind of contradiction or double talk is only prelude to the obfuscation of the next astonishing lines:

This sight was shown me, there and then, —   (405)
Me, one out of a world of men,
Singled forth, as the chance might hap
To another if, in a thunderclap
Where I heard *noise* and you saw *flame*   (thunder; lightning)
Some *one man knew God called his name.*   ("Saul, Saul," Acts 9.4)
For me, I think I said, "*Appear!*   (PU 3.3.148)
Good were it to be ever here.   (M't 17.4)
If thou wilt, let me build to thee   (M't 17.4 verbatim)
Service-tabernacles three   (truly memorials to Christ, Moses & Elias)
Where, forever in thy presence,
In ecstatic acquiescence,   (pagan)
Far alike from *thriftless learning*   (thematic)
And *ignorance's undiscerning,*   (thematic)
I may *worship* and remain!" . . .   (Prometheus)

All at once I looked up with *terror*   (430)
He was there.   (Prometheus)
He himself with his *human air.*   (contradicts "terror")
On the narrow pathway, just before,
I saw the *back of him*, no more — . . .   (Ex 33.23)
No face: only the sight   ("garment," light vest, Hom Sun 18; 437)
Of a *sweepy garment*, vast and *white*,   (M't 9.20-2, 14.36; PU 2.1.71)
With a *hem* that I could recognize.   (pun & irony)
I felt *terror, no surprise;*   (logic)
My mind filled with the *cataract*,   (PU 1.61)
At one bound of the mighty fact.
"I remember, *he* did say   (Jesus Christ)
    Doubtless that, to this world's end,   (irony)
Where *two or three* should meet and pray,   (M't 18.20)
    He would be in the midst, their friend;
Certainly he was there with *them!*"   (Zion Chapel's "sheep")
    And my pulses leaped for joy   (levity)
    Of the golden thought without alloy,

That I saw his very vesture's hem. . . .
And I hastened, cried out while I pressed   (453)
To the salvation of the *vest,*   (PU 2.5.55)
"But not so, Lord! It cannot be   (Ac 11.8 verbatim)
That thou, indeed, art leaving me —
Me, that have *despised thy friends!*   (PU 1.606)
Thou art the *love of God — above*
His power, didst hear me place his love,
And that was leaving *the world for thee.*   (Prometheus)
Therefore thou *must not turn from me*   ("demand," PU 2.4.8)
As [if] I had *chosen the other part! . . .*   (Lu 10.42; E-Day 304)
I thought it best that thou, *the spirit,*   (not "the Father"; 467)
   Be worshipped *in spirit and in truth*   (Jn 4.23)
And in *beauty,* as even *we* require it —   (Shelley & R.B.)
   Not in forms *burlesque, uncouth,*   (prayer-praise-sermon-song)
I *left but now,* as scarcely fitted   (Zion Chapel)
For thee [Prometheus] : I knew not what I *pitied* (PU 1.631, retraction)
But, all I felt there, right or wrong,
   What is it to *thee, who curest sinning?* (double entente: Prometheus
          abjures sin; Christ forgives, M't 18.16-8, Lu 7.21, Jn 5.10)
Am I not *weak* as thou art *strong?"*   (2 Cor 12.10; PU 2.3.93)

Only a burst of courage which prompted him to substitute
a spectral creature for Christ in the Vision, or desperation in
a program of deception which was deceiving both the simple
Christians and the wise pagans, could have misled Browning
into overplaying a hand so well disguised. For eleven or
twelve disjointed scriptural allusions in seventy sequential
lines are too many except for unrelieved burlesque and uncontrollable distraction. One can thus delete Browning's
exploits with St. Paul's vision on the road to Damascus, St.
Peter's vision of Moses and Elias with Christ, God's back
side, Christ's healing garment, Christ's presence with two or
three followers, St. Peter's vision of unclean animals, Mary's
honoring ointment, worship of God in spirit and in truth,
Christ's treating disease as if it were sin, and St. Paul's contrast of Weakness with Strength. But one cannot delete the
opposition these scriptural acts engender or the camouflage
they permit. As the Scriptures are filled with humorous or
strange references to "foot" and "garment," they are filled
with visions which are made dramatic by clouds, shadows,
light, voices, thunder (noise), lightning (flame) and rainbows.

In St. Paul's vision, for example, it was not only a light from heaven, brighter than the sun, and his being thrust to the ground; it was also a voice which unmistakably called him by name. Following Shelley instead, the disbelieving narrator decidedly prefers "Appear!" to such sham and deceit: "Now thou art thus restored. This cave is thine. / Arise! *Appear!*" (THE EARTH to Prometheus & Asia, PU 3.3.147-8). Similarly, his "Me, that have *despised thy* [Christ's] *friends!*" is a reversal of Prometheus' refusal to speak Christ's name since "it hath become a curse. I see, I see / The wise, the mild, the lofty, and the just, / *Whom thy slaves* [followers] *hate for being like to thee*" (PU 1.604-6). Even the "I see, I see" haunts the narrator's mind as he converts it into "For see, for see" in line 557.

Adapted quite awkwardly, "riven," "sprang," "cataract" and "vest" now seem unimportant as evidence, but they are as palpably a part of Shelley's contribution as "unexampled," "floundering," "soothe," "hiss" and "glozing" are a part of Aeschylus' contribution. Why Browning chose to make so much of the "hem" of a garment is not easily determined, but this is not the only time his wit, mockery and lightheartedness become fixed upon an undesirable aspect of Christ's ministry. There are only two scriptural references to "the hem" which attracted individuals to the healing power of Jesus, and unless Browning was using an obscure pagan tradition with innuendoes attuned to Landorian ears, the levity does not match that of "Easter-Day": "When the armed angel, conscience-clear, / His task nigh done, leans o'er his spear . . . / Till God relieve him at his post" (604-8); "As if a dragon's nostril split / And all his famished ire o'erflowed; / Then, as he winced at his lord's goad, / Back he inhaled" (536-9); "I fell to musing of the time / So close, the blessed matin-prime / All hearts leap up at, in some guise — / One could not well do otherwise" (377-80). Evidently Browning enjoyed creating *Christmas-Eve and Easter-Day*, but the lightheartedness of his avowal seems to be under pressure, suggesting that its spontaneity will be regained only in the shorter pieces where paganism is an inseparable and unlabored part of the character. Too much thought is now going into deception: "I will raise / My voice up to their point of praise! / I see the error; but above / The scope of error, see the love, — / *Oh, love of those first Christian days! / —* Fanned so soon into a blaze, / From the spark preserved by the trampled sect [Prometheans], / That the *antique sovereign Intellect /* Which then sat ruling in the world, . . . was hurled / From the throne he reigned upon" (645-55). One of Browning's very neatest reversals of Shelleyan diction without reversal of thought, he bemoans the glorious love of pagan days which was trampled out by early Christians.

In raising his voice Browning, like Shelley, made Christian not Classic Purity, Fear, Prize, Bear and Hope strategic to his pagan cause. To both poets Fear meant fear of Jehovah, which to them was unknown or absent. Prize meant attainment of the new Promethean day and Demogorgic Victory over Jehovah's tyranny. And because Christians are admonished "to bear" their pains and sorrows, Browning felt secure in adopting Shelley's favorite synonym for Courage. His emphasis, when sincerely intended, always reflects Shelleyan expropriation: "Death is a gate of dreariness and gloom, / That leads to *azure isles* and beaming skies / And happy regions of eternal *hope.* / Therefore, O Spirit! fearlessly *bear on*" (Q Mab 9.161-4). But of these five words Browning and Shelley made the most complete reversal in their contempt for Christian Purity: "The fountains of our deepest life, shall be / Confused in Passion's *golden* purity" (Epipsy 570-1); Pompilia's "purity of soul / That will not take pollution, ermine-like / Armed from dishonor by its own soft snow" (The Pope 676-9); Pompilia "would present you one *pure* glass . . . as God's sea, glassed in *gold*" (Caponsacchi 1142-3). Thus, for example, Colenso in "Gold Hair" is a typical diversion. For if the thirty double Louis-d'or were not "showered" by a divinity upon the Pornic girl, her parents had reason to question her purity. Like the wax-white Pompilia, she is seraphic and reminiscent of Danae whose own celestial visitor gave her Perseus who in turn taught Sun worship and founded the Magian priesthood.

"Easter-Day"

When in *La Saisiaz* (1878) Browning decides that he will "no more dare to *mimic* such responses in futile speech, / *Pass off human lisp as echo of the sphere-song out of reach*" (153-4), he is probably referring to his earlier introduction of Prometheus and Jehovah into the dramatis personae of *Christmas-Eve and Easter-Day*. Like the author of Job, Browning had first exhausted all available human challenges to God's providence before tempting Jehovah to speak as contestant to a battery of charges and complaints. "Easter-Day" is therefore thematically focused on the Last Judgment, not Christ's resurrection and promise of eternal life, in order to elicit answers by "the austere voice" to issues reiterated most recently in the companion poem on God's proper function, man's spiritual sovereignty, unjust imposition of flesh and ignorance on man, and the machine-like operation of pain and pleasure, joy and sorrow, reward and punishment. Distinguished from the narrator of "Christmas-Eve" (375), who only pretends to take or need Jehovah's help (1301-2), the narrator of "Easter-Day" is nonetheless as unperturbed and as unoffended as his fellow pantheist when in the Vision of Judgment he suddenly learns that pantheism accounts for his being banned from a Christian heaven. In the absence of faith in or fear of Jehovah, all else is peripheral to the apocalyptic event and it is not difficult any longer to imagine why two visions were published together when one is of Prometheus, the other of Jehovah. As with Guido Franceschini and other frustrated Browning characters facing divine judgment, the narrator had already resolved to say to Jehovah at the crucial moment, "So I was *framed* by thee, such way / I put to use thy senses here!" (564; Q Mab 9.22). And thus braced in self-consciousness, what with his trust in Art and Love still in premeditated reserve, the narrator leaves little space in the poem for the implication that "Easter-Day" is simply a debate between Browning's old, confident belief in God and a new, more exacting belief. Instead, the startling difference between the attitudes toward Jehovah of a Job and the narrator is to be observed in the degree of animosity each exhibits. Markedly shorn of the dignity of Job's God, but very much in character with the parsimonious and vindictive Jehovah of "Christmas-Eve," Browning's vulgar, talkative God in "Easter-Day" stands,

Like the *smoke*	(Faust 2.101; 640)
Pillared o'er Sodom, when day broke, —	
I saw him. One magnific pall	(Hard-to-be-a-Christian)
Mantled in massive *fold* and fall	(Milton)
His head, and *coiled* in *snaky* swathes	(PU 2.3.97; Milton)
About His feet: *night's black*, that bathes	(Milton)
All else, broke *grizzled* with despair,	(Milton)
Against the *soul of blackness* there,	(Job & Milton)

and speaks:

"All is come to pass.	(655)
Such *shows* are over for each soul	(Alastor 711, Q Mab 7.51)
They had respect to. In the roll	
Of Judgment which convinced mankind	
Of sin, *stood many, bold and blind,*	(graphic)
Terror must burn the truth into:	
Their fate for them! . . .	
This finite life, thou has preferred,	(Hard-to-be; 668)
In disbelief of God's plain word,	
To heaven and to infinity	
Thy choice was earth: thou didst attest	(679)
'T was fitter spirit should subserve	(ironically true & false)
The flesh, than flesh refine to nerve	
Beneath the spirit's play. Advance	
No claim to *their* inheritance	(Jehovah's followers)
Who chose the spirit's fugitive	
Brief gleams, . . .	
Thou saidst, — 'Let *spirit star* the dome	(PU 3.3.138; 693)
Of sky, that flesh may miss no peak,	
No nook of earth, — I shall not seek	
Its service further!' Thou art shut	(flesh's)
Out of the heaven of spirit; *glut*	(Death T 12, Q Mab 3.116)
Thy sense upon the world: 't is thine	
Forever — take it!"	

At which judgment the narrator, who has fallen "a mass, / No man now" before Jehovah's feet (654-5; Rev 1.17), is joyously transported by the thought that "Earth's exquisite /

Treasures" (702-3) are forever his. Nor does he contest the charge of disbelief in "God's plain word," loss of a heavenly inheritance or exploitation of the flesh by the spirit, since he knows from Shelley that flesh cannot pass the portal from life to Life. But Jehovah interposes and warns him in his euphoria that man's estimate of happiness falls so short of God's invention that an idolized earth may amount to no more than hell itself (705-11):

And thou, whose heaven *self-ordained*	(716)
Was, to enjoy earth unrestrained,	
Do it! Take all the *ancient shows*!	("shews," Shelleyan)
The woods shall wave, the rivers flow, . . .	(PU 1.122, 4.211)
Unvisited, as heretofore,	(727)
By God's *free* spirit, that makes an end.	(see "freely" below)
So, once more, take thy world! Expend	
Eternity upon its *shows*,	(Q Mab 9.155-7)
Flung thee as freely as one rose	(Jehovah's parsimony)
Out of a summer's opulence,	
Over the Eden-barrier whence	
Thou art excluded. Knock in vain!	

All part of a "horrid nightmare" (611) and projected thus to be read and interpreted, the narrator's description of Jehovah and his method of judging in "Easter-Day" differs in no fundamental details from the aspects of Jehovah's character to be found in *Paracelsus*, *Sordello* and "Christmas-Eve." Only in the severe symbolism of Jehovah's person is the Vision set apart, for to say that "night's *black* . . . broke, grizzled with despair, / Against the *soul of blackness* [Jehovah] " goes some distance beyond "strangle with a cross olive-stone" (Sord 2.422) or "at whose defection mortals starve aghast / As though heaven's bounteous windows were slammed fast / Incontinent" (Sord 3.929). Employment of such phantasmagoria to make Jehovah the very essence of blackness, accompanied by the slur at his parsimony in "Flung thee as freely as *one rose* / Out of a summer's opulence" and his vulgarity in "glut / Thy sense upon the world," no longer merely intimates that Jehovah is an evil force upon whose demise Browning earnestly waits. Especially since St. John, his supposed favorite scriptural writer, says, "God is light and in him is no darkness at all" (1 Jn 1.4). The "light" which only Paracelsus could look into without "blinkers" may now be assigned to Prometheus, for like Shelley's Jupiter, Browning's Jehovah is always to be clothed in darkness, blackness, shadow or cloud, ever suggesting secrecy, vapidity and evil. Since Browning was evidently thinking of Job and *Paradise Lost* as well as *Prometheus Unbound*, he might readily have turned to Job's classic "as darkness itself . . . where the *light* is as darkness" (10.22) or Milton's famous flames, emitting *no light* but making "darkness visible." Instead, and more consonant with his mood, Browning preferred Milton's description of Death in *Paradise Lost:*

<pre>
              The other *shape*,   (2.666)
If *shape* it might be call'd that *shape* had none
Distinguishable in member, joynt, or limb,
Or *substance* might be call'd that shadow seem'd,
For each seem'd either; *black it stood as Night,*   ("night's black," 645)
Fierce as ten Furies, terrible as Hell,   (PU 1.246)
And shook a dreadful Dart; what seem'd his head
The likeness of a Kingly Crown had on.
</pre>

Nor, as he searched for pictorial effects in *Paradise Lost* (2.629-870) beyond "night's black," was Browning hesitant in converting "thoughts inflam'd" into "writhed inflamed," "scaly fould" into "massive fold," "grieslie terrour" into "grizzled with despair" and "Snakie Sorceress" into "snaky swathes." Examples enough to substantiate Browning's indebtedness to Milton but not to define his vengeance toward Jehovah. For in addition to his monstrous shape Milton's *Death*, it should be recalled, is the son of Satan and Satan's daughter Sin who sprang a Goddess from Satan's head during the conspiratorial assembly in heaven. Most probably Milton was guided by the scriptural "Then when lust [Satan] hath conceived, it bringeth forth sin [Satan's daughter] ; and sin, when it is finished, bringeth forth death [Satan's son] " (Jas 1.15). Most probably Browning knew, if his vengeance is to be measured by his adaptation of Milton's lines, that he was striking immeasurably harder than Shelley at both the Christian God and his reputed Word.

Elated still over his possession of "all the world," the narrator picks "a leaf of fern" (738) and recollects how much from books he may learn of "earth's resources" and "exhaustless beauty." But Jehovah dismisses Nature's greatest success as mere antechamber to heaven's splendor, reminding the narrator that the fern leaf might have disarmed his "power to cope [Para 1.22] with God's intent" (766). Even with his trust thus removed in natural things, however, Browning's narrator holds up, bears on, "for *art* supplants, gives mainly worth / To nature; 't is *man stamps the earth* [Sord 2.163, PU 3.3.40-63] — / And I will seek his *impress*" (778-80). Upon which Jehovah speaks of Art's failure to obtain the one form with its single act, the one face with its one look, and then tediously reasserts his thoughts on Might and Judgment:

So, in God's eye, the earth's first *stuff*   (Shelleyan; 843)
Was, neither more nor less, enough
To house man's soul, man's need fulfil.
Man reckoned it *immeasurable*?   (Marenghi 133, 1-161)
So thinks the lizard of his vault!
Could God be taken in default,
Short of contrivances, by you,   (R.B.)
Or reached, ere ready to pursue
His *progress* through eternity? (thematic of God as of man)
That *chambered rock*, the lizard's world,   (Witch 63)
Your easy mallet's blow has hurled
To nothingness forever; *so,*
Has God abolished at a blow   (Caliban-like)
This world, wherein his saints were *pent,* — (PU 1.688)
Who, though found grateful and content,
With the provision there, *as thou* [R.B.], (dramatic irony)
Yet knew he would not disallow
Their spirit's hunger, felt as well, —
Unsated, — *not unsatable,* ("satiate," 814, C-Eve 367, Para 1.198,
As paradise gives proof. Deride PU 2.1.38, 3.35, Sord 2.438)
Their choice now, thou who sit'st outside!

With neither Nature nor Art presumably left to maintain his "boldness" (561) in the course of Jehovah's judgment, the narrator falls back on the Intellect. And note that when he cries, "Mind, mind, / So miserably cast behind, / To gain what had been wisely lost" (864), he boasts that Jehovah's heaven "had been *wisely* lost!" The pretended "anguish" cannot conceal the strong remaining courage: "I will seize *mind*, forego the rest, / And try how far my *tethered strength* / May crawl . . . till I strain / *Intoxicate* [PU 2.3.8], half-break my chain" (875-86). Nor does the sudden and "sickening" recognition of the limits of Knowledge, even of mythological verse, more than momentarily lessen the strife: "I cannot look back now, nor stake / Bliss on the *race*, for running's sake [1 Cor 9.24], / The goal's a ruin like the rest." So preemptorily, as if he were conversing with self-righteous friends, the narrator adopts Job's route of escape and cries, "Let me alone!" (891; Job 7.16 & 19, 10.20). And well he may briefly refrain from further exposure of the game, since backtracking on his report of God's speech opens up unremitting themes of Browning's poetry. Disclosing evidence of being extraneous and "planted," a practice the poet steadily flaunts in disregard of the reader's intelligence, "Could God be taken in default, / Short of contrivances, by you [R.B.], — / Or reached, ere ready to pursue his *progress* through eternity" is another way of accenting Jehovah's insecurity and need, under Demogorgon's law of Necessity which Browning here labels Progress, to renew his own fearful and guilt-laden pursuit through eternity. In thought as alternatingly primitive and sophisticated as Caliban's, Jehovah first crushes the world as the narrator would crush a lizard's rocky vault, then philosophizes on the difference between "unsated" and "unsatable." Already Paracelsus, Sordello and the narrator of "Christmas-Eve" have adopted Shelley's "satiate" to counter Jehovah's parsimony. Now through the manipulation of "dashes" in a long paragraph (783-863), Jehovah is made to assume guilt for even Michelangelo's unquenched "thirst, / *Titanically infantine*, / Laid at the breast of the Divine" (805). Defensively Jehovah asks, "Does it [Buonarroti's soul] confound thee . . . / Like the omnipotence [Prometheus'] which tasks / Itself to furnish all that asks / The soul it means to *satiate*?" And since one denial of his munificence deserves another, Jehovah is also made to utter, "But through / Life pierce, — . . . — drear / Deficiency gapes every side!" (823,

832). It is a deficiency identical with Jupiter's which THE EARTH sees corrected in Prometheus' rebellion (PU 1.159-79) and Shelley brings to an ideal state in Painting, Sculpture, Poesy and Arts which are "the mediators / Of that best worship" between man and Prometheus (PU 3.3.39-60).

Browning's knowledge of Shelley's poetry is now so complete that he honors the finest distinctions. His Jehovah is not "imageless" like Demogorgon, the Ultimate, but an "imaged vapor" (636) and like Jupiter a fiercely jealous but temporary interloper. When the narrator seizes "mind," a portion of the One Mind, Prometheus, his plans are for evasion of Jehovah and continued life on Earth, where Demogorgon's law of Necessity is operative in Nature. He understands that submission of his will is required by the One Power but it is, as with Asia and Panthea, a sweet surrender or assent ("The sweet desires within obey," PU 2.2.56) to a force whose impartial law favors Prometheus, not to self-abnegation among Jehovah's slaves. Committed to Mind and determined to task to the limit his "tethered strength [spiritual weakness]," how better could Browning's narrator show allegiance to Shelley than by straining "intoxicate," half-breaking his "chain" (PU 1.32)?

Hither the sound has borne us — to the realm   (PU 2.3.1)
Of Demogorgon, and the mighty portal,
Like a volcano's *meteor*-breathing chasm,   (thematic in Shelley)
Whence the oracular vapour is hurled up
Which lonely men drink wandering in their youth,
And call truth, virtue, love, genius, or joy,
The maddening wine of life, whose dregs they drain
To deep intoxication; and uplift,   ("strain/Intoxicate," E-Day 85-6)
Like Maenads who cry loud, Evoe! Evoe!   (bacchanal cry)
The voice which is contagion to the world.

If Hard-to-be-a-Christian has to be sent through the whole Vision of the Last Judgment to find difficulties in being a Christian, Common Sense, who had sternly warned against putting faith in intangibles, seems to have taught him little. For in one of the inescapably autobiographical vignettes of Browning's poetry, indemonstrable evidence suffers a lethal blow as Browning moves from childhood fearlessness of imaginary nightly intruders to adult rejection of the imbecility of Christian faith (398-501). Typically Browning diverts attention with the childish setting while bearing down on the adult persuasion. Typically his submerged thesis is planned to "note that I / Inclined thus ever" on the subject of faithful or faithless. That is, "The good bark answers to the helm / Where faith sits, *easier* to o'erwhelm"; "I wish indeed God's kingdom come — / The day when I shall see appear / His bidding, *as my duty*, clear / From doubt"; "At night it cometh like a thief. / I fancy why the trumpet blows; / Plainly to wake one"; "A bridge to cross, a dwarf to thrust / Aside, a wicked mage to stab — / And, lo ye, I had kissed Queen Mab! / So shall we marvel why we grudged / Our labor here, and idly judged / Of heaven, we might have gained, but lose!" How could one be more subtly deceptive than in Browning's "*idly* judged / Of heaven, we *might* have gained, but lose" through faith in a false and malicious promise by Jehovah? Browning surely means that he himself will never cease trying to break the chain of an unacceptable God, nor be drawn away from the Shelleyan intoxication of his youth.

Of course the narrator of "Easter-Day" holds Shelley's trump card all the while he pretends to suffer at Jehovah's denial of entrance to heaven, and that the card is Love now surprises only in that its potency is insufficient to persuade Browning's loved ones, masks and shows, to become "living men and women" in a pantheistic and pagan world:

<pre>
          Behold, my spirit *bleeds*,   (Shelleyan; 932)
Catches no more at broken reeds, —
But *lilies* flower those reeds above: (PU 3.3.99)
I let the world go, and take *love*!
Love survives in me, albeit *those*
I love be henceforth masks and shows   (sister, friends)
Not living men and women: still
I mind how love repaired all ill,
Cured wrong, soothed grief, made *earth amends*
With parents, brothers, children, friends!   (deceptive)
Some semblance of *a woman* yet   (R.B.'s mother died within the year)
With eyes to help me to forget,   ("semblance," Q Mab 1.133)
</pre>

Shall look on me; and I will watch
Departed love with love, attach
Old memories to *new dreams, nor scorn*
The poorest of the grains of corn
I save from shipwreck on this isle   ("isle," PU 4.200)
Trusting its barrenness may smile   ("bare," PU 4.179-82)
With happy foodful green one day,   ("green," PU 4.364, 404)
More precious for the pains. I pray, —   ("pray" to Prometheus)
Leave to *love, only!*   (not grace, mercy, faith)

Reminiscent of "while you turn upon your heel, / *Pray* that I be not busy slitting steel / Or shredding brass, *camped on some virgin shore / Under a cluster of fresh stars*" (Sord 3.857), the five italicized lines seem to mark a noticeable hardening in Browning's purpose. In perhaps the most intimate of all his rejections of Jehovah, Browning's devoutly religious and devoutly loving mother is associated with an unconquerable will to prove the paucity of Jehovah's providence and the indomitability of man's spirit. And the words grow harsher as a pitiless God, who is drawn without decorum or reserve, is poised in "his wrath" like a headsman, his "inflicting voice" smiting:

"Is this *thy* final choice?   (R.B.'s; 958)
Love is best? 'T is somewhat late!
And all *thou dost enumerate*
Of power and beauty in the world,   (uniquely an R.B. constant: Para 2.
        449,626; Luria 3.58; E-Day 766, 817,961; Saul 164; Lippo 283)
The mightiness of love was curled
Inextricably round about.   (Hom Merc 208-10)
Love lay within it and without,   (R.B. never admits Jehovah's love)
To clasp thee, — but in vain! Thy soul
Still shrunk from Him who made the whole,   (subtle double talk)
Still set deliberate aside   ("shrunk," Devil 26)
His love! — Now take love! Well *betide*   (R of Islam 3770-2)
Thy tardy conscience! Haste to take
The show of love for the name's sake,
Remembering every moment Who,
Beside creating thee unto
These ends, and these for thee, was said
To undergo death in thy stead
In flesh like thine: so ran *the tale.*
What doubt in thee could countervail
Belief in it? *Upon the ground*   (spoken by Jehovah)

'That in the story had been found   (spoken by R.B.)
Too much love! How could God love so?'
He who in all his works below   (spoken by Jehovah)
Adapted to the needs of man,
Made love the basis of the plan, — ...
Man thought man, for his kind's behoof,   (986)
Both could and did invent that scheme   ("invent," Q Mab 7.25)
Of perfect love."

Indeed it does sometimes appear in Browning's and in Shelley's poetry as if Love is thought to have sprung full-blown from man's brow and to be responsible, as with Asia and Prometheus, for the generation of truth and beauty and goodness. But to both poets human love is apparently only a portion of the anthropomorphic Prometheus' Love. Of all the words, other than Love, which permanently caught Browning's fancy, few compete with Power or Strength and Beauty or stem more certainly from Psalmic diction, possibly through Shelley. Wherever Browning wishes to symbolize youth, energy, love and god-like qualities altogether — Shelley's "truth, virtue, love, genius, or joy" — he is most likely to write Power and Beauty, Strength and Beauty, Beauty and Power, Beauty and Strength, or to intersperse the words in phrases or clauses thus assuring their juxtaposition. Seven times he uses Power and Beauty in the parleying with Christopher Smart, and through David and Fra Lippo Lippi he exults in the symbolic connotation of Beauty and Power or Strength. As there can be no doubt that it is Browning himself who "dost enumerate / Of power and beauty," there can be no doubt that it is Browning who says, "That in the story had been found / Too much love! How could God [Jehovah] love so?" Cowering "deprecatingly" (991), therefore, he asks only that he be allowed to die or granted the life he has known on earth. "Only let me *go on, go on,* / Still hoping *ever and anon* / To reach one eve the Better Land!" That is, the land better than Jehovah's heaven which he unreservedly turns down:

Then did the form *expand, expand* —   (1004)
I knew him through the *dread disguise*   ("After some *foul disguise* had
                    fallen, and ... / All things had put their evil nature off,"

As the whole God within His eyes   PU 3.4.70-7)
Embraced me.   (Alastor 431-3)

Embraced me? One cannot so soon forget the "revulsion new" (293) generated in "night's black, that bathes / All else, broke, grizzled with despair, / Against *the soul of blackness there.*" Nor as "the imaged vapor [Job 4.16], head to foot, / Surveying, motionless and mute, / Its work, ere, in a whirlwind rapt" (636) vanishes, can one forget that, dream or no, Browning has managed once again to depict the Christian God as hideous in appearance, pitilessly decreeing unjust laws and remorselessly exacting unjust penalties. These are not uncommon reasons for an agnostic or atheist to give. The peculiarity lies in the poet's Shelleyan belief that in the spiritual world Jehovah had not grown up to his potential or been touched by the qualities of Love, Truth, Goodness and Beauty which are the hallmark of Prometheus' care. The God whom Browning opposes is inordinately real but an unconscionable fraud, operating as temporarily and unmolestedly as Demogorgon permits Jupiter to operate on the edge of eternity, and vigorously to be resisted until he is unseated by juster and wiser spirits. See how joyously Browning concludes "Easter-Day":

```
            And so I live, you see,                        (1018)
Go through the world, try, prove, reject,         (all R.B. constants)
Prefer, still struggling to effect
My warfare; happy that I can                 (Para 1.200; 2 Cor 10.4)
Be crossed and thwarted as a man,                   (R.B. constant)
Nor left in God's contempt apart,               (Jehovah's sheepfold)
With ghastly smooth life, dead at heart,
Tame in earth's paddock as her prize [decay].  ("pasture," PU 3.3.110)
Thank God, she still each method tries            (Prometheus; earth)
To catch me, who may yet escape,                      (Cycl 478-82)
She knows, — the fiend in angel's shape!          (2 Cor 11.14-5)
Thank God, no paradise stands barred    (Prometheus; no true heaven)
To entry, and I find it hard         ("barred," Q Mab 7.202; impossible)
To be a Christian, as I said!
Still every now and then my head
Raised glad, sinks mournful — all grows drear             (levity)
Spite of the sunshine, while I fear
And think, "How dreadful to be grudged              (PU 2.2.91-5)
```

No ease henceforth, *as one that's judged.*
Condemned to earth forever, shut
From *heaven!*"   (Jehovah's)

   Clearly Browning is saying, now that his ire has abated,
that it is most uncivil to grudge his decision to avoid the
Christian heaven by remaining on earth. Undisguised in "the
fiend in angel's shape," his insistence upon being thwarted
"as a man" and his reference to "warfare" which falsely
echoes St. Paul's "I have fought a good fight" (2 Ti 4.7, 2
Cor 10.4) are repetitive arguments which substantiate Browning's escape from Christian servitude and divine tyranny:
"And no marvel; for Satan himself is transformed into an
angel of light. / Therefore it is no great thing if his ministers
also be transformed as the ministers of righteousness." Small
wonder the poet is so thankful that "no [true] paradise" is
barred to him and that no one has detected his subversive
warfare. Earlier he had complained that his "warnings" (353-
65) against being a Christian neither terrified nor converted
Londoners to his "purpose." Now he complains that he is
grudged his choice of earth by followers of Jehovah who are
too tame and too dead at heart to alter their uneventfully
smooth lives: "And *grudge* to sing those wise and lovely
songs / Of fate, and chance, and God, and Chaos old, / And
Love, and the chained Titan's woeful doom, / And how he
shall be loosed, and make the earth / One brotherhood."
Only at the very end of "Easter-Day" does Browning deign
to return to the ostensible reason for celebration: *"But*
Easter-Day breaks! *But* / Christ rises! Mercy *every way* / Is
infinite, − and who can say?" Yet even here his frustration
in not changing others to paganism is epitomized in "But, . . .
But," while his determination to "Go through the world, try,
prove, reject, / Prefer, still struggling to effect / [his] warfare" is reasserted in "Mercy *every way* is infinite." For
thereby Browning purloins all meaning from Mercy and substitutes a totally fulfilling Love.
   Nor is that quite all, since the excessively punctuated, con-
voluted elliptical thought of the first half of "Easter-Day"

becomes more nearly penetrable in the certainty of Browning's preference of earth to Jehovah's heaven. To "renounce the world" (142, 199) is to renounce the Mind (VII), and this is the rationale of the assault on Faith: "That faith might flap her wings and crow / From such an eminence!" (183-4). When Easy-to-be-a-Christian does not openly join the attack on Faith, he carefully prepares the way for expression of Hard-to-be-a-Christian's honest distrust of the Heart and full trust of the Head. Hard-to-be's complaint of the difficulty of faith (20, 30) is thus substantiated by Easy-to-be's "Prove to me, only that the least / Command of God is God's indeed" (34), and then for him martyrdom would be a negligible price to pay for "God's eternity of joy." Whereupon Hard-to-be's "could you joint / This flexile finite life once tight / Into the fixed and infinite, / You safe inside" (50) is first tempered by Easy-to-be's reservation that "You must mix some uncertainty / With faith, if you would have faith be" (71-2), but then indorsed by "But God, bethink you! I would fain / Conceive of the Creator's *reign* [Shelley's symbol of tyranny, PU 2.4.28] / As based upon exacter laws / Than creatures build by with *applause* [praise & prayer]" (87). Accepting the words as Easy-to-be's approval of a more reasonable pantheism, Hard-to-be praises the generosity of Nature and blames the groans and travail of Jehovah's creation. But his purpose is to expose the old story of human suffering in which all questions asked have been "flung back unanswered flat" (108). Blind, unanswered Faith seemingly disposed of, the disputants also agree on the absurdity of a scientific faith (124), but Easy-to-be injects a typical proviso. He would at least place faith in "a mere probability," provided it be "probable; the chance must lie / Clear on one side." Pretentiously taken aback by the elusiveness of faith, Hard-to-be then concludes that men believe what they want to believe (173). Demonstrable evidence to the contrary, men think in their search for truth that "the human heart's best" (185). Ignoring the Mind, men probe the heart for "its wants and needs, / And hopes and fears," and faithfully settle on the Christian creed without ever *puzzling* "out who Orpheus was,

/ Or Dionysius Zagrias" (193-4; Gisborne 51, Gen 4.22). Which is Browning's way of saying that on grounds of priority alone the suffering inflicted on Dionysius Zagrias, a Christ-figure, by the Titans should take precedence over the suffering inflicted on Jesus Christ by Jehovah.

Pleased that Easy-to-be accuses him of culling "briars, thistles, from our private plot, / To mar God's ground where thorns are not" (224), Hard-to-be pretends to summarize what has been said on Faith and on renouncing the world but emphatically states:

But there be certain words, broad, plain,	(257)
Announcing this *world's gain for loss,*	(Ph'p 3.7)
And bidding us reject the same:	
The whole world lieth (they proclaim)	(1 Jn 5.19)
In wickedness, — come out of it!	(2 Cor 6.17)

An injunction neither Hard-to-be nor Easy-to-be-a-Christian could any more countenance than do Paracelsus and Sordello, why does Hard-to-be expend so much energy on it? Browning knew that "renounce" (199) occurs only one time in the Scriptures and he could not have cared less: "But have *renounced* the hidden things of dishonesty, not walking in craftiness, nor handling the word of God deceitfully" (2 Cor 4.2). Browning knew that St. Paul was not given to the impossible in his missionary zeal: "I wrote unto you in an epistle not to company with fornicators: / *Yet not altogether* with the fornicators of this world, or with the covetous, or extortioners, or with idolators; *for then must ye needs go out of the world*" (1 Cor 9-10). So Browning is as ever engaged in saturating lines with easily recognizable scriptural admonitions to demonstrate acceptance before then covertly attacking them. For when Hard-to-be says, "The whole world lieth ... / In wickedness," he is quoting St. John's "And we know that we are of God, and *the whole world lieth in wickedness.*" When he says, "Announcing this world's gain for loss," he is thinking of St. Paul's "But what things [of this world] were *gain* to me, those I counted *loss* for Christ." And when he says, "come out of it," he is quoting St. Paul's "Wherefore *come out* from among them, and be ye separate, saith the

Lord." Here closely combined in disapproval are three restrictions of Christianity which require of the practitioner somewhat less than offensive rein on the joys of Nature, Art or human fellowship. But they are restrictions, whatever the degree, and incite Hard-to-be-a-Christian's sharpest scorn: "I who thrill through every nerve / At thought" (265-6) *of what* practicing Christians turn a deaf ear to.

On and on in "Easter-Day" one may go with Browning in his rejecting and preferring, but one final quotation will serve as a unifying example of his more daring thrusts, this time at St. Paul and Christian faith:

Hard-to-be.   Then begins   (292)
    To the *old point revulsion new* — ...   ("an old story, and its end /
            As old — you come back (be sincere)/ With every question
        you put here . . . / This time *flung back unanswered flat*," 103-8)
    If after all we should mistake,   (295)
    And so *renounce* life for the sake
    Of *death* and nothing else? . . .

Easy-to-be.   Who gains   (324)
    By that, I wonder? Here I live
    In *trusting ease;* and here you drive
    At causing me to lose *what most*
    Yourself would mourn for had you lost!

Hard-to-be.   But, do you see, my friend, that thus
    You leave Saint Paul for AEschylus?
    — Who made his *Titan's* arch-device   (Prometheus')
    The giving men *blind hopes* to spice   (Aeschylus 252; R.B.'s italics)
    The meal of life with, else *devoured*   (cf., Hom Merc 178)
    In *bitter haste*, while lo, death loured
    Before them at the platter's edge!
    If faith should be, as *I allege*,   (double entente)
    Quite other than a condiment ("faith, allege," Calderon 3.18, 1.136)
    To heighten flavors with, or meant ("condiment," cf. Fifine 1612-48,
    (Like that brave curry of *his* Grace [Jehovah's])   Aeschylus'
    To take at need the victual's place?   Thyestes)
    If, having dined, you would digest
    Besides, and turning to your rest
    Should find instead . . .   (R.B.'s ellipsis)

That for the martyr's gruesome and idiotic tale immediately preceding these lines (272-92; 1 Cor 15.32) Browning would deliberately take inspiration from St. Paul's infirmities of the flesh and his fighting with wild beasts is no longer shocking. He was probably thinking of "Now *faith* is the substance of things hoped for, the evidence of things not seen" (Heb 11.1). And that he would dare replace St. Paul's belief in rewards and punishments, taken solely on faith, with Prometheus' "blind hopes of good" is surprising only in that Shelley had made much of the same Aeschylean and scriptural phraseology. Readers would not know that Browning, like Shelley (PU 2.4.59), distinguished in his thought between "blind" (unknown, legioned) pagan hopes and "barren" (PU 1.8) Christian hopes. Browning knew that when Prometheus mercifully planted blind hopes in the dark breast of man, he also gave man Fire which made all the arts enjoyable and warned him "not to foresee harm [judgment] and forestall the Fates." But when Browning then added that Christian faith, like that brave curry Jehovah's Grace, is an incidental condiment and can scarcely be digested without the proper victuals of life, he simply defied the possibility of detection and got away with it. Hard-to-be-a-Christian is not any more faithful to the cause he falsely undertook to defend than was Shelley who openly set out to reverse the theme of Promethean submission in Aeschylus' lost play. But he is extraordinarily well informed on J. S. Blackie's Shelleyan translation (1850) of the *Prometheus Bound* and leaves the unforgettable impression that Browning and Blackie were not unacquainted even at this early date.

The so-called disquisition of "Easter-Day" is in reality a superior burlesque, planned to be as inconsequential as a quarrel in which two confirmed believers in the earth's roundness banter over why the earth is flat. Not even a moderately faithful Christian would speak of the Crucifixion in terms of "the all-stupendous tale" (233), scoff at the report of an earthquake accompanied by darkness or conclude that "all took place, you think, / Only to give our *joys* a zest, / And prove our *sorrows* for the best." Browning's total celebration of the birth and the resurrection of Christ is skillfully contrived, even to the craftily manipulated horror of the sacrifice of Christ (241-56) and the cruelly specified intent which amounts to an inversion of St. John's "For God so loved the world." But once the insincerity of the scriptural allusions is seen, the parody breaks through with increasing severity as Browning presses his warfare against the very same forces which encircled Paracelsus, Sordello and the poet himself in *Pauline*. The marshalling of Browning's arguments is revamped and strengthened by the introduction of two supposedly differing participants who nonetheless through reversal, juxtaposed contradiction and incomplete proposition unite not only to fault Jehovah's plan but also to amend it. More confident than his fellow pantheist, Hard-to-be-a-Christian understands how instead of a crucifixion it would have been more beneficial to man and more economic to Jehovah to "give license formal and complete / To choose the fair and pick the sweet" (255-6). Only pretentiously standing in a scriptural cloud (351; PU 2.5, stage direction; Ex 34.5) is he reluctant to tell his wild vision, "seeing that if I carry through / *My purpose*, if my words in you / Find a live actual listener, / *My story, reason must aver / False* after all — the happy chance!" (353-7).

SAUL

1855

Often considered the most beloved and the most profoundly religious of Browning's poems, "Saul" was published as a fragment in 1845, as a revised fragment in 1849 and as a completed poem in 1855. Whether Browning had unwonted difficulty in manipulating such familiar details, feared that his deceptive syncretism of pagan and Christian thought and diction was likely to be detected at any time or was mulling over a scenario which would accommodate a greater distortion than the visions of Prometheus and Jehovah in *Christmas-Eve and Easter-Day*, he was not to be rushed any more than he was on *Sordello* or *The Ring and the Book*. That he had given further thought to the direction of the fragment is substantiated in the 1849 revision, where by adding the symbolic Strength and Beauty of earlier poems Browning confirmed his trust in self-consciousness and his sympathy for pantheistic exhilaration, not Judeo-Christian mortification, of the flesh. But it is the completed poem which demonstrates how diligently Browning had searched the Scriptures to find the most nearly perfect allusions for atmosphere and tone. Without the long delay he may never have accumulated the many Christian overtones and pagan undertones which mesh so deceptively, though Browning may already have completed a "Saul" when he published the first fragment. Nor would he have had the same chance to compose what is probably his most convincingly Christian poem, though he had long before evolved the arguments he exploits in "Saul." Ironically it is also in "Saul" that Browning leaves his thought and diction most vulnerable to detection, for it is here that he is emboldened to transpose Christ's "for my strength is made perfect in weakness" into Shelley's "Resist not the weakness."

Predetermined by Browning's schematics, the traditional interpretation of "Saul" is a brilliant camouflage. After lovingly describing the evanescent joys of youth, David pretends to see his error in praising the comforts of the flesh and recommends instead the permanent fruits of the spirit. It is all very much like the old debates between body and soul with the time-honored resolution. But once David has said this he proceeds to ignore the whole matter, praising Saul to full consciousness in recital of his earthly and courageous physical acts. David would never truly be found guilty of depreciating the glory of man's life, even the mere living. So the total poem may more readily be placed in the context of Browning's deception if the indisputable evidence is pointed out before approaching Section XVI. For it is here that Browning conspicuously and characteristically announces the undisguised Truth which came upon David but later disguises in references to two distinctly different GODs. One is St. Paul's Jehovah, the other is Shelley's Prometheus, but their specific identities are not needed to determine the reversals and deceptive applications embodied in the decisive climactic lines:

'T is the *weakness in strength*, that I cry for! my flesh, that I seek
In the Godhead! *I seek and I find it.* O Saul, it shall be
A Face *like* my face that receives thee; a Man *like* to me,
Thou shalt love and be loved by; a Hand *like* this hand
Shall throw open the gates of *new life* to thee!

The unreliability of these strangely neglected words which sound so convincingly Christian is fourfold, but the key to Browning's deception rests in the daring reversal of St. Paul's reporting:

My grace is sufficient for thee: for my [Christ's] strength is made perfect *in* [your, Paul's] weakness.

Clearly Christ's words, which are based on a fundamental Old and New Testament concept, say that the weaker Paul is the greater will be the inflowing of Jehovah's or Christ's strength, and with a sufficiency for which Paul adds, "Most gladly will I rather glory in my infirmities [weaknesses] that the power of Christ may rest upon me." David's impassioned lines are then a pretense at acceptance of scriptural thought, entrusted to words which are rarely challenged because of their familiar ring. Their truth lies concealed in Browning's customary daring, which elsewhere in his poetry exceeds the bounds but perhaps not the openness. Having adopted Shelley's intolerance of the ignorant Christian masses, Browning dared to believe that his unsuspecting readers would never observe the reversal, much less recognize that in reversing St. Paul's "strength . . . *in* weakness" he was emptying Christianity of all its meaning. Browning could be equally confident that Christians, so ill informed of a doctrinal expression as major as their most intimate relationship with Christ, would least of all readers be suspicious of a Shelleyan intrusion with which Browning cancels the dependence of their faith in Christ and substitutes the independence of the human mind:

> Resist not the *weakness*   (PU 2.3.93)
> Such *strength* is in meekness   ("wisdom," PU 2.4.44)
> That *the Eternal, the Immortal,*   (Demogorgon)
> *Must* unloose through life's portal   ("demand," Will)
> The snake-like Doom coiled underneath his throne
> By *that* alone.   (weakness)

Like Shelley's Asia and Panthea who are similarly drawn to Demogorgon's cave, Browning's David is drawn through his own Love and Will to Prometheus. Call his exhilaration a mystical experience or grant it pseudo-scriptural sanction and it is still without Christian significance because the precedents of St. John's and St. Paul's being caught up to heaven were spiritual in nature; David's is starkly a physical invasion of the divinity: "my *flesh* that I seek / In the Godhead! *I seek and I find it.*" David's physical absorption by the deity, which is both repulsive and destructive to Judeo-Christian thought, Browning predicates on the belief that as Man is both flesh and spirit Prometheus is both Spirit and flesh or, to be more exactly Shelleyan, the race of mankind is "like" Prometheus: man's "spirit / Until it walked, exempt from mortal care, / *Godlike*"; "Man looks on his creation *like a God*" (PU 2.4.77-9, 102). Prometheus had long been a Christ-figure to the pagans, and as Shelley welded characteristics together until his Prometheus took on all the aspects of Jesus Christ's recorded nature, Browning interfused pagan and

Christian matters until the Hebrew David could exclaim without detection, "See the Christ [Prometheus] stand!" So the "pure white light," which has been an ambiguous object of perpetual concern to Browning scholars, is not to be found in Love or Truth or Wisdom or Beauty but in the fountainhead of all four absolutes, Shelley's Prometheus: "the overpowering light / Of that immortal shape was shadowed o'er / By love" (PU 2.1.71-3). Nor are Browning's capitalized Face and Hand any longer mysterious allusions. It is the Face of Prometheus which smiles on so many Browning characters: " 't is He, arrayed / In the soft light of his own smiles, which spread / Like radiance from the cloud-surrounding moon. / Prometheus, it is thine! depart not yet. / Say not those *smiles* that we shall meet again / Within that bright pavilion which their beams / Shall build o'er the waste world?" (PU 2.1.120-6). And it is the Hand of Prometheus which sustains and guides so many Browning characters, all in anticipation of the Promethean "new life": "I would fain / Be what it is my destiny to be, / The savior and the strength of suffering man" (PU 1.815-7); " 'God is one supreme goodness, one pure essence, / One substance, and one sense, all sight, *all hands*' " (Calderon 1.115-6, also 191-6).

Thus a cleverly implanted anachronism, which won reader acceptance by its implied reference to the Messiah or Anointed One, should no longer distract the reader. Jesus Christ, who claimed to be the Messiah, is as far removed from Browning's "Saul" as are his atonement or the Grace of his Father, an absence long remarked on by discerning critics. With Browning as with Shelley there is need neither for forgiveness nor atonement, since evil and sin are nonexistent except in the sense of erring or mistaking one's natural course, all out of thoughtlessness which Prometheus may lightly and lovingly check with a monitory touch. Browning would have been false to David's earlier conviction and his own fixed belief if King Saul had not been granted the same bliss permanently that David enjoyed briefly: "my voice to my heart / Which can scarce dare believe in what marvels last night I took part" (199). It was Browning's deception which demanded that he suddenly drop Saul from the action because any surcease to his sorrow would have been recognized by innumerable readers. As the poetic David's mind, reconstructed by Browning to conform to Shelley's philosophic idealism, is a part of the One Mind — Prometheus, so the poetic David's love is a part of Love — Prometheus, thus establishing the Shelleyan truth of the absence of any barrier whatsoever between a beneficent divinity and man. Because Demogorgon had promised that "all things thou *dar'st demand*" (PU 2.4.8) shall be granted, David's "dare" gave him the warrant to seek and to find his flesh in the Godhead. That is, provided the willful demand was sufficiently infused by love, a fact amply shown in David's love for Saul: "oh, all my heart how it loved him!"

All really diversionary prelude, the first fifteen long sections of "Saul" are followed by a section (XVI) of one verse. By emphatically announcing that the truth then came upon David, Browning intends to bring the palpable injustice of Jehovah, not the frailty of flesh, to a test:

<pre>
Then *the truth* came upon me. No harp more —   (Mab 8.236-7)
    no song more! outbroke —   (W Shelley Draft 14)
</pre>

Increasingly distressed by Saul's hopeless state and evidence that Jehovah did not care, offered no "sign" (scriptural & Shelleyan), David has yearned, "Could I help thee, . . . inventing a bliss, . . . I would give thee *new life* altogether, . . . had love but the warrant, love's heart to dispense." Now David will explain and instruct, albeit by retaining the disguise of GOD — Jehovah or Prometheus:

<pre>
I have gone the whole round of creation: (XVII, 238)
    I saw and I spoke:
I, a work of *God's hand* for that *purpose,*   (Jehovah's; to see & speak)
    received in my *brain*   (Mind)
And *pronounced* on the rest of his handwork —
    returned him again
His creation's approval or censure: (Jehovah's, Para 5.279)
    I spoke as I saw:
</pre>

```
I report, as a man may of God's work —              (a true God's work)
     all's love, yet all's law.      (Prom's Love, Demogorgon's Necessity)
Now I lay down the judgeship he lent me.   (Jehovah, 1 Sam 1.28, 2.20)
     Each faculty tasked
To perceive him, has gained an abyss,   (Jehovah; nothing, PU 1.369-70)
     where a dewdrop was asked.                              (so little)
Have I knowledge? confounded it shrivels                        (Mind)
     at wisdom laid bare.                                 (Prometheus)
Have I forethought? how purblind, how blank,     (meaning of "Prom")
     to the Infinite Care!                               (Prometheus)
Do I [even need to] task any faculty highest
     to image success?
I but open my eyes, — and perfection,        (condition of the One Mind)
     no more and no less,
In the kind I imagined, full-fronts me,               ("kind" of God)
     and God is seen God                              (Prometheus)
In the star, in the stone, in the flesh,
     in the soul and the clod.                           (pantheism)
```

The truth which comes upon David is the same rational truth that motivates other Browning characters — the truth of Prometheus' perfect Mind and perfect Love. If David has knowledge, it is still confounded by Prometheus' wisdom; if David has forethought, the meaning of the word "Prometheus," it is still purblind and blank before Prometheus' Infinite Care. Believing that "all's love, yet all's law," a perfect Christian and pagan syncretism, David would perceive Saul's Jehovah by these standards, but all that he gains is an unanswering (E-Day 108) abyss when a mere "dewdrop" was asked. Less volatile than Paracelsus who hurls Jehovah's imperfection back with scorn (5.279), David nonetheless vigorously contrasts Jehovah's unloving rejection of Saul with Prometheus' perfection which is seen in the star, the stone and the clod as well as in the flesh and the soul. And it is probable that his subtle use of "abyss" is an allusion to savage fiends in Jehovah's mind. David may have been created, like so many of Browning's masks, supposedly to pronounce approval or censure on God's work, but here he draws the kind of God he prefers from a contrast of Jehovah and Prometheus:

Yet with all this abounding *experience,*   (Mind; 255)
　　this *deity* known,   (Jehovah)
I shall dare to discover some *province,*   (faculty)
　　some *gift* of my own.   (Genius)
There's a *faculty* pleasant to exercise,   (third usage)
　　hard to hoodwink,   (Reason)
I am fain to keep still in abeyance,
　　(I laugh as I *think*)   (Mind)
Lest, insisting to claim and parade in *it,*   (intellect)
　　wot ye, I worst
E'en *the Giver* in one gift. — Behold,   (Jehovah)
　　I could love if I *durst*!   (Shelley's "dar'st")
But I sink the *pretension* as fearing   (Christian "presumption")
　　a man may o'ertake
God's own speed in the one way of love: (Jehovah's, through eternity)
　　I *abstain* for love's sake.   (momentarily)
— What, my soul? see thus far and no farther?

Clearly "this deity known" is not the perfect deity of
David's pantheism but the one who granted an abyss when a
dewdrop was asked. The David, however, upon whom the
truth came suspiciously late is the same David who cere-
moniously "knelt down to the *God of my fathers*" (15)
before Abner, not lovingly as to his own companionate
Prometheus. Fully informed of his mind's being a "gifted"
part of the One Mind, David further knows that his Will is
sufficient to the requirements of Demogorgon's "dar'st demand." So when he asserts that he could love ever so much
more than the unloving Jehovah, he is simply marking time,
not honestly restraining his confidence. When he laughs as he
thinks, the humor of his momentary abstention from "worsting" Jehovah for love's sake is anticipatory:

Do I find love so full in my *nature,*   (Myself, self-consciousness; 266)
　　God's *ultimate* gift,   (final & last, given forever)
That *I doubt* his own love can compete with it?   (E-Day 978-9)
　　Here, the parts shift?
Here, the creature surpass the *Creator,* —   (Jehovah, C-Eve 1005)
　　the end, what Began? (the demise of Jehovah; "In the beginning")
Would I fain in my impotent yearning   (PU 1.815-7)
　　do all for this man,
And dare doubt *he* alone shall not help him,   (Prometheus)
　　who yet alone can?   (R & B 6.1280)

Would it ever have entered *my mind*,
    the bare *will*, much less *power*,   (Shelleyan)
To bestow on this Saul what I sang of,
    the marvelous dower
Of the life he was *gifted* and filled with?   (Genius)
    to make such a soul,
Such a body, and then such an earth for
    insphering the whole?   (Shelleyan)
And doth it not enter *my mind*
    (as my warm tears attest)
These good *things being given*, to go on, (body, soul, earth by Jehovah)
    and give one more, *the best*?   (Love)
Ay, to save and redeem and restore *him*,   (Saul)
    maintain at *the height*   (divinity)
This *perfection*, — succeed with life's *day-spring*,   (Islam 493, Lu 1.78)
    death's *minute* of night?   (PU 3.3.113-4)
Interpose at the *difficult minute*(thoughtless mistake, not disobedience)
    snatch Saul the mistake,   (Death, Dial 39)
Saul the failure, the *ruin he seems* now, —   (PU 1.619, 768, 780)
    and bid him *awake*   (Adonais 39.2)
From the *dream*, the probation, the prelude,   ("dream of life")
    to find himself set
Clear and safe in *new light* and *new life*, —
    a new harmony yet   (PU 4.1-578)
To be run, and continued, and ended —
    who knows? — or *endure*!   ("who can say," E-Day 1040;
The man taught enough, by *life's dream*,   PU 4.562-75; Adonais 39.2)
    of the rest to make sure;
By the *pain*-throb, triumphantly winning
    intensified *bliss*,   ("pain of bliss," PU 3.4.125)
And the next world's *reward* and repose,   (Q Mab 2.65)
    by the *struggles* in this.   (against Jehovah)

Nowhere else in his poetry does Browning more exhaustively cover the catalog of his grievances against Jehovah. In Sections XVII and XVIII alone, words like believe, care, creature, crown, dare, death, doubt, dream, face, fear, flesh, gate, gift, hand, knowledge, law, love, new, perfect, poor, power, praise, prayer, redeem, repose, restore, ruin, reward, save, service, sorrow, soul, strong, spirit, submit, thou, truth, weak, will, wisdom and work make Browning's above syncretism seem almost effortless. Thematic in Christianity as well as in Shelley's Prometheanism, the words enable Browning to move back and forth between Jehovah, who is unwilling or unable to help Saul, and Prometheus, whose un-limited Love and perfect Will cannot fail. In spite of David's masterful dissembling, the contrast takes on characteristic focus: the munificence of Prometheus, the parsimony of Jehovah; the beneficence of Prometheus, the vindictiveness of Jehovah. It is thus Jehovah's arbitrary law versus Prometheus' infinite love, Jehovah's fearful speed through eternity versus Prometheus' calm wisdom, Jehovah's demand for prayer and praise versus Prometheus' offer of help and companionship, Jehovah's tyrannical will versus Prometheus' sympathetic will and Jehovah's dreadful might versus Prometheus' loving power. David's Prometheus, in contrast to the "God of his fathers," is an acceptable God because he grants man full credit for trying and imposes no punishment on waywardness. David then does not break Browning's continuum of approval or censure but follows in the path of his forerunners: "Make that creator which was creature" (C-Eve 1005).

Reminiscent of the evil Jupiter's being released on Prometheus, Saul's struggle seems to be directly with Jehovah, not with "an *evil spirit* from the Lord" after *the Spirit* of the Lord departed (1 Sam 16.14): "To betoken that Saul and *the Spirit* have ended their strife, / And that, *faint in his triumph* [over Jehovah], the monarch sinks back upon life" (9-10; cf., Gen 32.28). Slowly the exhausted Saul resumes his old motions and habitudes kingly (207-8). But Saul continues silent and the sight of his lost glory so distresses David that it is then he yearns for power to restore the former glory, even to give Saul a new life altogether. The intensity of David's "And oh, all my heart how it loved him," which symbolizes Prometheus' love as readily as Jesus Christ's but is truly David's, is therefore adequate to the successful completion of a spiritual and physical absorption by Prometheus. Perhaps Browning wished to convey a Christian impression that Saul was also caught up in David's mystical experience and derived the same "terrible glory." But the Truth of Section XVII is that an acceptable God would not, could not, fail to "snatch Saul" from the difficulty he faces and translate him to "in-

tensified bliss." As David's mind is occupied with thought of
Saul's great talents, it is also occupied with thought of the
triviality of his disobedient trip to the Witch of Endor. Life's
dream, of which Shelley makes so much, is at best probative
and worthy of endurance only because its end is the triumphant portal to new light, new life and new harmony, all
promised in Shelley's apocalyptic fourth act of *Prometheus
Unbound.* And all believed by Browning's David:

I believe it! 'T is thou, *God,* that givest,   (Prometheus; 286)
    't is I who receive:
In the first is the last, *in* thy will   (spirit of Spirit, will of Will)
    is my power to believe.
All's one *gift: thou* canst grant it moreover, (C-Eve 294-8; Prometheus)
    as prompt to my prayer
As I breathe out this breath, as I open
    these arms in the air.
From thy *will, stream* the worlds, life and nature,   (Shelleyan)
    thy dread *Sabaoth:*   (Rom 9.29, Jas 5.4)
I will? the mere atoms despise me!   ("mere atoms," diversionary)
    Why am I not [then] loth   (double talk)
To look *that, even that* in the face too?   (being despised)
    Why is it I dare
Think but lightly of such *impuissance*?   (weakness)
    What stops my despair?
This; — 't is not what man *Does* which exalts him,
    but what man *Would* do!   (effort & energy are all)
See the King — I would help him but cannot,
    the wishes fall through.
Could I *wrestle* to raise him from sorrow,   (Gen 32.24-30)
    grow poor to enrich,
To fill up his life, starve my own out,
    I would — *knowing* which,   (Mind)
I know that my *service is perfect.*   (fourth usage, cf., Heb 9.9)
    Oh, speak through me now!
Would I suffer for *him* that I love?   (Saul)
    So wouldst *thou* — so wilt *thou!*   (Prometheus)
So shall crown *thee* the topmost, ineffablest,   (Prometheus)
    uttermost crown —   ("topmost" & "utmost" Shelleyan
And thy *love* fill infinitude wholly,   superlatives)
    nor leave up nor down
One spot for the creature to *stand in!*   (rest idly)
    It is by no *breath,*   (prayer)
Turn of eye, wave of hand, that salvation   (praise)

> joins issue with death!
> As *thy Love* is discovered almighty,   (Prometheus')
>   almighty be *proved*   (propagated)
> *Thy power, that exists with and for it,*   (PU 4.395)
>   of being beloved!
> *He* who did most, *shall bear most;* the strongest   (Prometheus)
>   *shall stand the most weak.*
> 'T is the *weakness in strength,* that I cry for!   (PU 2.3.93-7)

Put as bluntly as Shelley ever phrased or dramatized them, when the obfuscation by diversionary word, impossible punctuation and double entente is eliminated, David enunciates Browning's understanding and advocacy of Will, Power, Love and Perfection. How Browning had the courage to be so forthright must therefore be attributed as much to his conscious skill at deception and his determination to advance trust in Prometheus as to his fearlessness of detection. The successful portrayal and warm appeal of David's character may hinge to a surprising degree on the poet's substitution of Dare and Pretension for Presume and Presumption, which to the Christian traditionally signify a lack of humility, a haughty spirit. But whatever the expression of hesitancy or forwardness before God, Browning's David finds in his smoldering will a determination to exercise a personal gift which does overtake Jehovah's "own speed in the one way of love," a province of his own which does "worst / E'en the Giver in one gift." In his willing, his extraordinary self-assurance, which are a denial of Jehovah's perfection and immutability and condemned by the Scriptures, David employs the Shelleyan "dare" seven times (99, 122, 200, 256, 260, 270, 293). Knowing that his will is part of Prometheus' Will, he can count on his excessive love and fierce energy to return him to Prometheus. To Browning as to Shelley, Love and Power are never to be separated (PU 4.395), and as David demonstrates, successful willing is impossible without the properly initiated or attendant love. Thus the confidence for David's saying "in thy *will* is my *power* to believe." The soulful address cannot possibly be to Jehovah, whom David has found deficient both in love and will. Nor can it possibly escape being directed to Prometheus since David's will is declared to be a part of the Will of Prometheus, the only deity disposed to do for Saul what Jehovah has failed or refused to do.

Inseparability of Love, Power and/or Will also explains why Browning's David four times associates Love with Perfection. David remembers Prometheus' words "I said all hope was vain but love; thou lovest" (PU 1.824). By the fullness of his love David knows that his "service is perfect" as he knows that the perfection of Prometheus, to whom he is drawn, is incontestable. Even THE EARTH's waiting cave exhales a "calm" perfection (PU 3.3.146), since it is to be the abode of Prometheus and Asia. First David spoke of the perfection to be seen in the star, stone, flesh and soul, and then of the perfection which must be found at the height (278); now he speaks of the perfection of his service (PU 4.168). All of which is projected on Shelley's metaphysics, first in the re-union of Prometheus and Asia which restores perfection to the deity, second in the sound of Proteus' shell which, unlike St. John's trumpet, introduces a new perfection to mankind (PU 3.4.1-204). Add to this apocalyptic "change" David's Weakness which resists not, indeed imposes on, Demogorgon's law of Necessity, and it becomes clear why Browning's David "dare / Think but lightly [that is, without fear] of such *impuissance* [weakness]" as permits him to surpass Jehovah's love and qualify for absorption by Prometheus. Even though Browning undoubtedly modelled his well-known "mystical experience" of David on Panthea's absorption by Prometheus (PU 2.1.62-89), there is probably nothing in Shelley or in any mystic which surpasses the convincing and artistic quality of David's mystical recollection in Section XIX. Yet it is a foregone conclusion that David rejects both the faith of his fathers and the faith required to believe that Jesus Christ's strength is made perfect in the weakness of a suppliant. David is a Promethean like his creator and he thus eagerly anticipates with the same irreversible trust the new light, the new life (PU 4.441) and the new harmony (PU 4.29) which Shelley promulgates in Act IV of *Prometheus Unbound*: "'T is love, all love!" (PU 4.369).

Like all of God's animals which were awakened by the sublimity of David's return to his sheep, David has felt the new law of love. He scarcely can await the new and diviner Promethean day.

It will be recalled that early in "Saul," after laughing (140) at his tardiness in seeing the futility of restoring Saul to mere consciousness, David alters his theme on the joys of earthly life and advises: "Leave the *flesh* to the fate it was fit for! the *spirit* be thine!" (160). But David is only pretending, for he then says, "Forget [do not believe] that man's *power* and his *beauty* forever take flight" (174); remember instead that as with the sun *nothing* has been produced in thy life beyond the measure of thine own deeds (166, PU 2.4.72-3):

so, each ray of *thy will*,	(Saul's; 167)
Every flash of thy *passion and prowess*,	("ray," Death, Dial 26, 31)
long over, shall thrill	
Thy whole people . . .	
With the *radiance thy deed* was the *germ of.*	(PU 4.387, Epipsy 223;
Carouse in the past!	Q Mab 5.9, 147; 171)

Although it is a repudiation of his scriptural heritage, such unqualified praise David knowingly predicates on "the *courage* that gains, / And the prudence that keeps what men strive for" (143-4). Thus it is a praise he foresees from all men in all time (220). Thanks to the energy with which Browning endows his aspiring characters, David does rapidly gain the warrant — "had love the warrant, love's heart to dispense" — and is permitted, in St. Paul's phraseology, to "report, as a man may of God's work — all's love [Prometheus], yet all's law [Demogorgon's law of Necessity]" (242). One of Shelley's favorite words for the exaltation of exceptionally talented individuals, Radiance may be given its most memorable play in "Epipsychidion": "As one sandalled with plumes of fire, / And towards the lodestar of my one desire, / I flitted, like a dizzy moth, whose flight / Is as a dead leaf's in the owlet light, / When it would seek in Hesper's setting sphere / A *radiant death*, a fiery sepulchre, / As if it were a lamp of earthly flame."

Somewhat oddly, Browning's introduction of the New

Law of Love (see also 331) is noticeably unobtrusive. Perhaps he did not choose to reflect Tennyson's "Who trusted God was love indeed / And love Creation's final law" (In Mem LVI, 1850), that is, "Strong Son of God [Jehovah], immortal Love." For the Promethean results of David's mystical experience were to be accentuated in the physical and the spiritual, in the ineffable Shelleyan Unity of the True, the Beautiful, the Good, and in the more subtle essence of David's "prayer" the morning after his absorption by Prometheus:

> but *O Thou* who didst grant me that day,　　(Prometheus; 191)
> And before it not seldom hast granted
> 　　thy help to essay,
> Carry on and complete *an adventure,* —(R.B.'s warfare against Jehovah)
> 　　my shield and my sword
> In that act where my soul was thy *servant,*　　(PU 3.3.1-4)
> 　　thy word was my word, —
> Still be with me, who then at the summit
> 　　of human *endeavor*　　(Ode to Liberty 243)
> And scaling the highest, *man's thought could,*　　(Mind)
> 　　gazed hopeless as ever
> On the new stretch of heaven above me — till,
> 　　*mighty to save,*　　(Isa 63.1, PU 4.408)
> Just one lift of *thy hand* cleared that distance —　　(Prom's, cf., 321)
> 　　God's throne from man's grave!

Messianic and Christian in so many of the overtones, David's words above, in what has been thought to be a prayer of thanksgiving to Jehovah, are inexplicable unless understood to be the opposite of prayer and addressed to a loving and beneficent deity who disdains praise or gratitude of any sort. The thirteen-line sentence, deliberately made incoherent by unintelligible dashes and jumbled impressions, is thoroughly in accord with the poet's normal practice of deception and illustrative of his regularly intruding his own personal persuasion despite the mask through which he enunciates and hopefully indoctrinates. Since the ideas confusingly repeat rather than advance the narrative, they are perhaps intended to say as much about Browning's own adventure in deception as about David's method of accomplishing a physical absorption by Prometheus. David has returned to his sheep in the hollow (Shelleyan) and can still "scarce dare believe in what marvels," in what "terrible glory," he had partaken the night before. And why not, since the emphasis here clearly falls on a protracted human endeavor which is totally dependent upon "man's thought" not faith, one scaling so high that the throne of Prometheus, the One Mind, consummates the aspiration of both David and Browning?

Fully representative of Browning's established litany of charges against Jehovah and praise of Prometheus, the ideas expressed in Sections XVII and XVIII are often alluded to in other sections of "Saul." One must search, however, for new indictments or approvals, and save for the distinctiveness of new phrase or imagery Browning's plan seems to have settled into a drive to perpetuate these fixed arguments in as many different settings as possible, with as many allusions to Shelley as possible. Like Paracelsus, David is fearlessly Shelleyan. As a pantheist, he is also a star-gazer and particularly impressed by the king-serpent's Shelleyan "change" as well as by the Shelleyan serpent that slid away silent, feeling the new law of love. David sees Saul's fame in the *light* it was made for and, because he is smitten by Shelleyan Radiance and Desire, he refuses to believe that Power and Beauty ever take flight. When in need of help David feels Prometheus' hand as intimately as do Pauline's lover, Sordello and Paracelsus. When contrasting the conditions of life, he describes the unfavorable ones in terms of hopes and fears or despair as persistently as do his fellow Browning characters. Like Shelley himself David is awed by great mountains and their snowy heights, and he is persuaded that Saul's genius, unlike Ozymandias' tyranny, will be perpetuated in the creative praise of sculptor, poet and scribe. David naturally rejects any intimation of Sin, believing with his creator and Shelley that whatever man's error it is not of his own making. And like his Browning forerunners David relishes all *thought* which permits him to speculate on life, Life, LIFE. Yet compassionately deceptive his "Didst thou see the thin hands of thy mother, . . . and hear her faint tongue" renews Browning's constant concession to the Christian faith of his own mother.

Why Browning decided to fashion his heroes and heroines Prometheans is more important than when he decided. For it makes no difference what period of history, what country or what age or sex a poem incorporates, the characters through which Browning speaks are Promethean, and possibly because he saw less chance of a fatal slip in a mask than in an imagined character. To doubt that he had the courage or temerity to make David a Hebrew Promethean is to forget that one of Browning's surest ways of deception was to dramatize the lives of the very historical characters least to be suspected of apostasy. One of the reasons for his selection of unknown, even unknowable, individuals was surely to aid his deception, but a better reason was his opportunity and ability to select individuals who in every historical case were of independent mind and strong belief or trust in the immortality of the soul. An example is that which Browning derived from his publicized Hebraic studies, started with "Saul" or as an outgrowth of that preparation. Apparently he wrote (1854) and released (1856) his first venture "Ben Karshook's Wisdom" too rapidly, for he exerted every effort to suppress this minor work for the future benefit of "Karshish," "Rabbi Ben Ezra" and "Holy-Cross Day." But the point here is that Rabbi Eliezer ben Hyrkanos (Karshook, meaning thistle & Shelleyan) was a famous and independently-minded teacher who, by the poet's conniving with Henry Fuseli's belief in the immortality of the soul, became a poetic "Hiram's-Hammer": "His [Hiram's] father was a man of Tyre, a worker in *brass*: and he [Hiram] was filled with wisdom and understanding, and cunning to work all works in *brass*" (1 K 7.14). Did Browning also fear that someone might remember he had threatened before naming a tenth of the wheels of opposition he planned for Jehovah to be busy slitting steel or *shredding brass* on some virgin shore under a cluster of fresh stars?

Oh, that it might be shown as quickly that as Karshook

was a recipient of Promethean metallurgy (including the stinging verbal retort), his fellow Hebrews were recipients of
multiple Promethean gifts. Browning knew that Abenezra
(Rabbi Ben Ezra, 1864) was a Neoplatonist, firmly believing
in the immortality of the soul; a distinguished scholar in
mathematics and astronomy, exhibiting originality and wit in
admirably crisp language; and a thinker in all of whose views
astrology held a prominent place. What better historical
figure could Browning have chosen to represent Shelley's
Radiance of Death and the joyous return of a partial but exceptional soul to the One Spirit, Prometheus? What better
historical commentator, as uniform misinterpretation of
"Rabbi Ben Ezra" attests, could Browning have chosen to
repeat: "Not that, admiring stars, / It yearned 'Nor Jove, nor
Mars; / Mine be some *figured flame* [Gisb 15-34] which
blends, transcends them all'" (10-2); "Not for such *hopes
and fears* / Annulling youth's brief years" (13-4); "Rejoice
we are allied / To *That* which doth provide / And not partake,
effect and not receive" (25-7); "Each *sting* that bids nor sit
nor stand but go! ... *Learn*, nor account the *pang*; dare,
never grudge the throe" (33-6); "Not once beat 'Praise be
Thine [Jehovah]! I see the whole design, / I, who saw power,
see now love *perfect* too: / *Perfect* I call Thy [Prometheus']
plan: Thanks that I was *a man*!'" (55-9). Thence shall Ben
Ezra pass, the poem continues, approved a man and forever
removed from the developed brute, a god though in the germ
(76-8). His rage was therefore right in the main, since acquiescence is vain, and he may face the Future because he has
proved the Past (100-2). It is enough if the Right and Good
and Infinite be named as one calls his hand his own with
absolute knowledge, subject to no dispute from fools that
crowded youth and forbade it to feel alone (115-20):

<pre>
      Be *there*, for once and all,   (Promethean new day; XXI)
      Severed great minds from small,
Announced to each his *station* in the Past!   (Adonais 5.2, Ode to
      Was I, the world arraigned,   Liberty 1.10, Hellas 74)
      Were they, *my soul disdained*,
Right? Let age speak the truth and give us *peace* at last!
</pre>

> *Fool*! All that is, at all,   ("vulgar mass," 133; XXVII)
>   Lasts ever, past recall;
> Earth changes, but thy soul and *God* stand sure: (Prometheus)
>   *What entered into thee*,   (from the One Mind, One Spirit)
>   *That* was, is, and shall be: (R.B.'s italics)
> Time's wheel runs back or stops: Potter and clay endure.

>   And I shall thereupon   (XIV)
>   Take rest, ere I be gone
> Once more on my *adventure* brave and new: (Saul 193)
>   Fearless and unperplexed,
>   *When I wage battle next*,   (against Jehovah)
> What *weapons* to select, what *armor* to *indue*.   (Saul 193; Gisb 175)

Irrespective of whether Browning's Ben Ezra or his David
responds more militaristically to the machinery of hopes and
fears, joys and sorrows, Abenezra, the historical Hebrew,
supplied Browning the chance in "Holy-Cross Day" (1855)
for one of his most unbelievable reversals. For in a translation
Browning claimed to have made of the famous "Song of
Death" he dared to convert the angel which appeared from
heaven to strengthen Jesus in Gethsemane (Lu 22.43) into
Prometheus, with the Titan then rescuing Jesus and replac-
ing him on the Cross:

> *Thou*! if thou wast He, who at *mid-watch* came,   (Prometheus;
> By the starlight, *naming a dubious name*!   PU 1.821; Jehovah's angel)
> And if, too heavy with *sleep* — too rash   (Disciples)
> With *fear* — *O Thou*, if that martyr-gash   (Jesus; Prometheus)
> Fell on *Thee* coming to take *thine own*,   (Prometheus; Jesus)
> *And we gave the Cross*, when we owed the Throne —   (Jews to
>   Prometheus)
> *Thou* art the Judge. We are *bruised* thus.   (Prometheus; Aeschylus' Io)
> But, the *Judgment* over, join sides with us!   (monitory touch)
> *Thine* too is the cause! and not more thine   (Prometheus or Jesus)
> Than ours, is the work of these *dogs and swine*,   (Christ's followers)
> Whose life laughs through and spits at their creed!   (Shelleyan)
> Who maintain *Thee* in word, and defy *Thee* in deed!   (Christ)

> We withstood *Christ* then? Be mindful how   (Jesus)
> At least we withstand *Barabbas* now!   ("Christian fellowship")
> Was our *outrage* sore? But the worst we spared,   (Q Mab 5.198)
> To have called these — Christians, had we dared!
> Let defiance to *them* pay mistrust of *Thee*, (Christ's slaves; Prometheus)
> And *Rome* make amends for *Calvary*!   (our rebellion; mistaking Prom)

We boast our proof that at least the Jew
Would wrest *Christ's name from the Devil's crew.*   (Christ from
Thy face took never so *deep a shade*   Christian; Marenghi 88, 144)
But we fought *them* in it, *God* our aid!   (Christians; Prometheus)
A trophy to bear, as we march, thy *band,*   (Blackie's PB 135)
South, East, and on to the *Pleasant* Land!   (not Promised Land)

Unintelligible unless read essentially as the marginalia suggest, these lines, supposedly written by an exceptional Hebrew scholar, must say that even in thought of death Abenezra remained proud that Jesus was withstood as the Christ by his people and sorrowful that Prometheus' vicarious act in rescuing Jesus from death on the cross was unrecognized by them. Otherwise, one needs to account for the marked similarity of Browning's diction in the first half of "Holy-Cross Day" with that of Shelley's *Oedipus Tyrannus; or, Swellfoot the Tyrant,* for the same rats, mice, dogs, pigs, swine, frogs, wasps, fleas and worms at joyous and vindictive play in filth and slime and stinking carcase and for the allusion of "bruised" to Io's experience with the rapacious Zeus as well as the related allusions in "Rabbi Ben Ezra" and "Karshish" (Lazarus) to pang, tang, itch and sting. Both poets delighted in reference to the stinging gadfly sent by Hera to persecute Io, partly because Io's "touch-born" son Hercules rescued Prometheus from Jupiter's enchainment. Nor can Shelley's influence be missed in harsh, strange, change, point or stranger-seed (R of Islam 2355) any more than in the thematic paraphrase of "When the slaves enslave, the oppressed ones o'er / The oppressor triumph for evermore" (R of Islam, ded, 13.6; 2.43.6, 8.15.9). But surpassing all else Ben Ezra's "Song of Death" reemphasizes the Shelleyan triumph of Death, the victory which exploits and belittles St. Paul's "sting" in contrast to Promethean radiance. It scarcely seems necessary to add that neither Moses nor Jesus left latitude for "joining sides" like children or dismissing judgment like momentary frowns. While J. S. Blackie probably provided "dubious name" and "band" and Shelley provided "crew" and "devil" (Triumph 184, Mask 190, Rosalind 683), Browning was devising "A trophy to bear, as we march, thy [Prome-

theus'] band, / South, East, and on to the Pleasant Land"
which also provided the most substantial 1863 addition to
the deception of *Paracelsus*: "A troop of yellow-vested white-
haired Jews / Bound for their own land where *redemption
dawns*" (5.345-6; Blackie's PB 103).

Browning's professed technical reasons for shuffling poems
about from edition to edition now seem much less reliable
than his ulterior thematic reasons. At least by the latter he
succeeded in placing "Holy-Cross Day" with its Christian
pogrom for the Jews finally next to the fiercely indignant
"The Heretic's Tragedy" with its "Middle-Age Interlude" of
a ghastly Church hanging. As Browning's deceptively re-
strained David offers only a foretaste of what the Hebrew
studies entailed, Browning's many other deceptively drawn
characters offer only hints of the probable abnormalities to
which he bent them to justify a commitment to Shelleyan
Love and to express opposition to Jehovah. Apparently the
startling "And yet God has not said a word!" means that
Prometheus approved of the method of winning Porphyria's
everlasting love. Apparently death to one's self (In a Gondola) and to an uncooperative husband (Pippa Passes) are
approved means of fulfilling physical love, as Browning's
earliest critics charged. Only inaction by the physically
attracted warrants a rebuke of any dimension by the poet:
"the unlit lamp [Promethean] and the *ungirt* loin" (Bion
Adonis 18). Thus in ordering his tomb the pagan bishop
merely regrets the end of his voluptuous physical existence
but takes deep consolation in a burial spot from which "to
see God [Jehovah] made and eaten all day long." In all
likelihood it is the saintly Brother Lawrence who is fully
deserving of the blast of uncontrollable and choking anger by
the libertine soliloquist.

A DEATH IN THE DESERT
1864

Presumably "A Death in the Desert" is an expression of St. John's fear that as memory of the actual life of Jesus vanishes daily around him so with his own death will all memory vanish, even of himself: "the Word of Life. / How will it be when none more saith 'I saw'?" In reality the poem is an imaginary manuscript recantation of St. John's faith, possibly owned by and possibly being read by the Gnostic Cerinthus who opposed the divinity of Jesus and, as legend has it, may have debated the issue publicly with St. John: "Cerinthus read and mused" (665). Though normally thought to be inspired by the Revelation and the Gospel of St. John, perhaps because Browning's John excitedly asks for his Gospel to handle rather than accept wine as a stimulant, the poem takes its impetus from and repudiates the epistles, as opposition to Jehovah, denial of his only begotten son and pretentious paraphrases (131-3, 186) attest. It is in 1, 2, 3 John that the apostle writes about the perfection of Jehovah's love, the need for genuine Christians to love one another not their enemies the heretics and Jehovah's promise of eternal life through faith in Christ Jesus. Scarcely a thought of Browning's John conforms to the recorded thought, not even to the historical John's attitude on love, because Browning's emphasis falls on a combined physical and spiritual love of the Shelleyan variety. Browning believed, and who can dispute him, that he could turn almost any idea, not just a religious one, topsy-turvy and go undetected if the proper setting were provided. To plant a whole system of alien thought in the mind of his John as if he were St. John, Browning reasoned that he needed only to scatter the most memorable incidents in the life of the beloved disciple among his and Cerinthus' heresies and to smother the heresies with distracting verbosities. Always a diversionary tactic, Piety in conjunction with misty and gibberish-like lines indicates that Browning thinks he has pushed one heresy far enough for the time being, not that he is ready to forsake its development.

Like Shelley, Browning was conversant with most if not all forms of Gnosticism and warmly addicted to many of the ancient beliefs. Their difference was that whereas Shelley was aggressively forthright Browning had to adopt a continuing subterfuge of pretending to distrust human knowledge when it was truly at the pinnacle of his faith. Each poet favored the very most primitive pagan thought, and with Browning the favor extended down to relatively late primitive religious forms such as those of Jacob Boehme, Cornelius Agrippa, Paracelsus and the Anabaptists and Primitive Baptists who retained an odd mixture of heretical and orthodox beliefs. Both poets had an inexhaustible grounding in Greek and still more ancient mythology, but while Shelley seemed to be nearer a purist in pagan adaptations, Browning like Agrippa revealed a predilection for the more shocking elements. Moreover Browning wandered far afield among the earliest interpreters of Gnosticism and the new Christology. A run-down of the ancient Gnostic authorities mentioned or alluded to in Browning's poetry uncovers an unusual breadth of curiosity and exploitation. The best known are probably Cerinthus, Valentinus, Ptolemaeus and Marcion, all made easily available through the syncretic Christianity of Agrippa if not the elaborate anti-heretical works of Irenaeus, Hippolytus and Epiphanius. A review of Browning's thought establishes a remarkably sympathetic acceptance of Gnostic forms which tended away from any particularly endowed human being, such as Jesus, and toward the most primitive pagan forms to which Shelley adhered. Browning was especially well versed in the time-honored antinomianism of Gnostic groups, in Manichean and Docetic practices which absorbed and gradually replaced Gnosticism per se, and in many gradations of opposition to and compromise with Gnosticism as the Church Fathers weeded out or absorbed rebellious groups.

Without knowledge beyond his own speculations on Gnostic rejection of the Moral Law, Browning would have been less effective in the surprisingly adaptable "Johannes Agricola." Without his earliest discoveries, probably in Agrippa, Browning could not have created the same Paracelsus. For Agrippa reflected Gnostic beliefs on the inertia of the flesh, freedom from which enables the enlightened soul not only to regain mastery over itself but also to win power over Nature, and on the fervency of love, lack of which seems to prevent Paracelsus' soul from becoming an image of God or God himself. Evidently Browning was untouched by the Docetic notion that Christ's body was merely a phantom or appearance, or that if real its substance was celestial. But Browning heartily indorsed Manichean emphasis on Wisdom and need for escaping the Kingdom of Darkness, that is, the body. And to the distinguishing Gnostic belief in two GODs Browning must have given his strongest approval: one, a God of love; the other, a God of justice and severity who soon became associated with Jehovah in the Gnostic mind. As Browning's reading became as diversified and knowledgeable as his father's and Shelley's, he had to reject the fideist Agrippa but he could pretend that his interest lay with the less rationalistic Agrippa, Paracelsus and other Reformation authors whose syncretisms of Neoplatonic, patristic, cabalistic and Hermetic thought stayed tenuously Christian. Browning was studiously familiar with the great debates which divided the Church Fathers into Platonists and Aristotelians, and his poetic allusions demonstrate that he was not uninformed on any of the famous disputants. But Browning's secret interest seemed to focus on such independents as Arius, Pelagius, the Socinians and Bruno whom he rarely mentions by name compared with the orthodox Albertus Magnus, St. Thomas and John Duns Scotus. For Pelagius' denial of original sin and need for baptism, denial of death as a punishment and need of divine grace for salvation accurately represent a very large part of Shelley's and Browning's opposition to Christian government. So do Socinian emphasis on freedom of thought and opposition to the trinity, original sin, depravity, predestination and the Roman Catholic Church conform to their beliefs. And Bruno's persuasion that the human soul may be reabsorbed by God contains the essence of their metaphysics. Browning was proudly though secretly of the Aristotelian party insofar as his allegiance weakened any dependence upon faith and neglect of the mind.

New Testament writers, given in almost every instance to condemnation of false or opposing prophets (Antichrists), strenuously opposed Gnostic attempts to blend Eastern mysticism, Greek and Roman thought with their new faith. Yet beyond its worldliness and its intellectualism which brought about the denial of Christ's divinity, Gnosticism probably aroused greatest opposition in its belief that spirit and matter are unaffiliated and that sin springs from the flesh only. More vehemently opposed to the Gnostics than St. John, Jude pinpoints their differences with early Christians: "Likewise also these filthy dreamers *defile the flesh, despise dominion, and speak evil of dignities*" (8). Clearly Jude and St. John could not condone a belief which maintained that only those individuals who cultivated their spiritual powers and ignored the body were truly immortal. The main object of 1 John is to safeguard its readers against the influences of false teachers (notably Cerinthus, if legend may be trusted). Because Browning's daring substitution of his and Cerinthus' heretical thoughts for St. John's scriptural teachings may seem more nearly impossible than his making the Hebrew David an apostate to Jehovah, one must remember Browning's threat of the number of wheels his imagination was to turn and his sole concern of life which was to advance the cause of a God who loves. Only a designingly determined person would venture to turn St. John totally against his lifelong struggle for Christ and supplant his goal of achieving eternal life with a search for earthly knowledge. Thus Browning cagily assigns single and indeterminate quotation marks to the most damaging hypothetical questions asked his John, and he confusingly permits his John to present two bodies of thought, the first of which is concluded with "This *might be* pagan teaching: now hear mine" (452). But Browning is so confident of his power to deceive that the thought of the first part nonetheless continues indistinguishable in the second part, or if any change is to be found the second part, supposedly the dying wish of St. John to his followers, is more completely the thought of Cerinthus and Browning than is the first part.

Who can doubt that Browning's dying John would suddenly sit upright on hearing exclaimed "I am the *R*esurrection and the *L*ife," be wary of the increasing number of Antichrists and express the belief that "Such ever was love's way: to rise, it stoops"? But these are diversions, just as John's "Plucking the blind ones back from the abyss" (641) diverts attention from the true abyss, Jehovah's heaven, and falsely conjures up Gnosticism and paganism as the beguiling entrapment. The poem first becomes seriously engaged with John's expressed disappointment at receiving no further commission after the Revelation and a more startling revelation that John has "grown" in wisdom and knowledge until his one desire is to teach "love" as the only way to godhood rather than formerly as the reason for Jehovah's sacrificial gift of his son:

With nothing left to my *arbitrament*	(free will; 143)
To choose or change: I *wrote*, and men believed.	(the Revelation)
Then, for my time grew brief, no message more,	
No call to write again, *I found a way*,	(self-determination)
And, *reasoning from my knowledge*, merely taught	(Myself, Mind)
Men should, *for love's sake, in love's strength believe*;. . .	(Shelleyan)
Since much that at the first, in deed and word [of Christ],	(168)
Lay simply and *sufficiently* exposed,	("Go ye into all the world")
Had grown (*or else* my soul was grown to match, . . .	
Of new significance and fresh result;	(173)
What first were guessed as points, I now knew stars, . . .	("stars," facts)
Ye brought me here, and I supposed the end,	(184)
And went to sleep with one thought that, at least,	
Though the whole earth should lie in wickedness,	(1 Jn 5.19,
We had the truth, might leave the rest to God.	E-Day 262; cf., 112-3)
Yet now I wake in such *decrepitude* . . .	(despondency)
Grasping the while for stay at *facts which snap*, . . .	(Cenci 5.1.82; 191)
Feeling for foot-hold through *a blank profound*,	(Hellas 870-8; 193)
Along with unborn people in strange lands,	
Who say — I hear said or conceive they say —	
'Was John at all, and did he say he saw?	
Assure us, ere we ask what he might see!'	(R.B.'s springboard)

All of which warns that in his supposed coma and long sleep Browning's John has changed (or enlarged) his mind and that his valedictory will be a denial of the faith 1 John 1-5 places in Jehovah's love and promise of eternal life. On his own John has found a Shelleyan way of "reasoning from [his] knowledge" that "men should, for love's sake, in love's strength believe." From out the "blank profound" of doubt, where his mind has been grappling with Fancy and Fact, now rise *stars* of knowledge he would not conceal from his followers. Not one thought here expressed typifies the real St. John, not even Browning's repeated use of a Johannine quotation which bitterly irritated Hard-to-be-a-Christian. For St. John does not say "the whole *earth* lieth in wickedness," disparaging to Shelley's praise of Earth; he says "the whole *world*," meaning the pagan counterpart to the Christian world. How Browning's John "assures" the impatient young of "the promise of [Christ's] coming" (177) thus institutes the advancement of heresies readily attributable to Cerinthus and Browning but deceptively assigned to St. John. Though the heresies have nothing to do with the Second Coming of Christ, they are made quite acceptable by the assurance of "What first were *guessed* as points, [John] now *knew* stars," and by the propitious placement of St. John's desertion of Christ at Gethsemane (310).

Can the impatient, John innocently asks, "who have *flesh*, a veil of youth and strength / About each spirit," share with me who "lie bare [dying] to the universal prick of light?" It matters little to Browning that St. John's only reference to youth appears in "I have written unto you, young men, because ye are strong, and the word of God abideth in you, and ye have overcome the wicked one" (1 Jn 2.14). While converting St. John into a resentful and unfaithful disciple who now thinks he has been misled by lack of knowledge which will teach youth to "see," Browning further adds a challenge by John to the fairness of old age and the validity of the Life and Death of Christ, each aspect of which belies the historical record:

Is it for *nothing* we grow old and weak,   (1 Jn 3.14; 206)
We whom God loves? When *pain* ends, *gain* ends too.   (Ph'p 1.21)
To me, that story — ay, that Life and Death
Of which I wrote 'it was' — to me, it is;
— Is, here and now: I apprehend naught else.   (gibberish-like, the last
                    three lines annul the whole of St. John's theology)
Is not *God* now i' the world *His power* first made?   (Prom, wisdom)
Is not *His love* at issue still with [imaginary] sin,   (Prometheus')
Visibly when a wrong is done on earth?   (diversionary)
Love, *wrong, and pain*, what see I else around?   (Jehovah's gifts)
Yea, and the Resurrection and *Uprise* . . .   (Eug Hills 73; PU 2.5.22)
And, as I saw the sin and death, even so   (218)
See I the need yet transiency of both,   ("sin & death")
The good and glory consummated thence?   (Q Mab 9.1-11)
I saw the power; I see the Love, once weak,
Resume the Power: and in this word 'I see,'
Lo, there is recognized the *Spirit* of *both*   (Prom; Love & Power,
That moving o'er the spirit of man, unblinds   PU 4.395)
His eye and bids him look. . . .
Just thus, ye needs must apprehend *what truth*   (235)
I see, reduced to plain *historic fact*,   (John has relinquished his faith)
Diminished into clearness, proved a *point*   (PU 3.3.41)
And far away: *ye would withdraw* your sense   (ye should withdraw)
From out eternity, strain it upon time,   (forget about eternal life)
Then stand before that fact, *that Life and Death*,   (of Christ)
Stay there at gaze, till it [Christ's life] *dispart, dispread*, (Q Mab 1.200;
As though *a star* should open out, all sides,   R of I 2519; PU 2.1.17)
Grow the world on you, as it is my world.   ("Love not the world, . . .
                    If any man love the world, the love of the Father is not in
                    him. / For all that is in the world, the lust of the flesh, and
                    the lust of the eyes, and the pride of life, is not of the
                    Father, but is of the world,"1 Jn 2.15-6; "Marvel not, my
                    brethren, if the world hate you," 1 Jn 3.13)

A Browning favorite, "pain and gain" was an unfortunate antithesis to employ since St. John's only use of either word for Christian edification is in the famous "And God shall wipe away all tears . . . neither shall there be any more *pain*" (Rev 21.4), where gain implicitly *begins* does not *end*. Obviously Browning is objecting to St. Paul's "For to me to live is Christ, and to die is *gain*" (Ph'p 1.21). Observe, though, after the false attribution of "Is it for *nothing* we grow old," since St. John faithfully wrote "We know that we have passed from death unto life," the mincing and pirouetting, the misleading assumption that Jehovah's love, not goodness or justice, is at issue with Sin. Gibberish-like and thus designed to be skipped, these lines accentuate the Shelleyan stress of intellectual choice on John's mind and effectively nullify his faith (fancy) of the past Was in the fact of the present Is. Browning knew that in all major modern religions Goodness, not love, is at issue with Sin: "Beloved, follow not that which is evil, but that which is good. He that doeth good is of God: but he that doeth evil hath not seen God" (3 Jn 11). It is in Prometheanism that Shelley pits Love against the imaginary evil and judgment of Christianity. As Shelley's "Uprise" betrays the ambiguity of GOD so Browning's capital letters in Resurrection and Life point to Prometheus, not Jesus Christ. But the poet's boldest inversion of New Testament thought occurs in John's statement that both Evil and Death are transient yet necessary concomitants of life, evil as necessary as good if man is to *learn*, to *progress*, to *accept God's gift* which is to "conceive of truth [fact] / And yearn to gain it, catching at mistake, / As midway help till he reach *fact* indeed" (605). Without regret Browning's John chooses the world as an *historic fact* and recommends that Christ's followers and his immediate followers forget about eternal life and learn how to become gods. Just how they are to do this involves three interrelated but sporadically presented acts: 1) recognize Jesus, best and good, as another man; 2) discover that Jehovah is not Love or beneficent; 3) exercise individual love and will (power) to become gods:

For *life*, with all it yields of joy and woe,	(leads to Shelley's Life)
And hope and fear, — believe the *aged friend*, —	(St. John; 245)
Is just our chance o' the *prize of learning love*, . . .	(Q Mab 9.5; 2 Jn 8)
But see the *double way* wherein we are led,	(Jn 14.6; 251)
How the soul learns *diversely* from the flesh! . . .	(S's Love, Hope 11)
Expect prompt teaching. Helpful was the light,	(255)
And warmth was cherishing and food was choice	
To every *man's flesh*, thousand years ago,	(vegetative existence)
As now to yours and mine; *the body sprang*	
At once to the height, and stayed: *but the soul, — no!* . . .	
The love that tops the might, the Christ in God.	(not God in Christ;
Then, as new lessons shall be learned in *these*	265; love & power)

Till *earth's work* stop and *useless time* run out,   (Q Mab 1.135-55)
So duly, daily, needs provision be
For keeping the *soul's prowess possible*,   (Hom Merc 544, 3 Jn 1.2)
Building *new barriers* as the *old decay*,   (PU 1.119; 4.550)
Saving us from evasion of *life's proof*,   (such as fire & sun, not faith)
Putting the question *ever*, *'Does God love*, (1 Jn 3.1,16,18,23; 4.16,18)
And will ye hold that truth [fancy] against the [whole] world?'
Ye know there needs no second proof with good
Gained for our flesh from any earthly source [like fire & sun].

To Browning, despite the careful employment of "learning love" to take the sharp edge off Will and Power toward which he is moving, love is not so much learned as united with power: "We must love,/ And what we love *most*, power and love in one" (373, PU 4.395). As the double way of learning contradicts "I am *the way*, the truth, and the life" (Jn 14.6), as the Love of Prometheus "tops" the Might of Jehovah, so "diversely" confirms Browning's alert exploitation of the 1862 publication of *Relics of Shelley*. Similarly, as Life is introduced in a Shelleyan frame, Browning counts on "learning love," which is as foreign to New Testament writers as Chance and Prize, to ameliorate the sudden question "Does God love?" which is then dropped to be reintroduced at line 549 as "What is God?" But the startling imposition on St. John, as Browning projected his John, is an acceptance of the knowledge that evil and good are required to protect the soul's prowess with new barriers against the decaying influence of Christian ethics, despotism and slavery. One searches in vain in St. John, St. Paul and other scriptural authors for confirmation of the body's perfection and the soul's stunted growth; to them both body and soul have either gone off after the world or in the soul's prosperity the body has become negligible. See how vast the distance is between Browning's John and the scriptural St. John on the function of love and care of the soul:

Beloved [only believers in Christ's divinity & Sonship], let us love one another: for love is of God; and every one that loveth is born of God, and knoweth God.

He [Cerinthus and/or other Gnostics] that loveth not knoweth not God; for God is love.

In this was manifested the love of God toward us, because that God sent his only begotten Son into the world, that we might live through him.

Herein is love, not that we loved God, but that he loved us, and sent his Son to be the propitiation for our sins.

Beloved, if God so loved us, we ought also to love one another.

No man hath seen God at any time. If we love one another, God dwelleth in us, and his love is perfected in us.

Hereby know we that we dwell in him and he in us, because he hath given us of his Spirit.

And we have seen [Christ] and do testify that the Father sent the Son to be the savior of the world.

Whosoever shall confess that Jesus is the Son of God, God dwelleth in him, and he in God.

And we have known and believed the love that God hath to us. God is love; and he that dwelleth in love dwelleth in God, and God in him.

Herein is our love made perfect, that we may have boldness in the day of judgment; because as he is, so are we in this world.

(1 Jn 4.7-14)

Nothing is anywhere said by St. John about "love's strength," "learning love" or "for love's sake." Nor is anything said about "loving one's enemies" in the epistles, for they portray solely the struggle between early orthodox Christians and their Gnostic opponents. One is the children of light and addressed as "beloved"; the other is the children of darkness and denied Jehovah's Spirit because they do not confess that Jesus is the Son of God. Unalterably opposed to such ignorance and slavery, Browning like Shelley transposes the whole matter, even to subsuming St. John's savior in Prometheus, and encourages his John to illustrate his new insight by recalling what he had "been used to hear the pagans own":

That fable of Prometheus and his theft,   (279)
How mortals gained Jove's *fiery flower*, grows old . . .   (Orpheus 94,
And out of mind; *but fire*, howe'er its birth,   Fire; 282)
Here is it, precious to the *sophist* now   (R of Islam 3244, 3235-52)
Who *laughs* the myth of AEschylus to scorn, . . .   (double-edged)
While were it so with soul, — this gift of *truth*   (fact; 287)
Once grasped, were this our *soul's gain safe*, and sure
To prosper *as the body's gain is wont*, —
Why, man's probation would conclude, his *earth*   (Christian)

Crumble; for he both reasons and decides,
Weighs first, then chooses: will he give up *fire*
For *gold or purple* once he knows its worth?   (PU 1.234-5)
Could he give *Christ* up were *His* worth as plain?   (double entente)

Browning's full purpose, as may be noted by jumping over to his second reference to *The Prometheus Bound*, is to replace St. John's blind faith and apostolic mission with his John's recognition of the hard fact of Promethean fire:

'Is John's *procedure* just the heathen bard's?   (new procedure; 530)
Put question of his famous play again
How for the *ephemerals'* sake Jove's fire was filched, . . .   (mankind)
The fact is in the fable, cry the wise,   (R.B.'s italics; 534)
Mortals obtained the boon, so much is fact,   (R.B.'s italics)
Though fire be spirit and produced on earth.   (R.B.'s italics)
As with the Titan's, so now with thy tale:
Why breed in us perplexity, mistake,   (2 Cor 4.8, PU 1.374)
Nor tell the whole truth in the proper words?'
"*I* answer, Have ye yet to argue out   (John)
The very *primal* thesis, plainest law.   (PU 2.4.35, Q Mab 9.79-81)
— Man is not God but hath *God's* end to serve,   (Prometheus')
A master to obey, a course to take,   (diversionary)
Somewhat to cast off, somewhat to become?   (diversionary)
Grant this, then man must pass from *old to new,*   (2 Cor 5.17, PU 4.49)
From *vain to real,* from *mistake to fact,*   (faith to reason)
From what once seemed good, to what now proves best.
How could man have *progression* otherwise?   (progress)

By separating his advocacy of Prometheus as true Christ and progress as growth of soul into godhood, Browning protects his daring and yet permits John to advance Shelleyan Love as if it were Christian. This he could do because St. John is thought more indulgent of the weakness of the flesh than St. Paul, but parallel severities are not uncommon or ever contradictory on the question of divine grace and human guilt. Browning repeatedly exhibits a distaste for judgment such as St. Paul's "Among whom also we all had our conversations in times past in the lusts of our flesh, fulfilling the desires of the flesh and the mind, and were by nature the children of wrath" (Eph 2.3). Yet he also knew that nothing in St. Paul's writings is really more unfavorable to human nature than St. John's "But Jesus did not commit himself unto them,

because he knew *all men*, / And needed not that any should
testify of man: for he knew what was in man" (Jn 2.24-5).
Like Jesus both St. Paul and St. John spoke to the foundling
Christians as to "little children," and their common purpose
seems consistently to be the admonition that even though
God's love is unlimited and first given, rapproachment with
God is independent of human strength or weakness.

Wishing to substitute Shelley's emphasis on Love, Power
and Life for the Gospel of St. John, Browning realized that
the witness of Christ to Jehovah's love was a serious obstacle.
Before he could nullify the love of St. John's God and advocate a proper will (power) to be administered by man's love,
Browning needed to show that with all his ethical words and
deeds Christ was still only a superior man. And this is what
his John next does:

Could [man] give Christ up were His worth as plain [as fire or sun]?
Therefore, I say, to test men, the proofs shift, . . .   (295)
And it is written, 'I forsook [Christ] and fled:'   (310)
There was my trial, and it ended thus.
Ah, but my *soul* had gained its *truth*, could *grow*: . . .   (Q Mab 9.83)
Well, was truth safe forever then? *Not so.*   (318)
Already had begun the silent work
Whereby *truth*, deadened of its *absolute blaze*,   (Christian)
Might need *love's eye* to pierce the *o'erstretched doubt.*   (Gisb 127)
Teachers were busy, *whispering* 'All is true   (Mask 69, 333)
As the aged ones report; *but youth can reach*
Where age gropes dimly, weak with stir and strain,   (Shelleyan)
And the full doctrine slumbers till to-day.'
Thus, what the Roman's lowered spear was found,
A bar to me who touched and handled *truth*,   (Fancy)
Now *proved the glozing* of some *new shrewd* tongue,   (PU 3.4.167)
This Ebion, this Cerinthus or their mates, . . .
Is this indeed a burthen for late days,   (337)
And may I help to bear *it* with you all,   (new truth [Fact])
Using my *weakness* which becomes your *strength*? . . .
What is the doubt, my brothers? Quick with it! . . .   (353)
And *no one* asks his fellow any more   (362)
'Where is the promise of His coming?' but
'Was he revealed in any of His *lives*,   (sardonic)
As Power, as Love, as Influencing Soul?'

The double entente of "give *Christ* up were *His* worth as

plain?" as fire and sun warns that new proofs have shifted John's allegiance from Jesus Christ to Prometheus, that his desertion opened his eyes to the more substantial knowledge of Prometheus' gifts and self-sacrifice. But the obvious exposure of Browning's reversal is the use of "Influencing Soul" which never reappears in John's developing thought on Power and Love. For it was in Christ's "Thy will be done" that both Browning and Shelley saw the unforgivable flaw, the unbelievable submission of will, of an otherwise perfect and godlike man. To Browning it was the daily testing — endless searching, evolving — for growth of soul which counted. He thus invites his John to take pride in the desertion of Christ, thereby changing St. John's long and arduous life for Christ into a prelude to growth through acceptance of the commentaries (glozing) of a new shrewd Cerinthus. Probably confused or unconcerned about calling Cerinthus an Ebion, Browning selected a foe of St. John and St. Paul who actually opposed them as a violent chiliast and judaizing Christian; Cerdo fits much better. But such inconsistencies never delayed Browning when he was intent on promoting Prometheus "as Power, as Love, as Influencing Soul." So the evidence that St. John's teachings on God's love are turned against him as readily as St. Paul's teachings on God's Strength are converted into Shelley's confidence in Weakness is less striking than Browning's own impetuosity which is running at full tide. First the aged soliloquist asks, "What's the doubt, my brothers? Quick with it!" That is, question no longer the promise of the Second Coming but whether Jesus Christ truly lived as Power, as Love, as Influencing Soul. Now Browning's dying John demands of his silent, disbelieving companions:

"Quick, for time presses, tell the whole mind out   (366)
And let us ask and answer *and be saved!* . . .   (by Prometheus)
'Here is a tale [Christ's life] of things done ages since;   (370)
What truth was ever told the second day?
Wonders, that would prove doctrine, go for naught.   (miracles, faith)
Remains the doctrine, love; well, we must love,
And what we love most, power and love in one,   (PU 4.395)

Let us acknowledge on the record here,
Accepting *these* in Christ: *must Christ then be?*   (only power & love)
Has he been? Did not we ourselves make Him?
Our mind received but what it holds, no more.   (Shelleyan)
First of the love, then; we *acknowledge* Christ —   (as superior man)
A proof we comprehend *His* love, a proof   (Prometheus)
We had such love already in ourselves,
Knew first what else we should not recognize   (Shelleyan)
'T is mere projection from man's *inmost* mind, . . .   (PU 2.1.119)
How prove you Christ came otherwise at least?   (388)
Next try the power: He made and rules the world: (so says Jn 1.3)
Certes there is a world once made, now ruled,
Unless things have been ever as we see. . . .   (Shelleyan)
While *will* and love we do know; marks of these   (power; 401)
Eye-witnesses attest, so books declare —   (ironic for St. John)
As that [O.T.], *to punish or reward our race,* (RB's "soul's abhorence")
The sun at undue times arose or set
Or else stood still; what do not men affirm?
But *earth* requires as urgently reward   (Christian)
Or punishment to-day as years ago,
And none expects the sun will interpose:
Therefore it was mere passion and mistake,
Or erring zeal for right, which changed the truth [of pagan fact]. . . .
First Jove's brow, Juno's eyes were swept away,   (416)
But Jove's *wrath,* Juno's *pride* continued long;
As last, will, power, and love discarded these,   (Prometheus)
So *law* in turn discards power, love, and will.   (Jehovah)
What *proveth God* is otherwise at least?   (Jehovah's unjust law)
All else, projection from the mind of man!' "   (Shelleyan)

Without break in continuity of thought, though the severest criticism of Jehovah is shunted off to an imaginary inter-
rogator (single quotes), Browning's John now takes up
company with the poet's shrewdest disputants. To the reader
it may become just another expression of Browning's resent-
ment at Jehovah's lovelessness and his unthinkable law, but
to Browning it became another "chance o' the prize of
learning love" through furtherance of Shelley's most persistent ground rule, the sovereignty of the Mind. While love
the human Jesus had, he was without will (power) to change
Jehovah's threat of rewards and punishments and thus failed
to become an "Influencing Soul." Moreover the so-called
Christian doctrine of love, which was no more Jesus' alone

than the air men breathe, does not make him Christ or raise him one whit above other loving men. Obeying Jehovah unto death meant no more, since a true and just God cannot both love and demand service, praise, prayers and slavish submission to his will. As beauty and truth, love and freedom were swept away by Jove's wrath and Juno's pride, so their wrath and pride were swept away by Prometheus' beneficent will, power and love. But then Jehovah's law discarded power, love and will, and Jehovah's fearful reign is now sustained by "mere passion and mistake, / Or erring zeal" of the ignorant masses. What proveth beyond his unjust law Jehovah's existence? All else is projection from the mind of man, whereas Browning's and Shelley's disbelief is "projection from man's *inmost mind*" (383). Taken as a piece, the lines are a lucid exposition of Shelley's "all things exist as they are perceived." Not that Browning believed any human mind is perfect, but he held with Shelley that free action was the only way through which an active and receptive mind could establish closer and truer unanimity with the One Perfect Mind.

By speaking of the inability of Christ's will to alter the unloving nature of his Jehovah, rather than of God's love in sending his Son to earth as a propitiation (1 Jn 4.10), Browning's John reaches the point at which men are separated according to their belief in Will:

"I say that man was made to grow, not stop; (doctrine of progress; 424)
That help, he needed once, and needs no more,
Having grown but an inch, *is withdrawn*: . . .   (withdrawn at creation)
Since all things suffer change save *God the Truth*.   (Fact; 431)
Man apprehends *Him* newly at each stage   (Truth)
Whereat earth's *ladder* drops, its service done;   (Witch 482)
And nothing shall prove twice what once was proved. . . .
What? Was man made a wheelwork to wind up,   (448)
And be discharged, and straight wound up anew?   (Jehovah's machine)
No! — grown, his growth lasts; taught, he ne'er forgets: . . .
I say, the acknowledgment of *God* in Christ   (divinity; 474)
Accepted by thy reason, solves for thee
All questions in the earth *and out of it*,
And has so far advanced thee to be wise. . . .   (Shelleyan)
Leave knowledge and revert to how it sprung?   (never)
Thou has *it*; use *it* and forthwith, or die! . . .   (knowledge)

```
With ignorance was surety of a cure.                     (488)
When man, appalled at nature, questioned first
'What if there lurk a might behind the might?'     (power without love)
He needed satisfaction God could give,
And did give, as ye have the written word:                 (ironic)
But when he [man] finds might still redouble might,
Yet asks, 'Since all is might, what use of will?'
— Will, the one source of might, — he being man           (Shelleyan)
With a man's will and a man's might, to teach
In little how the two combine in large, —      (will of Will, Prometheus)
That man has turned round on himself and stands,       (Epipsy 272-4)
Which in the course of nature is, to die.          (That is, if he fails to
                    recognize Jehovah's appalling & redoubled might as willed
                        and vindictive; thus Jesus Christ stands [dead] in "Saul"
                               while Prometheus is exalted by his defiance.)
```

According to Shelley it was Prometheus who altered man's vegetative existence by granting him a godlike power of reason, and it was this birthright which insured man's eventual wisdom. Prometheus is the GOD Browning disguises in "God the Truth," for he knew that the Scriptures speak only of a "God of truth" and "the truth of God" whereas Shelley virtually equates Prometheus with Truth. The only help Jehovah bestowed on man was his creation. Man was made to grow by the gifts of Prometheus, John argues. And because he never forgets, never needs anything proved a second time, man is not like an engine which runs down and must be rewound to repeat the same progress again and again within Jehovah's narrow circumscription. He may not have grown more than an inch, a millionth of Jehovah's stature, but he is potentially a god, becoming wiser and wiser as he uses his reason. This wisdom moreover enables man to know that the destructive might of Nature is not by chance but maliciously willed by a God devoid of love. Yet if one thinks that Browning's indictment of Jehovah may be unravelled that easily, he misjudges the poet's ingenuity and caution against detection. With perhaps his choice method of deceiving, Browning subtly places two matters together for emphasis between the subject and verb of a third matter, thus utilizing three not four dashes. As emphasis for the average reader is likely to settle on the secondary and illustrative matter, emphasis for

the more alert reader is unavoidable and falls properly on
"— Will, [which is] the one source of might" (495). But this
is only the first step since the reader must also pull the
surrounding or separated third matter together after a double
interruption. If he does, however, he reaches the whole
thought which is that the man who observes Jehovah's appal-
ling might redoubled and "Yet asks, 'Since all is might, what
use of will?' . . . / That man has turned round on himself and
stands, / Which in the course of nature is, *to die*." Is it not
unthinkable, John asks, to "Leave knowledge and revert to
how it sprung?" Reasonable acknowledgment of divinity in
Jesus, rather than faith in his Sonship, admits Jesus to the
company of godlike men and answers all theological questions both in and out the world. On the other hand, the man
who ignores or fails to use knowledge, deserts or fails to
apply his power of reason, "turns round on himself and
stands," the equivalent of mental or spiritual suicide: "Then,
as a hunted deer that could not flee, / I turned upon my
thoughts and *stood* at bay, / Wounded and weak and panting"
(Epipsy 272-4).

The histrionics, such as John's rationale for desertion of
Jesus and his daring introduction of the Promethean theft of
fire from Jove (Jehovah), if not the elaborate analogies have
disappeared in Browning's irresistible drive. Not his John but
Browning himself is now earnestly enjoined with St. John on
the validity of the disciple's sole thesis — the love of Jehovah.
The substance of Christ's life was love, Browning concedes,
but the tragedy of his love was Christ's refusal to challenge
the tyranny of his so-called Father. So the outcome for
Jehovah may be expected to be no less grim than that for
Shelley's Jupiter. The difference is that while Jupiter
(Jehovah) is ultimately withdrawn from being by Shelley's
Demogorgon, Browning's Jehovah, if the poet's will is sufficient, is to be withdrawn from the minds of his passionately,
mistakenly, erringly zealous followers. If one man is not too
"dead" (ignorant) to see that Jehovah's destructive might is
vindictively "willed," what of another man who then asks if
there be love behind the power and will? When Browning's

John asked three hundred lines earlier "Does God love?"
these were the lines which had been premeditated for the
answer:

<pre>
"And when man questioned, 'What if there be love   (500)
Behind the will and might, as real as they?' —
He needed satisfaction God could give,
And did give, as ye have the written word: (cf., 492)
But when, beholding that love everywhere, . . .
And since ourselves can love and would be loved,   (506)
We ourselves make the love, and Christ was not,' — . . .
Before the point was mooted 'What is God?'   (549)
No savage man inquired 'What am myself?'   (as Jehovah does)
Much less replied, 'First, last, and best of things.'   (Rev 1.11)
Man takes [accepts] that title now if he believes   ("I am that I am")
Might can exist with neither will nor love, . . .
While in himself he recognizes love   (555)
No less than might and will: and rightly takes.   (accepts, believes)
Since if man prove the sole existent thing   (subjunctive to indicative)
Where these combine, whatever their degree, . . .
He is surely higher in the scale   (cf., Ixion 92; 561)
Than any might with neither love nor will,   (Jehovah)
As life, apparent in the poorest midge, . . .   (Shelleyan)
Is marvelous beyond dead Atlas' self —   (565)
Given to the nobler midge for resting-place!   (Jehovah)
Thus, man proves best and highest — God, in fine,   (higher than might
                                        with neither love nor will)
And thus the victory [PU 4.578] leads but to defeat [for man who
   "takes that title" of "First, last, and best of things"],
The gain to loss, best rise to the worst fall,   ("God, in fine")
His life becomes impossible, which is death.   (man's)
</pre>

A skillful but bewildering manipulation of dashes, these
lines cannot mean less than: a thoughtful man, in his self-
consciousness (Myself), finds love and will and might a
normal endowment, thus proving that any less in Jehovah dis-
qualifies his claim to being "First, last, and best of things"; a
thoughtless man, who in himself may recognize love no less
than might and will, loses the Victory about which Demogorgon speaks when he does not expect love and will behind
Jehovah's might. In accepting St. John's "I am the Alpha and
the Omega," whereby Browning identifies Jehovah as the
nobler midge, this man's potential gain, being a god, leads
only to loss, the same as death. And should doubt persist that

"the nobler midge" is Jehovah, additional evidence resides in
the immediately juxtaposed man who gains godhood by
rejecting Jehovah's title of First and Last:

"But if, appealing thence, he *cower, avouch*   (cf., E-Day 991; 571)
He is *mere man*, and in *humility*   ("cower," Hellas 358)
Neither may know God nor mistake *himself*;   (Myself)
I point to the immediate consequence
And say, by such confession straight he *falls*   (really climbs)
Into man's place, *a thing* nor God nor beast,   (sacred to Shelley)
Made to know that he can know . . .
Creeps ever from fancies [faith] to the *fact*   (intellectualism; 583)
And in this striving, . . .
Finds progress, man's distinctive mark alone,   (586)
Not God's, and not the beasts': *God* is, they are,   (Prometheus)
Man partly is [in spirit] and wholly hopes to be [a god]. . . .
What he considers that he knows to-day,
Come but to-morrow, he will find misknown;
Getting increase of *knowledge*, since he *learns*
Because he lives, which is to be *a man*,
Set to *instruct himself* by his past self: (self-sufficiency)
First, like the brute, obliged by facts to learn,
Next, as man may, obliged by *his own mind*,
Bent, habit, nature, knowledge turned to law.
God's gift was that man should conceive of truth [fact]   (Prometheus')
And *yearn* to gain it, catching at mistake   (as did Paracelsus)
As *midway* help till he reach *fact indeed*. . . .   (PU 2.3.24, 40)
God only makes the live shape *at a jet*.   (623)
Will ye renounce this *pact of creatureship*?   (effective ambiguity)
The *pattern* on the Mount [Sinai] subsists no more, . . .   (Islam 3283)
But *copies*, Moses strove to make thereby,   (Unf Dr 93; 627)
Serve still and are *replaced* as time requires: (not by St. John)
By these, make newest *vessels*, reach the *type*!   (Q Mab 7.141; God)
If ye demur, this judgment on your head,
Never to reach the ultimate, angel's law,   (Epipsy 185, Q Mab 2.76)
Indulging every instinct of the soul   (Q Mab 8.200)
There where law, life, joy, impulse are one thing!   (PU 4.578)

The man who "appeals" to all mankind for the truth of
what Jehovah alleges thus saves his life. As he was "made to
know that he can know," he naturally and habitually applies
his reason and multiplies his knowledge into acceptable law.
He recognizes that his limitation, which requires trial and
error for progress, is real but temporary since Prometheus'

gift was that man should conceive of truth and yearn to gain it until he reaches "fact indeed." The sum of which accounts for Browning's circuitous analogy and explains how he deduced that Jehovah's might is vindictive because it is willed without love. Ever so briefly Browning would disguise the onslaught against Jehovah and his law with reference to "creatureship" and "vessel," but they are Prometheus' creatures, not Jehovah's, who are encouraged to place absolute dependence upon the mind, and "vessel" has stronger Shelleyan undertones than scriptural overtones (2 Ti 2.21). Foreign to St. John's total reliance on faith in man and love in Jehovah, Browning's thematic diction as well as the empirical data removes all prospect of accepting an unjust Jehovah as God. So the hiatus merely accentuates the momentum of saying that the Mosaic Law subsists no more. Instead, the laws of Jehovah may as readily be replaced as the inconsequential man of fancy (faith). And "if ye demur," a typical authorial intrusion, this judgment be upon your head: never to reach the angel realm in which the free and benevolent law of Prometheus subsists, never to indulge every instinct of the soul "where law [Empire], life, joy, impulse are one thing!" Not only does Browning dare to paraphrase and quote Demogorgon's final stirring words to Prometheus: "This, like thy glory, Titan, is to be / Good, great and joyous, beautiful and free; / This is alone *Life, Joy, Empire, and Victory*." He also takes the unprecedented chance of introducing Victory in "Thus the *victory* [of life] leads but to defeat [in Jehovah's law]" (568) and of utilizing Shelley's earliest draft of Demogorgon's speech: "Here now the human being stands adorning / This loveliest earth with taintless body and mind; / Blessed from his birth with all bland *impulses*, / Which gently in his noble bosom wake / All kindly passions and all pure desires" (Q Mab 8.198-202).

As he concludes "A Death in the Desert" with his mind demonstrably focused (669) on the strong defense of Jehovah's law in Romans 7, Browning seems increasingly depressed by the thought that the whole world has gone over to Jesus Christ and his vengeful Father. Like Hard-to-be-a-

Christian who fears that his warnings are converting no one
to Prometheanism, Browning's John leaves the impression
that the pale Galilean has indeed conquered all unless he can
be reduced to the status of *a man* and shown only to be on
the way to godhood. Despite the false pagan garb, Cerinthus
— who taught that Jesus was the human son of Joseph and
Mary, that the Christ descended on him at baptism and departed from him before the Passion and that his resurrection
and rule were to be in the future — is helpful chiefly in his
erratically stern criticism of the Old Testament law and its
origin. Perhaps that is why Browning attempts to draw
Cerinthus into the pagan fold by informing him so well on
John's earliest revelation of a new self-consciousness: "So is
myself withdrawn into my depths, . . . / Yet I *myself* remain;
I feel *myself*: / And there is nothing lost" (78-81) to which
Cerinthus adds the gloss "This is the doctrine he was wont to
teach, . . . / Three souls which make up one soul." The other
arguments of John are those of a confirmed Promethean, projected in a milieu which Cerinthus could probably have
understood no better than Browning's readers. Because St.
John taught that Jesus came to fulfill, not to annul or to displace, the law and because neither St. John nor Jesus
objected to rewards and punishments which symbolize
Jehovah's unjust law to Browning, Jesus Christ cannot now
be called "the illimitable God." Only Prometheus measures
up to that title, and even though his attributes are suddenly
disguised in square bracket, parallel scriptural and Shelleyan
illusions, capitalized pronouns, double entente, Cerinthian
musing and speculation on man's possessing an immortal soul,
the identity of Prometheus is unmistakable. For in order to
close his mechanically poorest deception, Browning feels
compelled to say that after Cerinthus had read and mused
over John's manuscript recantation "one [of his listeners]
added this":

"If *Christ*, as thou [Cerinthus] affirmest, be of men   (Jesus; 666)
Mere man, the first and best *but nothing more*, —   (mere matter)
Account *Him*, for reward of what *He* was,   (Jesus)
Now and forever, *wretchedest* of all.   (Ro 7.23-5)

<pre>
For see; *Himself* conceived of life as *love*,   (Prometheus)
Conceived of *love* as what *must enter in*,   (the spirit)
Fill up, make one with His *each soul* He loved: . . .   (all parts of One
That *He* will grow *incorporate* with all,   Mind; all return to Prom)
Groom for each bride! Can a *mere man* do this? (double entente; Jesus)
Yet *Christ* saith, this *He* lived and died to do.   (double entente,
Call *Christ*, then, the *illimitable God*,   PU 1.815; Prometheus)
Or [you are] *lost*!"   (to the "angel's law")
                    But 't was Cerinthus that is lost.]
</pre>

That is, if Cerinthus did not believe that all men, including
Jesus, have a spark of divinity which returns to Prometheus
at their death.

CALIBAN UPON SETEBOS

1864

Usually looked upon as the ruminations of a primitive mind on the nature of God, "Caliban upon Setebos" truly dramatizes the undesirable characteristics of Jehovah which inform Browning's previous poetry. Setebos is a counterpart of Shelley's Jupiter, the Quiet is the medium of Demogorgon, and Caliban is a masked voice for Browning's opposition to Jehovah, his parody of the superstitiously ignorant Christian masses and his advancement of the new Promethean day. When Caliban speaks about himself, the language is indeed suggestive of the primitive; when he speaks about Setebos, however, the language is indistinguishable from that of other Browning poems in which protest against Jehovah looms so large. Perhaps Caliban's strongest protest is lodged against Jehovah's spite, but Caliban neglects none of Browning's familiar complaints. Whether from Browning's confidence in the element of natural disguise or in surreptitious logical development, Caliban's words probably supply the poet's most lucid explanation of a doctrine of eternal progress.

Repeated some eight times, the divisional format of the poem offers a most visible structure: first, a statement of a flaw in Caliban's God; second, a comparison of the flaw with one Caliban possesses or knows about; and third, a conclusion that Setebos is different from Caliban only in that by tyrannical will he wields a stronger degree of power. Power then serves as a motivation to Caliban's speculations as to Browning's thought, while Strength and Weakness continue to perform their accustomed, informing roles. Why Browning deceptively added the superscription "Thou thoughtest that I was altogether such an one as thyself" (Ps 50.21) is of as much moment as why it was dropped, possibly inadvertently, from the 1868 collected edition. But the subtitle, "Or, Natural Theology in the Island," is the infinitely more subtle disguise, since it so accurately describes Browning's own pantheism. Not even the name Setebos, whether a god or a "greate [Patagonian] deuyill," proves so beguiling. If Browning erred at all in his calculations for the poem, it was in uniformly capitalizing the pronouns which refer to GOD, because Prospero, with whom Browning successfully planned to confuse the reader, cannot easily be the object of Caliban's positively identifiable protests. Yet why linger over these misleading acts of boldness and of testing the reader's intelligence, when the most daring of all, the skillful, condemnatory refrain indicating Jehovah — "So He" — eliminates the pretense of an undeveloped mentality in each of the poetic divisions? "So He" repeatedly leaves the God of Caliban's complex primitivism less spiteful, hateful, cruel or jealous than the Christian God of Browning's acquaintance:

And talks to his own self, howe'er *he* please,   (Caliban; 15)
Touching that *other*, whom his dam called God.   (Setebos)
Because to talk about Him, *vexes* — *ha*,   (Job, 1 Cor, Shelley)
Could *He* but know! and time to vex is now,   (Setebos, not Prospero)
When talk is safer than in winter-time. . . .

Setebos, Setebos, and Setebos!   (typically derogatory to R.B.; 24)
'Thinketh He dwelleth i' the *cold* o' the moon. . . .

'Thinketh, *it* came of being ill at ease;   (Setebos' condition; 31)
He hated that He cannot change His *cold*,
Nor cure its *ache*.

The first characteristic Caliban ascribes to Setebos is Hatred, generated by the coldness of his habitat and exemplified in his being ill at ease and achy. He reminds Caliban of an "icy fish" which longed for the "lukewarm brine" but on gaining it "sickened" (PU 1.675) and "flounced back from bliss she was not born to breathe, / And in her old bounds buried her despair [PU 3.3.95], hating and loving warmth alike: *So He* [Setebos]." Only ostensibly Setebos, "So He" is clearly accentuated to indicate Jehovah. And it is especially notable that the savage Caliban manages not to identify himself in the first division with a God whose irremediable coldness symbolizes decrepitude, jealousy and inability to love. The second characteristic Caliban ascribes to Setebos is Spite:

'Thinketh, He made thereat the sun, this isle, (44)
Trees and the fowls here, beast and creeping things. . . .
                        He made all these and more, (55)
Made all we see, and us, *in spite*: how else?
He could not, Himself, make a second self
To be His mate; as well have made Himself:
He would not make what he mislikes or slights,
An eyesore to Him, or not worth His pains:
But did, *in envy*, listlessness or *sport*, (Q Mab 6.109)
Make *what* Himself would fain, in a manner, be — (Man)
Weaker in most *points*, *stronger* in a few,
Worthy, and yet mere *playthings* all the while,
Things He *admires and mocks* too, — *that is it*. (rewards, punishes)
Because, *so brave, so better* though *they* be, (mankind)
It nothing *skills* if He begin to plague. (signifies, matters)

Reminiscent of Satan's "For what God after better worse would build" (PL 9.102), Caliban's sophisticated thought on Setebos' limitations and subjection to Necessity is too thoroughly Shelleyan to pass muster as genuine primitivism. It even allows that as Jupiter converted power surrendered by Prometheus into tyranny, Setebos converts his unavoidably worthy, better, braver creatures into objects of spite and envy, playthings he both jealously admires and mockingly plagues. So he, Jehovah.

Of Prometheus' mythological exploits, making men of clay possibly ranks next to stealing fire. Thus illustrative of God's Spite, Caliban imagines that he himself makes "a live bird out of clay" and "*wills* that he begin to live." Yet if a "leg snapped, brittle clay," Caliban would simply laugh:

And if *he*, spying me, should fall to weep, (a bird; 87)
Beseech me to be good, repair his wrong,
Bid his poor leg smart less or grow again, —
Well, as the chance were, this might take or else
Not take my fancy: I might hear his cry, . . .
Or pluck the other off, leave him like an egg (93)
And *lessoned* he was mine and merely clay. (PU 1.364-5)
Were this no pleasure, lying in the *thyme*, (bed of mint)
Drinking the mash, with brain become *alive*,
Making and marring clay at *will*? *So He* [Setebos].

Somewhat more disrespectful of the deity than asking Jehovah to swallow a cross-olive stone or describing Jehovah as flinging one rose over the wall of Eden's opulence, this picture of a besotted God registers the nature of Browning's animosity toward Jehovah. And yet as the intensity of the anger builds up to the poem's most famous part, as Browning adds motiveless malignity to Caliban's extraordinary breadth of thought, Caliban deduces that such cruel and spiteful treatment of God's creatures as he illustrates is neither right nor wrong in Setebos because Setebos is "strong and Lord." Pure Shelleyan doctrine of the unreality of evil, Power degenerates into vindictive Might only when divorced from Love and succumbing to the unnatural rather than to the Wrong ignorantly imagined by the moralists. Caliban too is strong when compared with yonder twenty-first crab he crushes: "Loving not, hating not, just choosing so. . . . As it likes me each time, I do: *So He* [Setebos]."

Yet suppose, Caliban muses, that Setebos is good in the main and placable if His mind and ways were guessed. What consolation is this to Setebos who is

rougher than His handiwork, be sure!	(111)
Oh, He hath made things *worthier* than Himself,	(Saul 59-60)
And *envieth* that, so helped, such things do more	(2 Cor 13.4)
Than He who made them! What *consoles* but this?	(2 Cor 1.5-7,
That *they*, unless through Him, do naught at all,	PU 1.820; mankind)
And must *submit*: what other use in things?	(PU 1.395)

Very likely Browning was thinking of St. Paul's frequent use of "consolation," and almost certainly he lifted "envieth" from "Charity envieth not; Charity vaunteth not itself, is not puffed up." But whatever the consolation Setebos demands, Browning rescores his point that Love is the missing ingredient which never requires submission or asks consolation. "Wot ye," Browning's David had similarly reasoned on love, "I worst / E'en the Giver in one gift." To demonstrate the tyranny of being subservient to God, or of having to do everything in God's name, Caliban thinks of a fowler's pipe he made and explains what he would do if the pipe itself were then to boast:

'I catch the birds, I am the crafty thing.   (123)
I make the cry my maker cannot make

With his great *round* mouth; he must blow through mine!'   (?)
Would not I smash it with my foot? *So He* [Setebos].

Thereupon Caliban reverts to his first impression, that of God's being cold and ill at ease, and ties it in with his impression of God's roughness. Wondering why — "Aha, that is a question!" — Caliban is thus given a chance to speculate on "the something over Setebos

That made Him, or He, may be, found and fought,   (the Quiet; 130)
Worsted, drove off and did to nothing, *perchance.*   (usually negative)
There may be something *quiet* o'er His head,   (PU 2.1.191)
Out of His reach, that feels *nor joy nor grief,*   (Q Mab 6.212-19)
Since both derive from *weakness* in some way.

A most lucid passage on Browning's Shelleyan ontology and eschatology, Caliban's words only divert by suggesting that supremacy in the world of spirits is gained by fighting and worsting one's superior or subduing one's competitor. The composure of the Quiet, reflected from Shelley's slumbering, dormant, tranquil and inaccessible Demogorgon, is as little disturbed by Setebos' making and tinkering with mankind as by mankind's unawakened spiritual potentiality. That is, until an act of Will arises sufficiently powerful to energize the Quiet out of its dreadful calm, no change can be effected in Setebos' reign of tyranny. Perfect in every way and outside the realm of being, "the secret *strength* of things" (Mt B 139), the Quiet cannot feel either joy or grief since both are derived from Weakness or spiritual immaturity. But when the Quiet does take cognizance of all over which fate rules, it seems to care for all but Setebos, a mettlesome power over his own creations who were made solely as objects of sport, and either fear and submit to Setebos' dictatorial manner or rebel and suffer his spiteful cruelty. Because of his unloving nature, his crippled power, Setebos can look up to the Quiet but never hope to soar to the remote and peaceful life of the "treasured spell" (PU 2.3.88).

To explain the difference, Caliban himself "joys" only because the quail come. He would have no reason for joy if he could bring them each time he had a mind to:

This Quiet, all it hath *a mind* to, doth.   (no mind; 137)
'Esteemeth stars the outposts of its *couch*,   (PU 1.75)
But never spends much *thought* nor care that way.   (cannot think)
It may *look up, work up,* — the worse for those   (subterranean)
It works on! 'Careth *but* for Setebos   (except)
The *many-handed* as a *cuttle-fish*,   (10; from which animals stole fire)
Who, making Himself *feared* through what He does,   ("hands,"
Looks up, first, perceives he cannot soar [figures of speech]   Calderon
To what is quiet and hath happy life;   116,184,193; Mt Bl 96-7, PU
Next looks down here, and out of very *spite*   3.3.146)
Makes this a *bauble*-world to ape yon real,   (trinket, fool's scepter)
These good things to match those as *hips* do grapes.   (rose apples)
'T is *solace* making *baubles*, ay, and *sport.* ("baubles," Death Vanq 17)

Although long paragraphs of examples would not exhaust Browning's manipulations of words, the above lines offer an exceptionally intricate and fine example. In conformity with the traditional placement of heaven above, Setebos looks up to the Quiet which is above him *only* in control, for the Quiet, like Demogorgon, "looks up, works up" from its subterranean quarters, being "o'er" Setebos' head and out of his reach only in a figurative way. Like Paracelsus and other Browning protesters, Caliban thinks that his world is a "bauble," a mere aping of spiritual reality, the few available good things approximating "yon real" as worthless rose apples approximate luscious grapes.

Then as if he has been illustrating the envious and spiteful sporting of Prospero not Setebos all along, Browning's Caliban is made to take out his vexation on Prospero by mimicking his careless and lofty lordship over the island. Caliban stitches a book of broad leaves and writes prodigious words therein, peels and names a wand, takes an animal skin for an enchanter's robe and makes a four-legged serpent cower and snarl and say that she is Miranda, Caliban's wife. His Ariel is a pouch-bill crane, and his "Caliban" is a blinded sea-beast and drudge which is penned in a hole o' the rock: "A bitter heart that bides its time and bites. / 'Plays thus at being Prosper in a way, / Taketh his mirth with make-believe: *So He* [Setebos]." Disagreeing with his dam who held that the Quiet made everything and that Setebos only vexed, Caliban further asserts, "Who made them *weak*, meant *weakness* He might vex." Else why not horny eyes no thorn could prick or plated scalp and armored flesh to ward off the snow or predator?

Ay, — so spoil *His* sport!   (Setebos'; 177)
He is the *One now*: only He doth *all.*   (while the Quiet slumbers)
'Saith, He may like, *perchance*, what profits Him.
Ay, *himself* loves what does him good; but why?   (Caliban)
'Gets *good* no otherwise.

A blinded beast, Caliban recalls in his attribution of absolute hedonism to Setebos, loves whoever places meat on his nose. Yet had he eyes he would want no help but love or hate as he chose. Setebos is worse, for he has eyes and uses them with "all His [ten] hands" craftily to profit only himself, but never for the sheer love of the work. Caliban too enjoys making something when all goes right and summertime suspends hunger and winter aches. Ever mindful of his doctrines of Work and of the Imperfect when they can be made to impinge on another pet idea, Browning has to twist things a bit here to allow for an obvious intrusion, but he thereby succeeds in adding contempt of creative work to the unloving nature of Jehovah. Thus Caliban sets to piling up squares of sod, covering the mounds with white chalk and then inscribing each with a moon: "No use at all i' the work, for *work's sole sake*; / 'Shall some day knock it down again: *So He* [Setebos]." It takes Cleon, the artist, to complete the doctrine: "Didst ne'er engage in work for mere work's sake — Hadst ever in thy heart the luring hope / Of some eventual rest a-top of it" (31-3, PU 3.3.49-61).

Caliban concludes that all the feats of his God are proof of how terrible (Ps 47.2) he is. Convinced that Setebos has a Spite against him and a mind to favor Prospero, Caliban cites a six-months' labor spoiled by a hurricane, wattles on which he wove half the winter washed away by a spiteful wave and a fiery meteor which fell where he lay half an hour before. Compared with such force, Caliban too well realizes how weak he is. He therefore wishes, in possibly Browning's most deceptive Caliban line (216), that he could both please and deceive Setebos [Jehovah] as Prospero does:

```
'Dug up a newt He may have envied once                        (214)
And turned to stone, shut up inside a stone.
Please Him and hinder this? — What Prosper does?
Aha, if He would tell me how! Not He!                        (Setebos)
There is the sport: discover how or die!         ("sport," cf., Para 4.693)
All need not die, for of the things o' the isle
Some flee afar, some dive, some run up trees;  (Setebos not omniscient)
Those at His mercy, — why, they please Him most    (rarely mentioned)
When . . . when . . . well, never try the same way twice!   (R.B. ellipses)
Repeat what act has pleased, He may grow wroth.
You must not know His ways, and play Him off.             (Ro 11.33)
```

But most prescient, Caliban knows that God's ways are "past finding out" and that without any reason he also favors and mistreats animals which are at his mercy. There is the sport! especially for a God who covets prayer and praise as Browning's ellipses seem to indicate. A thieving yet fearless squirrel Caliban spares, also a frightened urchin which curls up into a ball to play dead:

```
But what would move my choler more than this,         (graphic; 232)
That either creature counted on its life
To-morrow and next day and all days to come,
Saying, forsooth, in the inmost of its heart            (Shelleyan)
"Because he did so yesterday with me,
And otherwise with such another brute,
So must he do henceforth and always." — Ay?         (Heb 13.7-8)
Would teach the reasoning couple what "must" means!     (PU 2.4.8)
'Doth as he [Caliban] likes, or wherefore Lord? So He [Setebos].
```

That Browning permitted his disguise to slip with "move my choler" is less noteworthy than the subtlety with which Caliban represents an unpredictable and spiteful Jehovah. Clearly the poet is saying that Jehovah, like any bully, will continue to sport with his followers as long as they submit ("thy will be done") or take him for granted ("the same yesterday, and to-day, and for ever"). But Browning is also playing with "rule over us" from Hebrews 13 or a comparable scriptural passage, with Shelley's emphasis on Reason in "the reasoning couple" and with Demogorgon's "all things thou dar'st demand" in "what 'must' means!" Small wonder,

if rebellion against God is so spotty and ineffectual, that
Caliban conceives all things will continue as they are:

And we shall have to live in *fear* of Him   (& trembling," Ph'p 2.12-3)
So long as He lives, keeps His strength: *no change,*   (PU 1.24; 243)
If He have done His best, make no new world
To please Him more, so leave off watching this, —
If He surprise not even the Quiet's self
Some *strange* day, — or, suppose, grow into it   (Shelleyan)
As grubs grow butterflies: else, here are we,
And there is He, and nowhere help at all.

Clarity in Browning's perversive poetry is never served by
relaxed reading after an emotional outburst. The poet understood the inclination too well and often planted his most
devastating criticism of Jehovah where it was least to be
expected. He knew that Setebos (Jupiter) was not capable of
surprising the Quiet (Demogorgon), so his derision is intended for Jehovah who, like a butterfly grub, might grow
into the power beyond him. Nonetheless Caliban believes
that with the end of mortal life its spitefully imposed pain
shall stop. His dam believed otherwise, holding that after
death Setebos' friends were feasted (glorified), his enemies
plagued (damned). But such speculation is idle to Caliban,
for Setebos does his worst in this life, giving machine-like
respite to prevent death through pain and thus preserving the
last worst pain for death. Meanwhile Caliban decides that the
best way to escape Setebos' "ire" (PU 1.269, Q Mab 7.189) is
to avoid seeming too happy. It is as when he kills two happy
flies and aids two pain-ridden beetles. Even so he would have
Setebos misunderstand and believe that he strives hard,
suffers no less and envies Him. Caliban dances on dark nights,
moans at the sun, goes into a hole to laugh and speaks his
mind only as now concealed. If Setebos were to catch and
overhear him and ask "What chucklest at?" Caliban would
cut off a finger and prepare a burnt offering as appeasement:

While *myself* lit a fire, and made a song   (275)
And sung it, *"What I hate, be consecrate*   (R.B.'s italics)
To celebrate Thee and Thy state, no mate (repetitive "no mate")
For Thee; what see for envy in poor me?"   (R.B.'s italics)
Hoping the while, since evils sometimes mend, . . .   (PU 4.573)

That some *strange* day, will either the Quiet catch
And conquer Setebos, or likelier *He*   (Setebos [Jehovah])
Decrepit may *doze, doze,* as good as die.   (Hom Merc 385, Q M 6.125)

Expectedly God's cloudy curtain suddenly covers the world. Crickets cease "hissing" and all birds vanish except Setebos' raven which has informed on Caliban. "It was fool's play," first exclaims Caliban, "this prattling! Ha!" But as the peals of thunder and flashes of lightning increase, Caliban lies low, confesses his love for Setebos, cuts his teeth through his upper lip and promises to fast for a month to escape God's anger. Prepared for come what may in his correspondence, Browning's later pretended innocence in defense of Caliban's sacrilegious song is all of one masterful piece: "Then, as to the divergence from Shakespeare's Caliban — is it so decided? There is no 'forgetfulness of his love of music,' since *he makes a song and sings it*; . . . True, 'he was a very different being at the end of the Play from what he was at the beginning' but my Caliban indulges his fancies long before even that beginning." Indeed Caliban would need to have nursed his wrath as long as Browning had to wish to celebrate God's loneliness with dedicated hatred. Or to have Setebos *"misconceive,* suppose" (263) that Caliban always envies Him only because He is in a state of decay (PU 4.550). Browning very likely was thinking of Prometheus' response to Jupiter's final onslaught: "Never yet there came / Phantasms so foul through monster-teeming Hell / From the *all-miscreative* brain of Jove" (PU 1.446-8). Despite its secrecy and brute energy, Caliban's way of indicting Jehovah is as sophisticated and decisive as Asia's comparable indictment of Jehovah's tyranny: "To know nor faith, nor love, nor law; to be / Omnipotent but *friendless* is to reign" (PU 2.3.47-8).

Whether in his whole career Browning was enabled to gratify his animosity toward Jehovah more joyously than in "Caliban" is a question which spontaneously calls to mind "The Flight of the Duchess" (1845). More substantive to Caliban's reality is the fact that Browning was now constantly exploiting personal memories and current events which added immeasurably to the concealment of his subversive effort. The superficially grotesque ornaments of Caliban, what with the missing link of Darwinian days in the thoughts of so many, formed a perfect screen for the poet's willful mind and whatever scruples he wished to cast aside. He was thus blessed, as he would be again and again, with the chance to defend his Caliban mask with a beguiling innocence which must have increased his joy. Rarely then was Browning's wit enhanced as effectively by a generous mockery if not lightheartedness. More substantive to the Duchess' unreality is the fanciful art through which Browning conceals the deception to be found in "Caliban." So when the underlying thematic similarities of all Browning's poetry are admitted, it is interesting to speculate on why Caliban has not attracted and delighted as many readers as the Duchess. Is it because "The Flight" accentuates the love of Prometheus while "Caliban" accentuates the tyranny of Jehovah, though overlapping of the two themes is more prominent in the former? "The Flight" is also couched in a language as personalized and thus as distracting as Caliban's, its wild setting is almost as strange as Caliban's, and its atmosphere of superstition is as thoroughly barbaric or paganistic as Caliban's. Its Witch is just as unlikely a mask for Prometheanism as Caliban is an unlikely mask for opposition to Jehovah. Moreover, the structure of Browning's Shelleyan metaphysics is the same in both poems, and the disbelief of both characters in Jehovah's grace, mercy, love and justice hinges on the irreconcilable nature of justice and love as Shelley and Browning propounded it.

By employing or hinting at magic, white and black, from his earliest poems on, Browning gives the impression of being as deeply involved in magical if not arcane arts as his own Paracelsus. But that conclusion would ignore the many instances in which Promethean subtleties are subsumed in falsely implied magic. Because he permitted himself ever to be needled by St. Paul's "Casting down *imaginations*, and every high thing that exalteth itself against the knowledge of God" (2 Cor 10.5) and positively infuriated by his "No marvel; for Satan himself is transformed into an *angel of light*.

/ Therefore it is no great thing if his ministers also be transformed as the ministers of righteousness" (2 Cor 11.14-5), Browning could compose few lines without attempting to invalidate the one and validate the other. If the imagined Pied Piper is Prometheus or an envoy, as seems likely, he is nonetheless a most innocent and beneficent magical figure. If the imagined Pippa is a Promethean, as seems sure, she is nonetheless Nature's child, an angel of light and a minister of righteousness. And though the gipsy witch who negotiates the flight of the Duchess appears as anciently evil as the hoary cripple who supposedly but not really waylaid Childe Roland, she too proves to be beneficently assigned to guide the Duchess to the retreat awaiting all Promethean children (PU 4.26). Browning's Prometheus seems to operate through whatever agencies Jehovah disapproves, and his fiends or devils (including the poet) are always good or within the bounds of a mild reprimand and beyond the threat of a nonexistent hell. The only evil, the only enemy, is Jehovah with his misguided slaves. Thus the Duchess is rescued, not by chance of the Duke's scheme to teach her a lesson, but by the crone's own devising. When the narrating huntsman, serf and thrall, eavesdrops from the balcony, he sees his lady's maid in a trance on the floor and the Gipsy woman late, on the seat of state a queen (PU 2.4.3):

With head and *face downbent*	(Epipsy 292; 522)
On the *lady's* head and face intent:	(Duchess')
For, *coiled* at her feet like a child at ease,	(PU 2.3.97)
The lady sat between her knees . . .	
And her upturned face met the face of the crone	(Epipsy 295-301)
Wherein the eyes had grown and grown	
As if she could *double* and quadruple	(Sophia 6,7,9,14,16)
At *pleasure* the *play* of either pupil . . .	(Faust 322-3)
As up and down like a *gor-crow's flappers*	("gore," Devil 58, 43)
They moved to *measure*, or bell-clappers. . . .	(PU 4.77)
At once I was stopped by the lady's expression:	
For it was *life* her eyes were drinking	
From the crone's wide pair above unwinking,	
— *Life's* pure fire received without shrinking,	(Shelley's Life)
Into the heart and breast whose heaving	
Told you no single drop they were leaving,	

— *Life*, that filling her, passed redundant . . . (PU 2.5.48, 3.3.87, 4.578)
And the very tresses shared in the *pleasure*, (PU 4.79)
Moving to the *mystic measure*, . . . (PU 4.77, 129)
I could hear at last, and understand,
And when I held the unbroken thread,
The Gipsy said: —

"And so at last we find my *tribe*. . . . (PU 2.4.54, "crew," Ep 306; 567)
I *trace* them the *vein* and the other *vein* (Ghasta 142, Jane, Recoll 44;
That meet on thy *brow* and part again, Triumph 277-8, PU 2.5.23; 575)
Making our rapid *mystic mark*; (PU 3.3.10-75; Cenci 5.4.151)
　　And I bid my people prove and probe
　　Each eye's profound and glorious globe
Till they detect the *kindred* spark . . . (Q Mab 9.78)
　　Fit, when my people ope their breast, (592)
To see the *sign*, and hear the *call*, (scriptural & Shelleyan)
　　And take the *vow*, and stand the *test* (scriptural & Shelleyan)
　　Which adds one more *child* to the rest — . . . (PU 3.3.33)
Thou shalt victoriously *endure*, (PU 4.562)
If that brow is true and those eyes are sure; (601)
Like a jewel-*finder's* fierce *assay* (Shelleyan; R of Islam 1835)
　　Of the *prize* he dug from its mountain-tomb —
Let once the vindicating *ray* (PU 2.4.3)
　　Leap out amid the anxious *gloom*, (PU 2.4.3)
And steel and fire have done their part
And the *prize* falls on its finder's heart. (Q Mab 9.5)
So, *trial after trial* past, (Julian 472)
Wilt thou fall at the very last
Breathless, half in trance
With the thrill of the *great deliverance*, (Epipsy 277)
　　Into our arms for evermore;
And thou shalt know, those arms once *curled* (R of Islam 1120)
　　About thee, what we knew before,
How *love is the only good* in the world." (PU 1.824)

The setting for this centrally planned absorption or trance is as purely Shelleyan as the language of the incantation. What the Duchess — all fire, life and gladness — drinks from the Gipsy Queen's eyes is Promethean "Life," the sum total of Shelley's universe. Pine trees (PU 2.1.156-9) marching up the mountain like rows of black priests, birds and animals in alerted sympathy to the point at which one has instinctive knowledge of the flight's destination, iron ore and fiery smelting and sand all artistically embellished by gipsy moulding and glass blowing and pantheistic refusal of the Duchess to join the hunting-party to preside over the disemboweling — all these contribute to the druidical circle the Duke's huntsman draws for the execution of his little lady's adventure. In exchange for her conventional Church and State imprisonment, the Duchess is first promised by the Gipsy Queen that not a power of life will be unemployed in satisfying her nature's need. And then if she is not set on "blending" or union — apparently Browning's euphemism for marriage or human relationship — there "is *the other fate* in store, / And art thou fitted to adore, / *To give thy wondrous self away*, / *And take a stronger nature's sway*?" (642-5). Assured by passionate eyes that the Duchess wishes to take Prometheus' never indifferent sway (PU 2.4.35), the transformed witch lastly reveals that the final and best part of the choice is merciful Death and reabsorption by Prometheus: "And like *the hand* which ends a dream [life] , / Death, with the might of his [Prometheus'] sunbeam, / *Touches* the flesh and the *soul awakes*, / Then — " (686-9). Possibly Browning's most obvious use of THE EARTH's rationalization of Death (PU 3.3.103-23), these lines which may seem mischievously drawn out by the poet's ellipsis and a subsequent farfetched diversion on friendship are not incompatible with the helter-skelter of the whole poem. But the falsely imposed light-heartedness does not obscure pointed references to the "touch" given Io by Jupiter, serf and thrall not unlike Caliban, haters in the city's horrible streets and "green chapleted" forehead which bespeak Browning's opposition to Jehovah's tyranny as loudly as do the Shelleyan friend, yawn, shriek, myself, wheel-work, coiled, paling, ripple, dizziness, forethought, bruised, points, prize, gor-crow, mystic measure, kindred spark, sign, deliverance, charm and mind. Caliban is less explicit about the new Promethean day which will replace the pain of the present with the light, life and Love of the future: "Believeth with the life, the pain shall stop" (250). But like the Duke's huntsman who is inherited chattel Caliban would gladly search out "some snug corner / Under a hedge, like Orson the wood-knight, . . . / And sleep a sound sleep till the trumpet's blowing [Proteus' mystic shell, PU 3.3.65-84] / Wake me (*unless priests cheat us laymen*) / To a world where will be no further throwing / Pearls before [Christian] swine that can't value them. Amen!" (910-5).

THE RING AND THE BOOK
1868-69

Nowhere else in his poetry does Browning more successfully play the part of the double agent than in *The Ring and the Book*. Critics have long been uncertain of the poet's full intent, sometimes deducing opposite meaning from the same passages and lines. The truth is that Browning had so nearly perfected his art of deception that he was rarely in a strait for new or revamped machinations. And when detection seemed possible he could easily fall back on obscuration and prolixity in diction and punctuation. Increasingly emboldened by his genius and long proof of human indifference and ignorance, he could openly display ability at taking any side of any issue and yet so confuse in the meantime that even "Tertium Quid" is thought to be both objective and partisan to both causes. Consequently "The Pope," now obviously to be seen as the pivotal book for Browning's design, is so constructed that the Pope says and unsays whatever Browning wishes, threads negative statements through positive ones and emerges with either a positive or negative statement as he chooses. The major difference between "Easter-Day" and "The Pope" is the poet's probable substitution of different punctuation for the normal quotation marks which distinguish speakers. For like Hard-to-be-a-Christian Pope Innocent XII is a Promethean; so are Pompilia, Caponsacchi and the barefoot Augustinian worshipers of Shelley's Prometheus. And *The Ring and the Book* is Browning's magnum opus in advancement of Prometheanism. Thus it should be noted early that when Browning's Pope employs the word GOD he may mean either Jehovah or Prometheus, when he employs "Christ" or Master he may mean either Jesus Christ or Prometheus:

In *God's* name! Once more on this earth of *God's*, . . .   (Prom; 162)
I take *His* staff with my uncertain hand, . . .   (Prom; 164)

And forthwith think, speak, act, in place of *Him* —   (Prom; 167)
The Pope for *Christ*. . . .   (Prometheus)
While *hollowly* the avengers echo . . .   (PU 3.4.42; 178)
          "As for the weal or woe   (190)
Hereafter, *God* grant mercy! Man be just,   (Jehovah)
Nor let the felon boast he went scot-free!" . . .
Ay, and while thus I dally, dare perchance   (197)
Put *fancies* for a comfort 'twixt this calm   (faith)
And yonder passion that I have to bear, — . . .
Yes, though I flatter me with *fancy* thus,   (faith; 205)
I *know* it is but nature's craven-trick.   (Mind)
The case is over, judgment at an end,
And all things done now and irrevocable:
A mere dead man is Franceschini here, . . .
What other should I say than "*God* so willed: (Jehovah; 256)
Mankind is *ignorant*, a man am I:
Call *ignorance* my sorrow, not my sin!" . . .   (PU 3.4.43)
I shall face Guido's ghost nor blench a jot.   (263)
"*God* who set me to judge thee, meted out   (Jehovah)
So much judging faculty, no more:
Ask *Him* if I was slack in use thereof!" . . .   (Jehovah, graphic)
For I am ware it is the *seed of act*,   (271)
God [with-]holds appraising in *His hollow* palm,   (Jehovah; PU 3.4.42,
Not act grown great thence on the world below,   149, Isa 40.12)
Leafage and branchage, *vulgar* eyes admire.   (ignorant)
Therefore I stand on my *integrity*,   (Myself)
Nor *fear* at all.   (Jehovah)

Telltale Shelleyan words, practices and allusions are here
freely interspersed — calm, willed, ignorance, hollow, nor fear,
integrity, capitalized pronouns — but for purposes of collation a significant line is "And forthwith *think*, speak, act, in
place of Him [Prometheus]." For the Pope's "great self" is
described by Browning as one who had trod many lands,
known many deeds and probed many hearts beginning with
his own (1.296); as the first to bade leave in *peace* those Jan-
senists, re-nicknamed Molinists, "who may have other *light*
than we perceive; and as sagacious, resolute and prudent,
bringing his *intelligence* to bear, sitting with his *thoughts* for
company, cheering his lips to *benevolence* and receiving "all
his light" through the half-moon window (1.1214-53). By
Caponsacchi he is described as "a *strange* Pope, — 't is said, a
priest who *thinks*" (6.473). And by Fra Celestino he is

described as "an old good man / Who happens to hate darkness and love *light*, — / In whom too was the eye that saw,
not dim, / The *natural force* to do the thing he saw" (12.590-
3). Yet the earliest visible breech in the Pope's double talk
may appear in Browning's use of one of Shelley's cleverest
plagiarisms from or analogues with Christian theology: "He,
the Truth [Prometheus], is, too, / The Word. . . . / Whatever
we dare *think* we *know* indeed / — That I am I [Myself], as
He is He, — what else?" (375-80). Whereupon Antonio Pignatelli, the Pope now seven years, speaks to his "ancient self,"
the learned and the experienced in the ways of God and man:

Thou other *force* in those old busy days	(Shelley's Power; 387)
Than this gray ultimate decrepitude, —	(cf., Q Mab 7.66-275,
Yet sensible of *fires* that more and more	Ahasuerus becomes S's
Visit a *soul*, in passage to the sky,	Demogorgon; passion)
Left nakeder than when flesh-robe was new —	
Thou, *not Pope but the mere old man o' the world*, . . .	(wisdom)
Wilt thou, the one whose speech I somewhat trust,	(394)
Question the after-me, this self now Pope,	
Hear his procedure, *criticize* his work?	
Wise in its generation is the world.	(Lu 16.8)

Technically therefore it is not Pope Innocent alone who
speaks through the remaining lines but also Man of the World
whom the Pope trusts and considers wise in his generation.
Long unmeaningful words, broken coherence and excessively
disruptive "dashes" now fall squarely into place as the Pope
is identified as intervening throughout the "questioning" by
his "ancient self," Man of the World. To disguise his Dialogue
of the Mind, which is essentially the scheme of "Easter-Day,"
Browning resorts to the substitution of a comma and a dash
(, —) for normal quotation marks. All naturally runs unnoticed in Browning's habitual use of the dash, except for an
occasional, inexplicable "Proceed" (476), "I remark" (531),
"I see" (587), "note the point" (597), "See!" (656), "who
knows?" (1024), "Do I smile?" (1122), "you, you, our"
(1837-40), "ourselves" (1909), "we" (1911) and "when,
where" (1977) which clearly indicate two voices. That two
voices are speaking may also be detected by the language,

alternatingly urbane and clerical, but the dialogue is of one mind and Browning, the arbiter, permits only unchallenged disagreement, clarification or confirmation, one voice always charged with reason, the other often with religious clichés.

Although Browning's deceptive punctuation now has very little to do with confirmation of his Prometheanism, it does offer an occasional advantage in tangential matters. Unexpectedly the more prevalent the punctuation — four question marks or four exclamation points within three to four lines, to which is often added a plain dash (—), two commas with dash (, —) and a colon (:) — the less effective the deception becomes, simply because it does not any longer matter to understanding whether Pope or Man of the World speaks. But anyone who knows the difficulties of separating speeches by Hard-to-be and Easy-to-be-a-Christian can appreciate the variety of games Browning may play in his most skillful deception. Contiguous periods (.), question marks (?) or exclamation points (!), presumably within three consecutive lines, seem often to designate a change of speaker. So does it seem that contiguous colons (:), placed within a fixed number of lines, negate or alter normal deceptive patterns, and question mark or exclamation point with dash (? — ! —) may or may not have had meaning for Browning, though they appear to be mere red herrings. Hence apart from the comma and dash (, —), which may be separated at the ending and beginning of consecutive lines, the most satisfactory division of speakers is made through sightings of urbane or clerical diction. Yet even this method fails when Browning judges himself to be in a tight spot, for he then shades the diction or reverses his practice, thus allowing the Pope to speak urbanely or nondescript, Man of the World somewhat clerically or nondescript. So it is the Promethean Pope, the total man, to whom one must always turn when the illustrative examples of deceptive punctuation pass beyond reasonable acceptance.

Starting on the "unmanly" characteristics (398-571), Man of the World observes that Guido began life sufficiently helped — sound frame, solid intellect, wit, wisdom and courage — to cope with the implanted drawbacks and obstacles of earth. After all, as Browning himself soon intrudes, "Is this our ultimate stage, or starting-place, / To try man's foot, if it will creep or climb?" Hence to the Pope's ancient self Greed, not tortuous murder, is unseemly, not wicked or sinful, in one who began life "fortified by propitious circumstances," and Guido's belief in "just the *vile* of life," not its evil, is his "black mark." The marriage, Guido's last deliberate act, exemplifies an habitual creed and it should therefore be used to show the "very sum and substance of [Guido's] soul," not his life. Without an acceptable motive for marriage, Guido exhibited "what sinks man past level of the brute . . . / All is lust for money: to get gold." Thus Pompilia became "his *slave*, his chattel, to first use, then destroy. . . . undertaken in God's [Prometheus'] face / With all these lies so opposite God's [Prometheus'] truth, / For end so other than man's end." Agreeing that Guido accepted the Church's base of doctrine, both voices hold him strictly to "Man is born nowise to content himself, / But to please God [Jehovah]." So to Man of the World when Guido's scheming is met by counterscheming, he "soars to the *zenith* whence the *fiercer* fowl / May dare the inimitable swoop" (Ode W Wind 21-2). He draws on the *curious* crime (Ye Hasten 6) to satiate malice and institutes the love-intrigue, thus stripping Pompilia's parents of the one possession they held dearest. As when in our Campagna *fire* overruns a *hut* (R of Islam 1024, 2788, Q Mab 2.164-81), even to the *ivy and wild vine* (Epipsy 500), and exposes an old malicious tower, some obscene tomb, the dwellers believed a temple in their ignorance and clung about and thought to lean upon:

POPE.
    There laughs *it* o'er their ravage, —   (pagan tower; 628)
MAN OF THE WORLD.   *where are they?* (PU 4.8, 48, 55)
    So did his cruelty burn life about, . . .
    Upon the wife, that, at extremity,   (632)
    Some crisis brought about by *fire and flame,*   (Prometheus)
    The patient *frenzy-stung* must needs break loose, (R of Islam 2881)
    Fly anyhow, find refuge anywhere,

Even in the arms of who should front her first,
No monster but a man — while nature *shrieked*   (PU 1.80)
'Or thus escape, or die!' The *spasm* arrived,   (PU 2.1.203)
Not the escape by way of sin, —

POPE.   *O God*,   (Prometheus)
Who shall pluck *sheep* Thou holdest, from Thy hand?   (deceptive)
Therefore she lay resigned to die, — ...

MAN OF THE WORLD.
Whereby the *man* so far attains his end   (Guido; 655)
That *strange* temptation is permitted, —   (Shelleyan, cf., 830)

POPE.   see!
Pompilia wife, and Caponsacchi priest,
Are brought together as nor priest nor wife
Should stand, and there is *passion* in the place,
Power in the air for evil as for good,
Promptings from *heaven and hell*, as if the stars   (Prom & Jehovah)
Fought in their courses for a *fate* to be.   (close periods)

MAN OF THE WORLD.
Thus stand the wife and priest, a *spectacle*,   (1.498, Cenci 5.3.38)
I doubt not, to *unseen assemblage there*.   (spirits, Shelleyan)
No lamp will mark that window for a *shrine*,   (Shelleyan)
No *tablet* signalize the terrace, *teach*   (Q Mab 7.53)
New generations which succeed the *old*,   (thematic)
The pavement of the street is *holy ground*;
No bard describe in verse how *Christ* prevailed   (Prometheus)
And *Satan* fell like lightning! *Why repine?*   (Jehovah; cf., 7.894)
What does the world, told *truth*, but lie the more?   (Promethean)

A second time the plot is foiled; nor, now,
By corresponding sin for counter*check*,
No wile and trick that baffle trick and wile, —   (graphic)

POPE.
The play o' the parents! here the blot is *blanched*   (Q Mab 7.158)
By *God's* gift of a *purity* of soul   (Prometheus'; Q Mab 7.154)
That will not take *pollution*, ermine-like   (Q Mab 4.151)
Armed from dishonor by its own soft snow.
Such was this *gift* of God who showed *for once*   (see gift below)
How He would have the world go white: it seems
As a *new* attribute were born of each   (thematic)
Champion of truth, the priest and wife I praise, —   (PU 1.443)

MAN OF THE WORLD.
As a *new* safeguard sprang up in defence   (thematic)
Of their *new noble nature*: so a thorn

<pre>
Comes to the aid of and completes the *rose* —   (symbol of secrecy)
Courage, to wit, no woman's *gift* nor priest's,   (PU 3.3.2)
I' the crisis; *might* leaps vindicating right.   (Prometheus)
See how the *strong* aggressor, bad and bold,   (as opposed to *weak*)
With every advantage, preconcerts surprise,
Leaps of a sudden at his victim's throat
In a *byeway*, —. . .   (Cenci 3.1.60, 5.3.33)
POPE.   There skulks crime   (695)
Behind *law* called in to back cowardice!   (Church's)
While out of the poor *trampled* worm the wife,   (PU 1.214, 386)
Springs up a *serpent*!   (always salutary in Shelley)
</pre>

Such lines amply demonstrate the latitude Browning could exercise with exceptions to the comma and dash (, —), with run-on paragraphs and with change of speaker at paragraph break or within a prearranged number of lines. And as subsequent dialogue unfolds, those latitudes are probably exercised on all of the poet's possibilities, even to separating ? — or ! — at the end and beginning of consecutive lines. It should also be noted that while continuity of thought between voices is often evident, there are instances of thought by Man of the World smoothly carrying on as if no interruption had been injected by the Pope. Of much greater interest than the technical deceptions, therefore, is the evidence that urbane responses, once isolated, may rightly be assigned to Browning who makes sure that no thought expressed accords with, no success gained stems from, Church practice or doctrine. Through Man of the World the stage is set for Browning's habitual onslaught against the Church and for Browning's most elaborate and most determined effort to advance the cause of Shelley's Prometheus. It is the absence of "the manlier sin," not the presence of the deadlier sin, which rouses Man of the World's indignation, and it is Nature — bramble-finch, our Campagna, holy ground — which provides suave analogies seen always in rougher, cruder light by the Pope. Thus Nature, properly incited by Guido's unmanly cruelty, "shrieks" to Pompilia, "Escape or die," after which Browning's Man of the World adds, "The *spasm* arrived, / Not the escape by way of sin." Truly Browning saw no diminution to Pompilia's gloriously drawn virtue in sharing her life with Caponsacchi, and Shelley's ECHOES inspire the diction: "Where the earth reposed from spasms, / On the day when He [Prometheus] and thou [Asia] / Parted, to commingle now" (PU 2.1.203-5).

Nor does Browning fail soon thereafter to eulogize the spot where "soul meets soul" (PU 4.451) in the loveliest of lines: "No lamp will mark that window for a shrine, / No tablet signalize the terrace, teach / *New* generations which succeed the *old* [see 11.1860-8], / The pavement of the street is holy ground; / No bard describe in verse how Christ [Prometheus] prevailed / And Satan [Jehovah] fell like lightning! Why repine? / What does the [Christian] world, told [pagan] truth, but lie the more?" As one may be sure that the exclamation point after "lightning" indicates that "Satan" refers to Jehovah, the Church or enemy of Prometheus, one may also be sure that "Why repine" indicates Browning's, as well as Pompilia's (7.894), unconquerable Will to believe that Shelley's Promethean Truth would eventually wash the earth clear and pure. Expectedly Man of the World prescribes a heroic entry for Caponsacchi. Champions of truth "by gift of God," as the Pope elevates them, Pompilia and Caponsacchi are miraculously rescued "as a *new* safeguard [Prometheus] sprang up in defence / Of their *new noble nature*." Courage, not gift of Jehovah, is then the *new* attribute "as might [Power] leaps vindicating right." Strong aggressor with every advantage including surprise, Guido is no match for the Weakness which by Will "must unloose through life's portal" (PU 2.3.96) the union and rescue of Pompilia and Caponsacchi. Always in Browning, it seems, "a thing / I doubt not, *nor fear for*, secure some god [Prometheus] / To save will come in thunder from the *stars*" (*Pauline* 665-7).

Somewhat more discreet in recounting her experiences with Caponsacchi on the flight from Arezzo than Pope or Man of the World, Pompilia emphasizes psychical as well as natural union with her "deliverer" almost as if they were Prometheus and Asia (PU 1.807-11) or Prometheus and Panthea (PU 2.1.78-82): "So was that minute vouchsafed [fated] me, so / The manhood, wasted then, was still at watch / To save me yet a second time: no *change* / Here, though all else *changed* in the *changing* world!" (7.1399-1402). "Otherwise / Here alone would be failure, loss to me — / How much more loss to him, with life debarred / From giving life, *love locked from love's display*, / The day-star [Sun — Prometheus, 2 Pet 1.19] stopped its task that makes night morn!" (7.1764-8). But Caponsacchi is not yet fully attuned to the refinements of Shelley's spirits or their dedication to unrestricted Life. So he must await Prometheus' instant of Change before he can respond differently from Man of the World to Pompilia's physical attractiveness:

Into *another* state, under *new rule*	(6.949)
I knew *myself* was passing swift and sure;	(Myself)
Whereof the *initiatory* pang approached,	(cf., 10.1206)
Felicitous annoy, as bitter-sweet	(cf., 10.589)
As when the virgin-band, the victors chaste,	
Feel at the end the earthly garments drop,	(Q Mab 1.128-38)
And rise with something of a rosy shame	
Into mortal nakedness: so I	
Lay, and let come the proper throe would thrill	
Into the *ecstasy* and *outthrob* pain.	(Q Mab 1.176)

Next addressing the Pope's reference to fowlers who hawk, shoot and snare yet eschew *vile* practice, Man of the World asks how Guido hunts Pompilia and quickly replies with "the fraudful trap" (722, Oedipus 1.1.183). Craft, greed and violence complot his revenge, and violence bespeaks all three when Guido's son and heir, Pompilia's babe, is born. Other men free their *souls* from care at new birth, "*fly up* in thanks / To God [Prometheus], reach, recognize His love for once: / Guido cries '*Soul*, at last the mire is thine!'" (752-4). "So man / *Wills* good to man, so Guido makes complete / His murder!" (787-9).

MAN OF THE WORLD.

, — off *they* fly!	(the murderers; 794)

So is the murder managed, *sin* conceived	(deceptive)
To the full: and why not crowned with triumph too?	
Why must the sin, conceived thus, bring forth death?	(Yet why)

I note how, within hair's-breadth of escape,
Impunity and the thing supposed success,
Guido is found when the *check* comes, the *change*, (PU 1.125;3.4.76)
The *monitory touch* o' the tether — felt   (P's warning,PU 3.3.85)
By few, not marked by many, named by none   ("tether," Serchio 6)
At the moment, only recognized aright   (cf., La S 109)
I' the fulness of the days, for *God's*, lest sin   (Prometheus)
Exceed the service, leap the line: such *check* —   (PU 1.125)
A secret which this life finds hard to keep,   (R.B.'s secret)
And, often guessed, is never quite revealed —
Needs *must* trip Guido on a stumbling-block   (fated)
Too vulgar, too absurdly plain i' the path!
Study this single oversight of care.   (Reason)
This *hebetude* that marred sagacity,   (obtuseness)
Forgetful of all the man best *knew*, —   (wisdom)

Man of the World implies that Guido's carelessness in not securing a simple pass for "change" of horses was his downfall — when Guido and his four accomplices in murder fled Rome to reach the first stopping place from which fresh horses would have put them scot-free in Arezzo and friendly territory. But Browning, through Man of the World, talks about GOD and thinks about Prometheus who, when asking that his curse of Jupiter be repeated, reminds all friendly spirits that it was he, the Titan, who made his agony the barrier to Jupiter's punishment of them:

> me alone, who *checked*,   (PU 1.125)
> As one who *checks* a fiend-drawn charioteer,
> The falsehood and the force of *him who reigns*   (Jehovah who tyran-
> Supreme, and with the groans of pining *slaves*   nizes; Christians)
> Fills your dim glens and liquid wildernesses:
> Why answer ye not, still? *Brethren*!

This rare monitory check or Touch, initiated by Prometheus and unloosed by Necessity, explains why, when the Pope interjects "Why thou [Guido] fool and blind, / It is the mercy-stroke that stops thy fate, / Hamstrings and holds thee to thy hurt," Man of the World may compassionately ask:

> , — but how?   (853)
> On the edge o' the precipice! One minute more,
> Thou hadst gone farther and fared worse, *my son*, . . .   (deceptive)
> Thy comrades each and all were of one mind,   (857)

Thy murder done, to straightway murder thee . . .
So, to the last, *greed* found itself at odds   (860)
With *craft* in thee, and, proving conqueror,
Had sent thee, the same night that crowned thy hope,   (cryptic)
Thither where, this same day, I see thee not,
Nor, through *God's* mercy, need, to-morrow, see.   (Prometheus)

As rigidly opposed to capital punishment as Shelley, Browning answers once and for all how he and Man of the World felt about Guido's beheading. To them man's spirit is part of the Spirit of Prometheus and indestructible beyond all culpability. Yet once Browning had interpolated "A secret which this life finds hard to keep, / And, often guessed, is never quite revealed," it behooved him to avoid unnecessary risk in the last three lines. Instead, he boldly unites Prometheus' monitory touch or Check with a mercifully divine love which preserves even the murderer.

Found "midmost blotch of *black*" (865) by Man of the World, Guido nonetheless stands honest in the red of the flame beside the "yellow" (879) which would pass for white in his brother Paul, the Abate, who is all craft but no violence. And the younger brother Girolamo, priest and canon, will either blend his currently hybrid violence and craft into greater crime

MAN OF THE WORLD.   Or subside   (898)
    And let the *simple* quality emerge,   (ignorant)
    Go on with *Satan's* service the *old* way?   (Jehovah's; Church)
    Meanwhile, what promise, —

POPE.   what performance too!
    For there's a new distinctive touch, I see,
    Lust — lacking in the two — hell's own *blue* tint
    That gives a character and marks the man
    More than a match for *yellow* and *red*. Once more   (thematic)
    A case reserved: *why should I doubt*? Then comes
    The gaunt gray nightmare in the furthest smoke,
    The hag that gave these three abortions birth.

One would expect Browning to assign to the more outspoken Pope, not Man of the World, the task of characterizing Guido's mother, in spite of Shelley's approving "And women too, ugliest of all things evil" (PU 3.4.46; "changed," 3.4.155ff). Yet a better reason for the Pope's unusually venomous words is not to be overlooked in the way Browning carefully develops "Huddling together [mother & sons] in the *cave* they call / Their palace" with "pitchy furnace stirred / At the centre" (867, 874). For there is a permissible exception to following Prometheus' "I wish no *living* thing to suffer" (PU 1.305) since to Shelley all Churchmen were the same as dead. Hence in preparation for Man of the World's (R.B.'s) most insensitive utterance, even Guido's four ignorant companions in murder suffer unreasonably through the Pope's harsh "God-abandoned wretched lumps of life" (922; Cyclops 388). Now other unnoticed individuals, including complacent onlookers, claim to be classed subordinately *vile* (961) by Man of the World, but when he speaks in deadly seriousness it is the Archbishop of Arezzo who draws his fiercest condemnation because he sent Pompilia back to Guido unhelped. Browning would have the reader believe the passage applies to the mother and her three abortive sons, but Guido (dead) and Paolo (fled) are no longer available to cluster round an imagined pitchy furnace in the impoverished, cave-like palace:

MAN OF THE WORLD.
        , — *thou,* chosen of *both*   (Archbishop; Church & God)
To do the shepherd's office, feed the sheep —   (985)
How of this lamb that *panted* at thy foot   (Shelleyan)
While the wolf pressed on her within crook's reach?
Wast thou the hireling that did turn and flee?
With thee at least anon *the little word*!   (fire)

Such *denizens* o' the cave *now* cluster round   (Churchmen)
And heat the furnace *sevenfold*: time indeed   (Isa 30.26; M't 13.42)
A bolt from heaven should cleave roof and clear place,
Transfix and show the world, *suspiring flame,*   (pierce thru; dying)
The main offender, scar and brand the rest   (the Church)
Hurrying, each miscreant to his hole: then flood
And purify the scene with outside day —
Which yet, in the *absolutest* drench of dark,   (blackness)
Ne'er wants a witness, some stray *beauty-beam*
To the despair of *hell.*   (Jehovah's heaven; 999)

After all the precaution Man of the World has taken to honor
Prometheus' compassion and absence of hate, he could not
be remotely prone to ask heaven to pierce Guido's tribe
through with a bolt of lightning. Such denizens as he speaks
of are "now" clustered round with clerical threats of hell,
and they are exactly as "black" as the Jehovah of "Easter-
Day." The "main offender" is the Church, where miscreant
priests fearfully await their last long gasp of breath.

It is a far cry from Browning's "denounce" to "pronounce," but Pope Innocent now reassumes his preeminence
and begins a formal pronouncement of Pompilia's innocence.
Rather than interjecting comments, he seems to be the main
speaker, periodically interrupted by Man of the World or, as
Browning dissembled, the Pope's ancient self (Eze 8.12-16):

<pre>
POPE.   First of the first,   (999)
    Such I pronounce Pompilia, then as now
    Perfect in whiteness: stoop thou down, my child, . . .   (purity)
    Let me look at thee in the flesh as erst,   (1004)
    Let me enjoy the old clean linen garb,   (Man of the World's)
    Not the new splendid vesture! . . .   (the Pope's)
                    Everywhere   (1008)
    I see in the world the intellect of man   (Shelley's Mind)
    That sword, the energy of his subtle spear,
    The knowledge which defends him like a shield —
    Everywhere; but they make not up, I think,   (deceptive)
    The marvel of a soul like thine, earth's flower
    She holds up to the softened gaze of God!   (Prometheus)
</pre>

Because he is Pope, which Man of the World calls "a necessity
of times," and dares not grant clerical privilege to Guido in
opposition to public demand, Innocent must be responsible
for the death sentence and fracture of Promethean pity.
Therefore he and Man of the World cannot be totally fused
into Antonio Pignatelli at this ideal juncture or at any later
one. But that the Pope speaks from the secular side of his
nature is seen in the preference of clean linen garb of his
former self to splendid vesture of his present papal self. That
the speaker is the Pope, rather than possibly Man of the
World, is also seen in the slight subordination of man's intellect, despite the noticeable Shelleyan emphasis on mind,

thought and knowledge. As Pompilia's spirit is part of the Spirit of Prometheus, so Pompilia's mind is part of the One Mind, and Browning's alter ego could never truly place act above actor. Moreover, Man of the World is presently needed to remind the Pope of Promethean virtues a "reforming" pantheist might thoughtlessly neglect:

POPE.
    Yet if in *purity* and *patience*, if   (Shelleyan; 1018)
    In faith held fast despite the *plucking fiend,* . . .   (Jehovah)

MAN OF THE WORLD.
          , — if in *right* returned   (1021)
    For *wrong*, most *pardon* for worst injury,   (PU 4.571)
    If there be any *virtue*, any *praise*, —   (Ph'p 4.8)

POPE.
    Then will this woman-child have proved — *who knows?*
    Just the one prize *vouchsafed* unworthy me.   (fated)

With St. Paul impudently exhibited in "any virtue, any praise," it should be said that Browning was less a master at reading meaning out of words or reading new meaning into words than Shelley. Each of them exploits "Finally, *brethren*, whatsoever things are true, whatsoever things are honest, whatsoever things are just, whatsoever things are pure, whatsoever things are lovely, whatsoever things are of good report; if there be any virtue, and if there be any praise, think on these things." Yet Shelley's exploitations always ring thoroughly pagan while Browning's never seem to lose their Christian flavor, partly no doubt because of his intended ambiguity. Even when Browning's use of St. Paul's most familiar words seem adopted from or through Shelley, including either favorable or unfavorable implication, his words lose the pristine quality of Shelley's paganism. Both poets were fully aware of St. Paul's being influenced by the diction of Euripides and other pagan writers as well as of the initial syncretism of pagan and Christian thought which was drawn by the Church Fathers. Yet it is as likely that Browning and Shelley simplified their task by plundering the hymns of Isaac Watts, Charles Wesley and Martin Luther as that Browning plundered Shelley for "the plucking fiend" ("pitiless, prolific fiend," Q Mab 4.30; 6.69-71, 109-10). At any rate, the hymns popularize all the syncretic words and rhymes and *The Revolt of Islam* (1149-51) gives the Pope chance to castigate Jehovah in whom he is revealing greater and greater distrust.

Three times now Pope Innocent has expressed momentary doubt of an unexplained origin, probably in Prometheanism rather than in Christianity, and each time the worldly, thinking side of his nature seems to counter the misgivings of "Why should I doubt?" (906), "Who knows?" (959), and "who knows? — / Just the one prize vouchsafed unworthy me," the last of which enables Man of the World to speak of Pompilia as a Rose, a chance-sown, cleft-nursed seed which sprang up by the wayside beneath the foot of the enemy (the Church, 1038; "cleft," Orpheus 23):

MAN OF THE WORLD.

My rose, I gather for the breast of *God*,	(Prometheus; 1042)
This I praise most in *thee*, where all I praise,	(PU 3.4.153-63)
That having been obedient to the end	
According to the *light* allotted, *law*	(Promethean)
Prescribed thy life, still tried, still standing test, —	(old-new)

POPE.

Dutiful to the foolish parents first,	
Submissive next to the *bad* husband, —	(Shelleyan)

MAN OF THE WORLD.   nay,

Tolerant of those meaner miserable	
That did his hests, eked out the dole of pain, —	

POPE.

Thou, patient thus, could *rise from law to law*,	(old-new; 1050)
The *old* to the *new*, promoted at one cry	(Jehovah's; Prom's)
O' the trump [shell] of *God* to the new service, . . .	(Prometheus)
Oh child that didst despise thy life so much . . .	(1059)
Thou didst . . . *how shall I say?* . . . receive so long	(all R.B.'s)
The standing ordinance of *God* on earth,	(Jehovah; 1064)
Why wonder if the *novel* claim had clashed	(Dante Conv 1-9)
With *old* requirement, seemed to supersede	(cf., 1550)
Too much the *customary* law? But, brave,	(the Church's)
Thou at first promptings of what I call *God*,	(pantheism)
And fools call Nature, didst hear, comprehend, . . .	
To worthily defend the trust of trusts,	(1075)
Life from the Ever Living: — didst resist —	(PU 2.5.48)

Especially identifiable as the Pope's speech by the papal use of "Oh child," the absence of urbanity and the prevalence of scriptural allusions, lines 1051-80 above are the first in which the Pope speaks of moving from an "old" (Catholic) to a "new [Promethean] service," of how it would be difficult for Pompilia long accustomed to the old requirements to allow the new, "novel claim" which too much supersedes the customary Church law. These lines also provide the Pope's first admission of being a pantheist: "What I call God / And fools call Nature." Small wonder that he praises Pompilia's brave response to Prometheus at first prompting, a natural response identical with that of brute, bird, reptile, fly, tree and plant (1070-4). Though, as will be seen, Pompilia herself places service to Prometheus above rescue of her unborn child.

Pope Innocent and his ancient self are only slightly less impressed by Caponsacchi's than by Pompilia's bravery, once "my son," "my warrior-priest" has been touched by Pompilia's spirit. The Pope thinks peradventure Caponsacchi's being an "irregular noble scapegrace" results from Churchman "who will misteach, mislead."

<pre>
                    Better bear   (1100)
The King of Pride go wantoning awhile, . . .   (PU 3.4.91)
Through deep to deep, followed by all that shine, (PU 3.4.86-96;1103)
Churning the blackness hoary: He who made   (Prometheus)
The comely terror, He shall make the sword   (fire, PU 2.4.66-7)
To match that piece of netherstone his heart,   (PU 2.3.70, Hellas 415;
Ay, nor miss praise thereby; who else shut fire   Jehovah's; Prom,
I' the stone, to leap from mouth at sword's first stroke,   cf., 7.1385)
In lamps of love and faith, the chivalry   (P's emblem, PU
That dares the right and disregards alike   3.3.170, 4.92)
The yea and nay o' the [Christian] world? Self-sacrifice, —   (2 Cor 1.
                17-9, PU 3.4.150: "which makes the heart deny the
                     yes it breathes," before the Promethean change)
</pre>

Knowing that the Pope alludes to the wantonness of the SPIRIT OF THE EARTH, the "self-sacrifice" involved in Prometheus' filching fire for man and the glorious "change" (PU 3.4.71-204) to be brought about by the new Promethean day, Man of the World interposes to ask about the Church's idolized Madonnas, turned Christian idols from pagan

Venuses despite the perversely lingering purblind love of poor
Rome (1112-22), before returning to the courageous conduct
of Caponsacchi. While "our adversary" the Church may
prefer to condemn Caponsacchi's blameworthy and prolonged youth, Man of the World would "rather chronicle the
healthy rage, —

POPE.
   When the first moan broke from the martyr-maid   (1134)
   At that uncaging of the beasts, —   (Mary, who died 1-24)

MAN OF THE WORLD.   made bare
   My *athlete* on the instant, gave such *good*   (Naples 122)
   Great undisguised leap over post and pale . . .   (PU 4.577)
   There may have been rash *stripping* — every rag   (Naples 122; 1139)
   Went to the winds, —

POPE.   infringement manifold
   Of laws prescribed *pudicity*, I fear,   (chastity)
   In this impulsive and prompt *self-display*!   (Myself)
   Ever such tax comes of the foolish youth;
   Men *mulct* the wiser manhood, and suspect   (penalize)
   No veritable *star* swims out of *cloud*.   (passion, Epipsy 81,79)
   Bear thou such imputation, undergo   (Shelleyan, third quick use)
   The penalty I nowise dare relax, —   (unavoidable to a Pope)

MAN OF THE WORLD.
   Conventional chastisement and rebuke.
   But for the outcome, the brave *starry* birth   (passion, Epipsy 81)
   Conciliating earth with all that *cloud*,   (passion, Epipsy 79)
   Thank heaven as I do! Ay, such *championship*   (PU 1.443)
   Of *God* at first blush, . . .   (Prometheus)

POPE.   In thought, word and deed,   (1164)
   How throughout all thy warfare thou wast *pure*,   (Shelleyan)
   I find it easy to believe: and if
   At any *fateful* moment of the *strange*
   Adventure, the strong *passion* of that strait,   (Epipsy 77-85)
   Fear and surprise, may have revealed too much, — . . .
   The perfect beauty of the body and soul   (1176)
   Thou savedst in thy *passion* for *God's* sake,   (star & cloud; Prom)
   He who is *Pity*. Was the trial sore?   (Prometheus; PU 1.53)
   Temptation sharp?

MAN OF THE WORLD.
        Thank God a *second* time! . . .   (first, 1151)
   Yea, but, *O Thou* whose servants are the *bold*, . . .   (Prom; 1184)

POPE.

> *Thou*, whose sword-hand was used to strike the lute,   (Cap; 1196)
> Whose sentry-station graced some wanton's gate,
> Thou didst push forward and show mettle, shame
> The *laggards*, and retrieve the day. Well done!   (Church-trained,
> Be glad thou hast let *light* into the world   PU 1.301)
> Through that *irregular* breach o' the boundary, —   (unconv'al)

MAN OF THE WORLD.   see

> The *same* upon thy path and march assured   (light)
> Learning anew the use of soldiership,
> *Self-abnegation, freedom from all fear*,   (Promethean)
> Loyalty to the life's end! *Ruminate*,   (Shelley's Think)
> *Deserve the initiatory spasm*, —   (cf., 6.951)

POPE.   once more

> Work, be unhappy but *bear* life, my son!   (fourth use, PU 4.562,
>   573)

In absolute agreement on Pompilia's and Caponsacchi's right conduct and Guido's conventionally unavoidable death sentence, the Pope and Man of the World now assert that their unconventional approval is directly dependent upon Prometheus:

> Yet my poor *spark* had for its source, the *sun*;   (PU 3.1.24; Prom)
> Thither I sent the great looks which *compel*   ("All things thou dar'st
>   [Will to] demand," Demogorgon, PU 2.4.8)
> *Light* from its fount: all that I do and am   (thought; 1282)
> Comes from the *truth*, or seen or else surmised,   (Prometheus)
> Remembered or divined, as *mere man* may:
> I *know* just so, nor otherwise. As I *know*   (cf., La S 179)
> I speak, —

MAN OF THE WORLD.

> What should I *know*, then, and how speak
> Were there a wild mistake of *eye or brain*   (rational, T of Life 201)
> As to recorded *governance* above?   (Epipsy 361, Mt B 140)
> If my own *breath*, only blew coal alight   (PU 2.3.84)
> I styled *celestial* and the *morning-star*?   (Q Mab 1.105,213,2.60,

POPE.

> I, who in this world act resolvedly, . . .   Islam 356, 485, 501)
> Shall I dare try *the doubt* now, or not dare?   (1302)

Antonio Pignatelli does then try the simulated doubt in Browning's most famous simulated prayer, and Shelley's Prometheus thereafter stands firmer than ever in his intellect:

<pre>
O Thou, — as represented here to me   (Prometheus; 1303)
In such conception as my *soul* allows, —   (spirit of Spirit)
Under Thy measureless, my atom width! —   (cf., Saul 292)
Man's mind, what is it but a convex *glass*   (PU 1.657-63, 4.382; 2 Cor
Wherein are gathered all the scattered *points*   3.18; PU 3.3.40-63, 138)
Picked out of the immensity of sky,
To re-*unite* there, be our heaven for earth,   (PU 4.80-3, 93-128, 273)
Our known unknown, our *God* revealed to man?   (Prometheus)
</pre>

Here and in the remainder of the Pope's long miscontrued words (1303-42) Browning expounds Shelley's theory of the One Mind. To Shelley only thought or mind is immortal, or even existent, and as thought "is the measure of the universe" (PU 2.4.73) so Prometheus, the One Mind, is the God of the universe. Yet Browning's syncretism is so warily arranged that almost every aspect of the Pope's Prometheanism is balanced by a correspondingly acceptable scriptural allusion. "O Thou," suggesting Jehovah, is symptomatic of Browning's adoration of Prometheus, and as ever it is intended to say that man's soul and his mind are as atoms to the measureless dimension of the One Mind, the mass of whose perceptions is the universe. Notwithstanding, even the lowest form of life — "*insect* or angel" — knows (thinks), else it could not love. Since all thought eternally resides with Prometheus, shared though it be with all living things in varying degrees of purity, all human thought originates with and returns re-united to Prometheus, clearly echoing Shelley's "They [men] behold ... as in a *glass*, / The future" and "Leave Man, who was a many-sided *mirror*." The lucid next lines — "Existent somewhere, somehow, as a whole; / Here, as a whole proportioned to our sense, — / There, (which is nowhere, speech must babble thus!) / In the absolute immensity [Q Mab 1.266], the whole / Appreciable solely by Thyself, — / Here, by the little mind of man, reduced / To littleness that suits his faculty, / In the degree appreciable too; / Between Thee and ourselves" — boldly confirm Browning's acceptance of Shelley's separation of mind and matter, his agreement with Shelley on the fragmentary value of speech (cf., 346-97) and his nearest approach to indorsing Shelley's Prometheanism as idealistic. Pope Innocent believes that "even the creation [Jehovah's] fades / Into a puny exercise of power" when compared with Prometheus' choice of the Pope's world (Heb 1.2, 11.3; PU 1.2) as scene of "Thy transcendent act of self-sacrifice" and of himself (cf., Boy and Angel) as Prometheus' representative. "Both emanate alike from Thy [Demogorgon's] dread play ... / Incomprehensibly the choice is Thine! / I therefore bow my head and take Thy place." Browning tends to merge the functions of Prometheus and Demogorgon, but he well knew that Prometheus had to will the particular world for his impalement and the particular Pope in Rome before Demogorgon could effect the results.

"A tale of Thee" (1343), which has been thought to be a devout euphemism for the life and death of Jesus Christ, is not then accepted on faith by the Pope as expected; in fact, the tale is unsatisfactorily loved until tried by his reason. Then it is pronounced "sound," because "Mind is not matter nor from matter, but / Above [Prometheus] , — leave matter then, proceed with mind!" Even the very best minds are not strong, intelligent and good up to their potentials, however. So when the human deficiency is explored, the cause (Jehovah, the creator) for the effect (man), it is found that God's ample strength and intelligence are not matched (cf., La S 301) by an observable goodness without the instance of unlimited love in Prometheus' self-sacrifice for man. "Then is the tale true and God [Prometheus] shows complete." Beyond the tale and the Pope's reason, but not as hinted into an unanswering darkness, Browning supplies Shelley's "Feel," which rather ironically enables the Pope to remain faithful to Prometheus if the intellectual and spiritual dynamo of Shelley's Feel and Browning's Myself is eternal. Otherwise "this dread machinery / Of sin and sorrow ... else, / Devised," that is, devised by Jehovah, would confound the Pope. Only from self-sacrificing love, the new Promethean machinery, evolve the missing moral qualities of man, making him love and be loved, become creative and self-sacrificing and eventually a god himself. Thus man "wrings" from all earthly pain all heavenly pleasure for a common eternal heritage. It is a matter of indifference to the Pope whether "all pleasure," all pain having been revealed, be surmised as an independent truth "or only truth reverberate, changed, made pass / A spectrum into mind." As intelligence is increasingly "filled," truth becomes more and more conceivable. Actually, though he often accents moral quality, the Pope does not overemphasize. Browning assumed with Shelley — his doctrine of the imperfect is indeed none other than Shelley's doctrine of perfectibility — that morality is significant only for imperfect man and gradually dissipates as man is initiated into Godship. Moral and material universe are thus a single beneficent environment which entices man and nature toward ultimate perfection.

Believing that human life, moral and material simultaneously, is training and passage (1406), the Pope now speculates on the death of Pompilia and concludes that it is no tragedy at all, "this irrelevant circumstance / Of inquisition after blood." Since Browning is clearly prompted by Shelley, both of whom paraphrase or abstract St. Paul's well-known apostrophe to Death (1 Cor 15.55), Pope Innocent reflects on Life as a spiritual value not at all unlike Shelley in "Death is the veil which those who live call life: / They sleep, and it is lifted" (PU 3.3.113-4). So does Caponsacchi reveal that he is consciously motivated by Shelley's thought: "Death was the heart of life, and all the harm / My folly had crouched to avoid, now proved a veil / Hiding all gain my wisdom strove to grasp" (7.939-41). And this is also what the Pope means in "We . . . feel that life is large and the world small, / So, wait till life have passed from out the world" (1422-4). Thus creating the impression that another individual soul has gone to heaven, joined Jehovah, while truly saying that Pompilia's soul or spirit has been reabsorbed into the spirit of Prometheus. Rather impersonally the Pope is not astonished that whereas he can "so receive and trust," others like himself reject and disbelieve, subordinating the future to the present. But this attitude is assumed in order that he may be overwhelmingly surprised in a very complex double entente at the "haply [intelligent] found and known and named," touched to terror at "these [intelligent] ones" who also turn their backs on the Promethean future. "Enough / O' the dis-believers [in Prometheanism]," therefore; "see the faithful few [in Christianity]," a sorry contingent in whom Jesus Christ must give up his gains:

POPE.
 Can it be this is end and outcome, all   (1527)
 I take with me to show as stewardship's fruit,
 The best yield of the latest time, this year
 The seventeen-hundredth since God died for man?
 Is such *effect* proportionate to *cause*? (cf., 1355; Q Mab 6.212,
 And still *the terror* keeps on the increase R of Islam 3237)
 When I *perceive* . . . how can I blink *the fact*? (R.B.'s ellipsis)
 That the fault, the obduracy to good, (Islam 1486, cf., Pope 1873)
 Lies not with the impracticable stuff (Ugolino 49-54)
 Whence man is made, his very nature's fault, . . . (thematic)
 This terrifies me, thus compelled *perceive* (1533 above; 1541)
 Whatever *love* and faith we looked should *spring* (PU 4.557-61)
 At advent of the *authoritative star,* (Prometheus, see 6.998)
 Which yet lie sluggish, *curdled* at the source, — (Love, Hope 25)

MAN OF THE WORLD.
 These have leapt forth profusely in *old time,* (pagan times)
 These still respond with promptitude to-day,
 At challenge of — what unacknowledged powers
 O' the air, what un*commissioned* meteors, *warmth* (PU 1.368;
 By *law,* and *light* by rule should supersede? 3.3.89; cf., 1066)

In full accord in these climactic lines, the Pope and Man of the World speak almost as if Browning intended them to re-emerge as Antonio Pignatelli. Whatever love and faith they had expected to spring from the advent of Prometheus, the authoritative star, yet lay sluggish and curdled at the source, no competitor to the love and faith which "leapt forth pro-fusely in old time" and which respond today at challenge (demand) of Demogorgon's law of Necessity and Prometheus' Light, that is, warmth of "assent" and rule of love. But Prometheanism still deserves to supersede Christianity since the impracticable stuff of man's obdurate nature, which pre-cludes a fruitful Christian stewardship by the Pope, is the fault of man's creator, Jehovah. While Prometheus' powers

are yet unacknowledged by the world, at least they are not
"commissioned" as are the vindictive acts of Jehovah on an
arbitrary basis of rewards and punishments. Indeed such
cause (Jehovah) as Pope Innocent perceives is proportionate
to effect (man); like Browning he thus perceives a different
God who knows that "Life is probation and the earth is no
goal / But starting-point of man" (1431-2).

Whereas Caponsacchi sprang forth blind, brave, obedient
at Pompilia's first summons (1551), "blind? / Ay, as a man
would be inside the *sun*, / Delirious with the plenitude of
light," the Christians were slunk into corners and the Churchmen were pursuing selfish ends like tyrannical emperors.
Despite himself, how can the Pope avoid speaking loud what
truth (Prometheus) speaks low?

> "Or better than the best, or nothing serves!   (1574)
> What boots deed, I can cap and cover straight
> With such another doughtiness to match,
> Done at an instinct of the *natural man*?"
> Immolate body, sacrifice soul too, —

MAN OF THE WORLD.
> Do not these publicans the same? Outstrip!
> Or else stop race you boast runs neck and neck,
> You with the *wings*, they with the feet, —   (deceptive, see 715)

POPE.   for shame! . . .
> And is this little all that was to be?   (1609)
> Where is the *gloriously*-decisive *change*, . . .   (2 Cor 3.18, Ph'p 3.21,
>   Q Mab 1.192, Witch 179)
> Of human *clay* to *divine gold*, we looked   (Epipsy 160, St Epips 17)
> Should, in some poor sort, justify its price? . . .   (1613)
> What is it when suspected in that *Power*   (Jehovah; 1621)
> Who undertook to make and made the world,
> Devised and did effect man, body and soul,
> Ordained salvation for them both, and yet . . .   (R.B.'s ellipsis)
> Well, is the thing we see, salvation?

MAN OF THE WORLD.   I
> Put no such dreadful question to *myself*,
> Within whose *circle* of experience burns   ("the earth," Isa 40.22)
> *The central truth, Power, Wisdom, Goodness, — God*:   (Prom)
> I must outlive *a thing* ere know it dead: (Jehovah)
> When I outlive the *faith* there is a *sun*,   (double entente)
> When I lie, *ashes* to the very soul, —   (Shelleyan)

POPE.
    Someone, not I, must *wail* above the *heap*,   (Dirge 8; PU 1.595)
    While I see day succeed the deepest night —
    How can I speak but as *I know?* — my speech
    Must be, throughout the *darkness,* "It will end: (Christian era)
    The light that did burn, will burn!" Clouds obscure —   (pagan)
    But for which obscuration all were bright?
    Too hastily concluded! *Sun*-suffused,   (Prometheus)
    A cloud may soothe the eye made blind by blaze, —

MAN OF THE WORLD.
    Better the very clarity of heaven:
    The soft streaks are the beautiful and dear.
    What but the *weakness* in a faith supplies   (PU 2.3.93)
    The incentive to humanity, no *strength*   (PU 2.3.94)
    Absolute, irresistible, comports?
    How can man love but what he *yearns* to help?   (R of Islam 3044)
    And that which men think *weakness within strength*   (reversal)
    But angels know for strength and stronger yet —
    What were it else but *the first things made new,*   (paganism)
    But the repetition of the *miracle,*   (cf., 7.1418)
    The divine instance of *self-sacrifice*   (Prometheus')
    That never ends and aye begins for man?
    So, never I miss footing in the maze,
    No, —   (habitual with R.B.)

POPE.   I have light nor fear the dark at all.

MAN OF THE WORLD.
    But are mankind not real, who pace outside
    My petty *circle,* world that's measured me?   (cf., 1627)

Man's obduracy to Good being the fault of Jehovah, Pope Innocent can deduce from Christian conduct no reliable reason for trusting scriptural promises such as "Who shall change our vile body that it may be fashioned like unto his glorious body." So with Jehovah's ordained salvation rejected by the Pope as an unconscionable ruse, Man of the World enunciates the poet's classic reversal: within his worldly circle of experience and knowledge "burns / The central truth, Power, Wisdom, Goodness, — God [Prometheus]," all of which is denied Jehovah by Browning (La S 335-48, Calderon 1.114-46). Man of the World has outlived Jehovah to know that he is dead, but it is as unlikely that he will outlive Prometheus as it is that he will ever doubt the reality of the *sun* (Prometheus). Eagerly rejoining, the Pope also *knows* that the light which did burn, will burn when "first [pagan] things are made new" again. Thus they can both subscribe whole-heartedly to Shelley's advocacy of human weakness within Prometheus' strength, an unqualified reversal of Jesus Christ's "For my strength is made perfect in [thy] weakness." The divine instance of self-sacrifice now attributed to Prometheus is then the beginning of self-sacrifice by man, not the atone-ment made once and for all by Jesus Christ.

Not one but a combination of ingenious strokes enables Browning to create the impressive speech by Euripides, gym-nast, bard and philosopher. Through little stretch of the imagination Browning could envision Euripides a dedicated Promethean, and by interpolating inverted Pauline thought from Romans 1-3 as if it were Euripidean thought he could interweave immemorial strands of Christian thought with his and Shelley's syncretism of Christianity and paganism. Thus with considerable duplicity Browning was able to incorporate the personality of Euripides, some of the most nearly univer-sal of St. Paul's words and graphic allusions to *Prometheus Unbound* into a whole which brilliantly disguises the frontal assault on Jehovah by Euripides:

Regard me and that *shake* I gave the world!	(PU 2.4.74-5; 1676)
I was born, not so long before Christ's birth . . .	
Pope Innocent, *who art to answer me!* — . . .	(PU 2.4.124; 1681)
Whose lot fell in a land where *life* was great	(1702)
And *sense* went free and beauty lay profuse,	(thought)
I, *untouched* by one adverse circumstance,	(Hope, Fear 9)
Adopted *virtue* as my rule of life,	(truth, beauty, goodness)
Waved all reward, *loved but for loving's sake,* . . .	(Shelleyan)
How much of temperance and righteousness,	(Acts 24.25; 1713)
Judgment to come, *did I find reason for,*	(none by R.B. or Shelley)
Corroborate with my strong style that spared	
No sin, nor swerved the more from *branding brow*	(of Jehovah)
Because the *sinner* was called Zeus and God?	(Shelleyan)

All of which is truly Shelleyan but intended to be miscon-strued as Christian in order that Jehovah, like every other living thing, may be resubjected to the same criticism which Browning has successfully disguised for thirty-six years:

I saw that there are, *first and above all,*   (Demogorgon; 1728)
The hidden forces, *blind necessities,*   (law of Necessity)
Named *Nature,* but the thing's self unconceived:
Then follow, — how dependent upon these
We know not, how *imposed* above ourselves,
We well know, — what I name the gods, a power
Various or one: for *great* and *strong* and *good*   (PU 4.577)
Is there, and *little, weak* and *bad* there too,   (Jehovah)
Wisdom and *folly*: say, these make no God, —   (Prom vs Jehovah)
What is it else that rules outside *man's self?*   (Myself)
A *fact* then, — always, to the naked eye, —
And so, the one *revealment possible*   (logical deduction)
Of what were unimagined else by man.
Therefore, what gods do, man may criticize,   (thematic)
Applaud, condemn, — how should *he* fear the truth, —   (man)

Repetitive though it be, the above is probably Browning's
most succinctly worded reason for opposing the little, weak
and bad folly of Jehovah, for advocating the great and
strong and good wisdom of Prometheus. All that now remains unsaid in Browning's proselytical zeal is the projection
of Euripides' choice of the new Promethean day:

You have the *sunrise* now, joins truth to truth,   (Prom; 1757)
Shoots life and substance into death and void;   ("The warmth of an
            immortal youth [Prometheus] *shoots* down," PU 3.3.89)
Themselves compose the whole we made before:
The forces and *necessity* grow God, —
Proved just His *operation manifold*   (Faust 1.106; R of Islam 349)
And *multiform,* translated, as must be,   (PU 3.4.93)
Into *intelligible* shape so far
As suits our *sense* and sets us *free to feel.*   (Shelley's three constants)

Unthinkable heresy to the humble or exalted Christian,
Pope Innocent's belief, like David's, that man may applaud or
condemn God's action is muted by the ambiguous part given
Euripides and by his opening words: "The inward work and
worth / Of any *mind,* what other *mind* may judge / Save God
[the One Mind] who only knows the thing he made." But
this is a rank alteration of Romans 2.28-29 which Browning
expected to be associated readily with "For when Gentiles,
which have not the law, do *by nature* the things contained in
the law, these, having not the law, are a law unto themselves"

(Ro 2.14). If St. Paul was apparently so inconsistent as to
allow that pagans were by nature a law unto themselves, how
could it be detected that Browning was pointing toward
"God forbid: yea, let God [Prometheus] be true, but every
[disbelieving] man a liar" (Ro 3.4)? For these memorable
words were to be the text of a sermon Pompilia's confessor
was to preach on the non-interference of loving and munifi-
cent (1744) Prometheus, the interference of unloving and unjust Jehovah:

— Hear *law*, appointed to defend the just,	(the Church's; 12.577)
Submit, for best defence, that *wickedness*	
Was bred of flesh and innate with the bone	(original sin)
Borne by Pompilia's *spirit* for a space,	
And no mere *chance* fault, passionate and brief:	
Finally, when ye find, — after this touch	
Of man's *protection* which intends to mar	(the Church)
The *last pin-point of light* and damn the *disc*, —	(sun)
One wave of the hand of *God* amid the worlds	(Prometheus)
Bid vapor vanish, darkness flee away,	
And let the vexed *star* culminate in peace	
Approachable no more by *earthly* mist —	(churchly)
What I call *God's hand*, — you, perhaps, — mere chance	(Prometheus')
Of the true instinct of an old good *man*	(Pope Innocent)
Who happens to hate darkness and love *light*, —	
In whom too was the eye that saw, not dim,	
The *natural* force to do the thing he saw, . . .	
I *demand assent*	(PU 2.4.8, 124; 595)
To the enunciation of my text	
In face of one proof more that '*God* is true	(Prometheus)
And every *man* a liar' — . . .	(disbeliever; 602)
That only *strength* is true: while man is weak,	(Prometheus)
And, since truth seems reserved for heaven not earth,	
Plagued here by earth's *prerogative* of lies,	(Q Mab 7.226, 214)
Should *learn to love* and long for what, one day,	(Shelleyan)
Approved by *life's probation*, he may speak.	

When placed in context (456-643) Fra Celestino's words
are even more revealing, for they follow Browning's longest
exposition on the endurance of ancient pagan practices PRO
CHRISTO (Prometheus) and precede a bold assertion to his
Catholic audience that he has "long since renounced *your*
[Christian] world." Who better than Pompilia's confessor

could advance the poet's belief, not only that Pompilia was innocent in the elopement as she was innocent throughout her life but also that the Church doctrine of original sin was thus rightly abrogated by Prometheus' own hand? Especially since through its unjust repressiveness beauty was made blank and innocence destroyed, strangled save for one Pompilia who was "plucked from the [Christian] world's calumny, / *Stupidity, simplicity,* — who cares?" Nor is this the end of Browning's insistence upon the innocence of Pompilia. Caponsacchi and Pompilia herself are as insistent as the Pope on the purity of her nature: "When Don Celestine bade 'Search and find! / For your soul's sake, remember what is past, / The better to forgive it,' — *all in vain!*" (7.591-3). "When I was taken first to my own church . . . / And bid confess my faults, I interposed / 'But *teach me what fault to confess and know!*'" (6.1326-9). "One pure glass, . . . the perfect soul Pompilia" (6.1142-4). Even the bibliophile Cencini is impressed by the "impertinence" of the barefoot Augustinian's sermonic broadside and urges his correspondent to "remember it, as I engage to do!" (455).

Just how should Euripides be answered then, if not by the Pope's wish for return of the thrill of dawn, when the whole truth-touched man burned up assured the fire would, from his little heap of ashes (embers, sparks, PU 2.3.84, Ode W Wind 66-7, Triumph 201ff), lend wings (PU 4.219) to the world's conflagration (PU 271-318, Q Mab 9.1-22, St Epipsy 147) which Christ (Prometheus) awaits before he makes all things new (1785-94)? So should their ghosts ("the frail," PU 1.241), rapt from Christian glory of pain to Promethean glory of joy, feel the finite love blent and embalmed with the eternal life (1795-1803). But, deplore both Pope and Man of the World, we have become too familiar with the Light. Faith now points the politic, the thrifty way. Not even the Christian act could have succeeded without Nero's cross and stake to challenge saints and martyrs. Thus what is required for the propagation of Prometheanism is a formidable danger, unlikely in a world where ignoble confidence and cowardly hardihood make the old heroism impossible. "Unless," the

Pope confidently interjects, it be the mission of the age
ushering in my death to shake

This torpor of assurance from our *creed*	(Christian; 1848)
Re-introduce *the doubt discarded,* bring	(by Christianity)
That *formidable danger* back, we drove	(natural insecurity)
Long ago to the distance and the dark? . . .	(by a false Faith)
And man stand out again, pale, resolute,	(1856)
Prepared to die, — which means, *alive at last?*	(self-sufficient)

As the old dependence in pagan gods was broken up by
faith in Christianity, so now Christian faith must be broken
up; it has grown to be faith in the mere report (myth), not
faith in Jesus. Whence men need bravely to disbelieve the
Christian report through increased trust in Prometheus whom
the report belies (1862). Like the Molinists, men must deny
the recognized (manipulated) truths of the Church and become obedient to truths yet unrecognized but perceptible.
Thus, and thus only, may "Man's God," that is, the Church's
God, be corrected by the living "God's God in the mind of
man." For "the few" that rise to the new Prometheanism,
multitudes will blindly fall away to the old Christian depth.

a few,	(1871)
E'en ere *new law* speak clear, may keep the old,	(Promethean)
Preserve the Christian level, call good good	(Islam 1489, cf., Pope 1534)
And evil evil (even though *razed and blank*	(Fiordis 13; Zucca 32)
The *old titles,*) helped by custom, habitude,	(the Church's)
And all else they *mistake for finer sense*	
O' the fact that reason warrants, —	(fact, reason)

As before, "the few" hope, fear not impossibly, that at least
one Pompilia will say, "I *know* the right place by foot's *feel,*
/ I took it and tread firm there; wherefore *change?*" But what
a multitude will surely fall through the crumbling Christian
truth and rest upon the lust and pride of human nature. A
multitude whose very souls even now seem to need re-creat-
ing, whose future we dispose of with shut eyes and whisper,
"They are grafted, barren twigs, / Into the living stock of
Christ [Jesus]: may bear / One day, till when they lie death-
like, not dead" (1891-3). So if those who with all the aid of

Christ succumb, how will it be for those without Christ who unaided sink (double entente: Jesus or Prometheus)? Futile though the future sound, Pope Innocent has no intention of blocking the way of the new Prometheans, what with expectant pantaloon, sock, plume (Shelleyan) and castanet. Both he and Man of the World thank the chance and praise the self-sacrificing act which brought Caponsacchi safely through. Joyously encouraged, they wonder whether he can repeat the prodigy of rescuing Pompilia, even teach others why his Promethean step was right while their Christian step was wrong. As for Abate Paul and Guido, they attain their ends by force and guile, looking to the pragmatism of tomorrow. As for Pietro and Violante, there they lie, "first effect of the *new cause of things*" (1943), with the ONE Christian [Promethean] mother, wife and girl,

— Which three gifts seem to make an angel up, —	(1947)
The *world's* first foot o' the *dance* is on their heads!	(PU 4.60-179)
Still, I stand here, not off the stage though close	
On the exit; and my last act, as my *first*,	(Para 5.543; exposure of papal
I owe the scene, and *Him* who armed me thus	cruelty; Prometheus)
With Paul's sword as with Peter's key. I *smite*	(R of Islam 810)
With my whole strength once more, ere end my part,	
Ending, so far as man may, this *offence*.	(Christianity)

Nor will Pope Innocent be deterred by Church followers who continue to beg, "let *mercy* rather pile up *pain on pain* / Till the *flesh* expiate what the *soul pays* else!"

Nowise! Remonstrants on each side commence	(1969)
Instructing, there's a new tribunal now	(verboten to R.B.)
Higher than *God's* — the educated man's!	(Prometheus)
Nice sense of honor in the human breast	
Supersedes here the *old coarse oracle* —	(pagan)
Confirming none the less a point or so	
Wherein blind *predecessors* worked aright	(Gentiles, Ro 2.14-6)
By rule of thumb: as when *Christ* said, — when, where?	(Prometheus)
Enough, I find it pleaded in a place, —	(PU 1.395-400)
"All other wrongs done, patiently I take:	
But *touch my honor* and the case is *changed*!	(Myself, PU 1.492)
I feel the due *resentment*, — *Nemini*	(Cenci 5.2.30)
Honorem trado is my quick retort."	(Isa 48.11-3)
Right of *Him*, just as if pronounced to-day!	(Prometheus)

Dependent on an endless array of scriptural and Shelleyan correlatives, Browning expected discerning Christian readers to associate "touch my honor" with "for how should my name be polluted? and I will not give my glory unto another." But his Pope alludes to an Aeschylean conversation between Prometheus and Io and Prometheus' defiance of Jupiter, and merely pretends to wander aimlessly through a number of supposedly disconnected thoughts. All along he has been duly informed on Shelley's indebtedness to Virgil, Epicurus, Lucretius and Silenus, particularly with reference to a universally pervading mind, thus a pagan principle with which Shelley could easily identify his law of Necessity (2083, PU 2.2.41-63). Now he gives the impression of being most weary yet determined to stand on "the Lord's [Jehovah's] side" while slyly negating the Christian concept of death in "God [Prometheus] unmakes but to remake [Guido's] soul / He else made first in vain; which must not be." A risk Browning remedies with an overshadowing description of a powerful lightning storm at Naples and a pontification the Pope dare not allow Guido to live. But the Pope, not to be denied a conclusion on his culture-hero as apocalyptic as that of *Prometheus Unbound*, has already made his stand through ambiguous imaginings. Observe how carefully he distinguishes between soft culture (2082), which he rejects, and the spirit of culture (2011), which he indorses for the future guidance of man, in order that he may truly end on Shelley's Monarch (Emperor) of the World and the return of the Golden Age ("This is alone Life, Joy, *Empire*, and Victory" PU 4.578; 2.4.126-8):

```
But herein lies the crowning cogency — ...              (2009)
That in this case the spirit of culture speaks,         (2011)
Civilization is imperative.
To her shall we remand all delicate points          (spirit of culture)
Henceforth, nor take irregular advice       (cf., 7.667; "sly," Homer Mer
O' the sly, as heretofore: she used to hint ...     318; spirit of culture)
But why be forced to mumble under breath                (2019)
```

What soon shall be acknowledged as plain fact,
Outspoken, say, in thy successor's time?
Methinks we see the *golden age* return!
Civilization and the *Emperor*   (Monarch, Prometheus)
Succeed to Christianity and Pope.

POMPILIA AND CAPONSACCHI

Because Pompilia and Caponsacchi so often now sound like Asia and Prometheus, one can more easily imagine them sitting in front of the destined cave talking "of time and change, / As the world ebbs and flows, ourselves unchanged" (PU 3.3.4) than as they appear in Court or on death-bed. From first sight of each other they seem mutually disposed to reject the material world, attributing every aspect of their unhappiness and deprivation to its organizational tyranny. Thus when Pompilia approaches Caponsacchi and the waiting carriage, the blackened night is charged with the expectant atmosphere of Asia's return to Prometheus. On the flight from Arezzo Pompilia gains the same strength from holding another woman's new baby that Asia gains from the ever-loving EARTH SPIRIT in whose childish innocence is thought to be a self-portrait of Shelley. Only just awakened to the new, "novel" faith, Caponsacchi is solely dependent upon Pompilia's love, which is as effusively unselfish as Asia's for Prometheus. And in their separation Caponsacchi vividly reflects the sadness and longing of Prometheus for reunion with Asia: "I said all hope was vain but love" (PU 1.824). So the recounting of Shelley's curative and creative effects of Love and Mind, the promised Promethean "change" to come over the earth, as well as Shelley's repetition of the faults inherent in the "pride of kings and priests" is as prevalent as Browning could make it. Each character ascribes the new grace of life to the self-sacrifice of Prometheus, and neither can well bear the delay in passage from this dream world through the veil of death to Life. Nor is the urgency strange to them, for in Shelley's "changes and chances" they see only a fair restoration of joys and pleasures, an escape from pains and sorrows. Knowing the pagan belief that souls are derived from stars, Pompilia dares frequently to call her rescuer "my star"; borrowing the only beautiful and sad part of his Church affiliation, Caponsacchi dares as often to call Pompilia a saint or angel. Yet, whether Browning intended the analogy of characters to be so exacting or not, Pompilia's affinity for and strong inducement to follow Prometheus, Caponsacchi's chanced but fated conversion to Prometheanism and their total trust in eventual reunion beyond death with Prometheus are now much more interesting to the reader than the sordid facts of the *Old Yellow Book*.

Like the youthful Browning the child Pompilia is made magically aware of the beauty, heroism and romance of the pagan world. Mt. Zion chapel had been as drab and uninviting to the young Browning as playtime at home was colorful and exciting, largely because of the visual aids in mythology delighted in by his father. And playtime to Pompilia is similarly distinguished from hasty trips to damp and dismally lighted San Lorenzo, largely because of an exciting wall tapestry at home overflowing with mythological and legendary figures. Tisbe, a neighbor child, becomes Diana with a half-moon on her hair-knot, spear in hand, indicating that the precocious girls knew Diana who, as goddess of the moon and light, presided most favorably over childbirth and "slaves." Pompilia becomes a hamadryad with green leaves flourishing out of her fingertips, portending that she is to be the object of a hunt and a slave to Guido. Nor is that all the playmates glean from the tapestry, for when Pompilia is told that a "cavalier" is arriving the next day, she then remembers Tisbe had said that the slim young man with wings at head, wings at feet and sword threatening a monster was a cavalier, confirming their knowledge of Perseus' rescue of Andromeda from the sea-monster and possibly of the "resplendent mirror" lent to Perseus by Athene. Otherwise why would Browning implant in Pompilia's memory the dragon and St. George, a figure whose famous shrine at Lydda lay near the scene of Andromeda's rescue by Perseus? Or Michael, whose "pair of wings will arrive first / At Rome, to introduce the company, / And bear him from our picture [tapestry] where he fights / Satan, — except to have the dragon loose / And never a *defender*"? Or the naming her son Gaetano after a *new* saint without also knowing that it was Cajetan, the overseer of Luther at the

Diet of Augsburg, who said a pope should be "the *mirror* of God on earth"? One may suspect that at some point Pope Innocent and Pompilia had consulted on "O Thou ... / *Man's mind, what is it but a convex glass* / Wherein are gathered all the scattered points / Picked out of the immensity of sky, / To *re-unite* there, be our heaven for earth, / *Our* known unknown, *our* God revealed to man?" (cf., Shelley's fascination with glass, mirror, Ode to Heaven 21, Hellas 806, PU 1.662, 4.382).

Though not fully conscious of the potential strength her pagan knowledge promised, Pompilia was really better qualified than has been thought to cope with the miserable desertion of her parents or the tragically insensitive advice of both Governor and Archbishop. At least Guido "never did by speech nor act imply

'Because of our souls' yearning that we meet   (768)
And mix in soul through flesh, which yours and mine
Wear and impress, and make their visible selves, . . .
Let us become one flesh, *being one soul*!' . . .   (Shelleyan)
                              But when he spoke as plain —   (774)
Dreadfully honest also — 'Since our souls
Stand each from each, a whole world's width between,
Give me the fleshly *vesture* I can reach   (Fiordispina 79)
And *rend* and leave just fit for hell to burn!' —   (Cenci 5.2.167-8)
Why, *in God's name*, for Guido's soul's own sake   (Prometheus)
Imperilled by *polluting* mine, — I say,   (Eze 16, PU 1.34, 160)
I did resist; would I had overcome!

So when against my own guidance I obeyed the Archbishop the worst befell. "My husband's hatred waxed nor waned at all, / His brother's boldness grew effrontery soon, / And my last stay and comfort in *myself* / Was forced from me: henceforth I looked to God [Prometheus] ... / Henceforth I asked God counsel, not mankind" (845-53).

I admit that I was *blind* to so much, even the feigned letters Guido conceived, but that is the fruit of "all such *wormy* ways, / The indirect, the unapproved of God [Prometheus] : / You cannot find their author's [Jehovah's] end and aim, / Not even to substitute your good for bad, / Your straight for the irregular; you stand / Stupified, profitless, as cow or sheep that miss a man's *mind*" (663-9). Yet Guido had no right in the "whole sad strange plot, the grotesque intrigue / To make me and my friend *unself* ourselves, / Be other man and woman than we were" (701). "I felt there was just one thing Guido claimed / I had no right to give nor he to take; / We being in estrangement, *soul from soul*" (715-7). "So we are made, such *difference in minds* [PU 3.3.39], / Such *difference* too in eyes that see the *minds*! / That man [Caponsacchi], you misinterpret and misprise — / The glory of his nature, I had thought, / *Shot* itself out in *white light, blazed the truth* / Through every atom of his act with me: / Yet where I *point* you, through the crystal shrine, / *Purity* in quintessence, one dew-drop, / You all descry a spider [primitively thought a guise for Prometheus] in the midst" (912-20; "dew-globe," PU 4.424-43).

Then I must lay my babe away with Prometheus, nor think of him again in gratitude. My last breath shall be wholly spent in one more attempt to disperse the stain and mist from a lustrous and pellucid soul. So when I am gone, though sorrow stay, and people need assurance in their doubt that Prometheus has a servant, man a friend, the weak a saviour and the vile a foe, let Caponsacchi be invoked. "There, / *Strength* comes already with the utterance!" (935-6). Strength sufficient too for Pompilia to rehearse in detail the experience of first looking on Caponsacchi, the threatening scene Guido created at supper after the theater and the traitorous involvement of a household maid. Almost as if paraphrasing the "changed" Prometheus (PU 1.53-8, 70), Pompilia answers Guido's importuning mistress, "Let it suffice I either feel no wrong / Or else forgive it" (1121). Thus frustrated by Pompilia's goodness, her inability to read and her distrust of the false letters which had been shuttled back and forth, Margherita changes her tactics and says, "Now that Easter is past, everyone leaves for Rome; even Caponsacchi resigns himself and follows" (1196-9). Next morning Pompilia awakes with child, calls Margherita and joyously asks the disbelieving maid to send Caponsacchi to her:

                    He will come.   (Caponsacchi; 1370)
And, all day, I sent *prayer like incense* up   (pagan)
To God the *strong*, God the *beneficent*, . . .   (Prometheus)
Till at the last He puts forth *might* and saves.   (Power, Will)
An old rhyme came into my head and rang   (1376)
Of how a *virgin*, for the faith of God   (vestal)
Hid herself, from the Paynims that pursued,
In a cave's heart; until a *thunderstone*,   (PU 4.355)
Wrapped in a flame, revealed the couch and prey   (Shelleyan, Islam
And they laughed — "Thanks to lightning, ours at last!"   4666)
And she cried "Wrath of God [Jehovah], assert His [Prom] love!
Servant of God, *thou fire*, befriend His child!"   (Demand)
And lo, the fire she grasped at, *fixed its flash*,   (tamed fire, PU 2.4.66)
Lay in her hand a *calm* cold dreadful sword   (Shelleyan)
She brandished till pursuers strewed the ground, . . .
She walked forth to the solitudes and *Christ*:   (Prometheus; 1389)
So should I grasp the lightning and be saved! ("solitudes," Mont B 137)

But as the day wore on trouble grew whereby I guessed there
would need be born a star. At dusk I "started up, *was pushed
[by Prometheus]*, I dare to say, / Out on the terrace, leaned
and looked at last / Where the *deliverer* [Epipsy 277, Islam
1553] waited" with the same silent and solemn face:

Friend, foolish words were borne from you to me;   (Shelleyan; 1405)
Your soul behind them is the pure strong *wind*,   (PU 4.561)
Not dust and feathers which its breath may bear:
These to the *witless* seem the wind itself, . . .   (Mind-less)
I speak to the strong soul, no weak disguise.   (1414)
If it be *truth*, — why should I doubt it *truth*? —   (Shelleyan)
You serve *God especially*, as priests are bound,   (Prometheus)
And care about me, *stranger* as I am,   (Shelleyan)
So far as wish my good, — that *miracle*   (Vita Nuova, cf., 10.1650)
I take to intimate *He wills* you serve   (Prometheus)
By saving me, — what else can *He* direct? . . .
Now I imperil something more, it seems,   (1425)
Something that's trulier me than this *myself*   (self-awareness)
Something I trust in *God* and you to save.   (Prometheus)

So did my star rise, the first word ever from his lips, as
Caponsacchi breathed, "I am yours," and then added, "Have
you the *will*? Leave God [Prometheus] the way!" Thus commissioned, Caponsacchi became "mine, thank God! / He was
mine, he is mine, he will be mine" (1442-3). Nor was there

pause in the leading and the light, though a cloud the next night was broken by prayer to let the "wavering" Caponsacchi shine through the darkness of expected rumor and revenge. I saw my white star turning red, but a word from me and the white was back:

No, *friend*, for you will take me! 'T is *yourself*   (1457)
Risk all, not I, — who let you, for I *trust*
In the *compensating* great God: enough!   (not Jehovah)
I *know* you: when is it that you will come? . . .
And *this man*, men call sinner? *Jesus Christ*! (Caponsacchi; oath; 1468)
Of whom men said, with mouths *Thyself mad'st once*,
"*He hath a devil*" — say he was *Thy* saint,   (double entente; Prom)
My Caponsacchi! *Shield and show* — unshroud   (Shelleyan)
In *Thine* own time the glory of the soul   (Prometheus')
If aught obscure, — if ink-spot, from vile pens
Scribbling a charge against him.

As for me, it is otherwise. Let men sift my thoughts which I throw like the flax for sun to bleach; I did pray, do pray, in the prayer shall die, "Oh, to have Caponsacchi for my guide!" (1480). Ever the face turned up to mine, the hand holding my hand across the world, a sense signifying peradventure Pompilia be divine, yet aware that "weakness" mars the print men see but not Caponsacchi, who from his soul rewrites "love and strength," mending the *obliterated charter* (Alastor 329, Q Mab 6.55):

"So kneels a *votarist*,   (1490)
Weeds some poor waste traditionary plot
Where shrine once was, where *temple* yet may be,   (pagan)
Purging the place but worshipping the while,   (Q Mab 7.138)
By faith and not by sight, *sight clearest so*, —   (Reason)
Such way the *saints* work," — says Don Celestine.   (double entente)

I could believe that by his "strong will" Caponsacchi had woven around me the world we travelled in, all things helped so well (1544). Though it was unnatural that such comfort should be sustained throughout the journey, I remember it all as one milky way, so

Do *new* stars *bud* while I but search for old,   (PU 4.368, Islam 3162)
And fill all gaps i' the glory, and *grow him* —   (PU 2.1.81, C'sacchi)

Him I now see make the shine everywhere.   (1554)
Even at the last when the bewildered flesh,
The cloud of weariness about my *soul*
Clogging too heavily, *sucked* down all sense, —   (Shelleyan)
Still its last voice was, "*He* will watch and care;   (Prometheus)
Let the strength go, I am content: *he* stays!"   (Caponsacchi)

Believing as I fainted that the red eve was a red morn, I let them crush together into a *solid fire*. When I suddenly saw Guido in my room at the inn, I did spring up, attempt to thrust aside that "ice-block" (Islam 851-2) between the sun and myself, lay low the "neutralizer" of all good and truth. And if that were sin, never obey voice more of the Just and Terrible (Demogorgon), who bids, "Bear!" [PU 4.573] / Not — "Stand by, bear to see my angels bear!" (1583). "I am clear it was on impulse to serve God [Prometheus] / Not save *myself.*"

But when at last, all by *myself* I stood   (1598)
Obeying the *clear voice* which bade me rise,   (Nature)
Not for my own sake but my babe unborn,
And take the *angel's hand* was sent to help —   (Caponsacchi)
And found the *old adversary* athwart the path —   (Church, Law)
Not my hand simply struck from the *angel's*, but   (double entente)
The very angel's self made foul i' the face
By the *fiend* who struck there, — that I would not bear,   (Jehovah)
That only I resisted! So, my first
And last resistance was *invincible.* . . .   (Promethean)
This time, the *foolish prayers* were done with, *right*   (1616)
Used might, and solemnized the sport at once.   (Will & Power)
All was against the combat: vantage, mine?
The runaway avowed, the accomplice-wife,
In company with the plan-contriving priest?
Yet, shame thus rank and patent, I struck, bare,
At foe from head to foot in *magic mail*,   (legal & church protection)
And off it *withered*, cobweb-armory   (Shelleyan)
Against the *lightning*! 'T was truth singed the lies   (Promethean fire)
And saved me, not the vain sword nor *weak* speech!   (prayer)

You see, I *will not* have the service fail!   (Will, Power, Love)
I say, the *angel* saved me: I am safe!   (double entente)

The judges judged aright in the main. And gave my bird (babe) the life among the leaves God meant him! "Weeks and months of quietude, I could lie in such *peace* and *learn* so much — / Begin the task, I see how needful now, / Of *understanding* somewhat of my past, — / *Know* life a little, I should leave so soon." Therefore, because Caponsacchi has restored my soul, I have gained, enjoyed and suffered, nay got *foretaste of better life beginning where this ends:*

```
All through the breathing-while allowed me thus               (1655)
Which let good premonitions reach my soul    (Prom's monitory touch)
Unthwarted, and benignant influence flow                 (beneficent)
And interpenetrate and change my heart,                   (Shelleyan)
Uncrossed by what was wicked, — nay, unkind. . . .
                       till my boy was born,                 (1663)
Born all in love, with naught to spoil the bliss . . .
Christmas before me, — was not that a chance?      (Shelleyan; 1673)
I never realized God's birth before —                (double entente)
How He grew likest God in [simply] being born.
```

My parents, if they too much affected frippery, have been punished and submit themselves. "Say no word: all is over, they see God [Prometheus] / Who will not be extreme to mark their fault / Or He had granted respite: they are safe" (1685-9). As for that most woeful man, my husband, I give him for his "good" the life he takes. We shall not meet in this world nor the next,

```
But where will God be absent! In His face       (Prometheus; 1703)
Is light, but in His shadow healing too:
Let Guido touch the shadow and be healed! . . .          (deceptive)
So he was made; he nowise made himself: . . .       (thematic; 1714)
His soul has never lain beside my soul:                     (1716)
But for the unresisting body, — thanks! . . .          (Reviewer 5)
Still but for Guido; I am saved through him                 (1721)
So as by fire; to him — thanks and farewell!             (lightning)
```

Even from my death there is safety for my babe. The little life, the fact which means so much, shall not Prometheus stoop the kindlier to his work, now that my hand he trusted to receive and hold must let the treasure fall perforce. The better, Prometheus shall have an *orphanage* his own way, if Gaetano lives beyond my last breath. Why should I doubt Prometheus will explain in time what I *feel* but cannot find

the words to express. So seems so much else, not explained
"but known!" I now withdraw from earth and man to my
own soul, to compose "myself" for Prometheus. Yet there is
more! Yes, I shall end my breath in being true to my soul:

He is still here, not outside with the world,   (Caponsacchi; 1756)
Here, here, I have him in his rightful place! . . .
O lover of my life, O *soldier-saint*, (Man of the World's term; 1769)
No world begun shall ever pause for *death*!   (mere veil to Life)
Love will be helpful to me more and more
I' the coming course, the new path I must tread —
My weak hand in thy strong hand, *strong for that*!   (Love)
Tell him that if I seem without him now,
That's the world's insight! *Oh, he understands*!
He is at Civita — do I once doubt
The *world* again is holding us apart?   (Christian)
He had been here, displayed in my behalf
The broad brow that reverberates the *truth*,   (Promethean)
And flashed the *word God* gave him, back to man! (Love; Prom)
I know where the *free soul* is flown! My fate (to "here, here" above)
Will have been hard for even him to *bear*:
Let it confirm him in the trust *of* God,   (not *in* God)
Showing how holily he dared the deed! . . .
It was the name of him I sprang to meet   (1791)
When came [Guido's] knock, the summons and the end. . . .
I would have sprung to *these*, beckoning across (Cap's heart & hand;
Murder and *hell gigantic and distinct*   1794)
O' the threshold, posted to exclude me heaven: (Christian heaven)
He is *ordained* to call and I to come! . . .   (fated)
I think he would not marry if he could.   (1806)
Marriage on earth seems such a counterfeit,
Mere imitation of the inimitable:
In *heaven* we have the real and true and sure.   (Promethean)
'T is there they neither marry nor are given
In marriage but are as the angels: . . .
Be as the angels rather, *who, apart,*   (1816)
Know themselves into one, are found at length (one Soul)
Married, but marry never, no, nor give
In marriage; they are man and wife at once
When the true time is: *here we have to wait*
Not so long neither! . . .   (if Promethean)
So, let him wait *God's instant* men call years; (Prometheus')
Meantime hold hard by truth and his great soul,
Do out the duty! Through such souls *alone*
God stooping shows sufficient of *His light*

For us i' *the dark* to *rise* by. And I rise.   (the earth; "I am the Earth, /
Thy mother; she within whose stony veins, . . . / Joy ran,
as blood within a living frame, / When thou [Prometheus]
didst from her bosom, like a cloud / Of glory, *arise*, a
spirit of keen joy!" PU 1.152-8)

More melodramatic in isolation than in context, these Shelley-laden lines are abstracted and quoted to illustrate the exceptional ingenuity with which Browning submerged their pagan veracity in the total monologue. Because none of the characters in *The Ring and the Book* relates an experience in sequence, it was easy enough for Browning's inconsistencies and contradictions to be ricocheted off each other and left dangling. Because Pompilia, like David and Pippa, is drawn as a child of God, it was rightly assumed that her extraordinary perspicacity at seventeen would be noted and dropped. Browning's greater accomplishment was in knowing intimately the sentiments of the Christian faith and exposing their religious and theological nuances as subtly as Shelley's nuances are hidden. He could not have been disappointed in the masterful subterfuge despite the ironic turn Christian acceptance gave to Pompilia's disguised Shelleyan beliefs. Still and all, even Pompilia's most obvious thoughts are simply not Christian thoughts. She possesses a goodness and a forgiving spirit which are really only Promethean. She believes in the Oneness of Soul, depends on the truth both of herself and God and exhibits a mind which warrants remarkable self-consciousness and determination to *know*, to *understand*, even to the accurate paraphrasing of Shelley's famous passage on "such difference in minds." Clearly Browning balances Pompilia's retention of her "Myself" in Prometheanism against her loss of all Christian hope including "the frightfulness of [her] despair in God [Jehovah]" (845-53, 1274). Like the poet himself in *La Saisiaz* Pompilia is now "held up, amid the nothingness [the Church], / *By one or two truths only* — thence I hang, / And there I live, — the rest is death or dream, / All but those *points* of my support" (598-601). That is, Myself and Prometheus.

Pompilia's vocabulary is equal to Browning's most exhaustive use of Shelley's unbelievably repetitive diction. Like her creator she is rationally insensitive toward the witless and she instinctively associates their ignorance with Jehovah, whose ends and aims are *wormy*, fiendish and impossible to learn. She would therefore dare spring through Jehovah's hell, itself posted to keep her out of his heaven, to be reunited with Caponsacchi. Only the benevolent Prometheus then is absolutely good and wise and true. Friend, savior of man and foe of vileness, he is Pompilia's Christ and compensating God who pushed her onto the terrace for the fateful encounter with Caponsacchi. It is also Prometheus who tames fire and makes it an expression of his love through the sword Pompilia chances to seize; it is Jehovah who always employs fire as a fearful thing and a means of human enslavement or destruction. Unreservedly Pompilia will not have the service of Caponsacchi to Prometheus fail, and she dares "demand" that the rescue be consummated, even though she understands the necessity of sweet assent to a fate over which not even Demogorgon has control. As for Death Pompilia looks upon it as the supreme moment. The brave, the beautiful and the talented should have no fear, for in the loss of the fleshly hindrance Death unveils an eternity of freedom, love and creative splendor, all awaiting Pompilia and Caponsacchi in their eternal reunion. Thus believing in the indestructibility of the soul, Pompilia recalls that not even Guido's soul can be totally separated from Prometheus since he is everywhere human souls abide. Death is truly the rewarding Life.

Called as a witness for the second trial, this time from relegation for complicity in Pompilia's flight, Caponsacchi is alternately rational and emotional, but the disparity is merely part of Browning's plan to deceive. Only pretentiously is Caponsacchi less well versed in the Promethean faith which gives Pompilia unearthly strength or more distrustful of his own guidance than hers. So as with Shelley and Browning in their personal rescue of oppressed daughters Caponsacchi measures up in every detail to all the implications of rescuer, defender, deliverer, soldier-saint and savior. He is indeed "love's slave, / Looking no farther than his liege [Prometheus] commands" (*Pauline* 948-9).

Men of the Court who have recalled me as witness to Guido's latest crime, what do you want? "I have paid enough in person at Civita, / Am free . . . / Thank you! I am rehabilitated then, / A very reputable priest. But she — / The *glory* of life, the *beauty* of the world, / The *splendor* of heaven, . . . well, Sirs, does no one move?" (105-24). "The glory, I say, / And the beauty, I say, and splendor, still say I, / Who, priest and trained to live my whole life long / On *beauty* and splendor, solely at their source, / God [Prometheus] , — have thus recognized my *food in her*" (Epipsy 580). So I did become a fribble and coxcomb by direction of the Church, I broke no word to make you disbelieve me now. I need that you should know "my" truth, though I did listen to:

<pre>
"Therefore, don't prove so indispensable . . .   (at sanctitude; 361)
Arezzo's just a haven midway Rome —   (364)
Rome's the eventual harbor, — make for port,
Crowd sail, crack cordage! And your cargo be
A polished presence, a genteel manner, wit
At will, and tact at every pore of you!
I sent our *lump of learning*, Brother Clout,
And Father Slouch, our piece of piety,
To see Rome and try suit the Cardinal.
Thither they clump-clumped, beads and book in hand,
And every since 't is meat for man and maid
How both flopped down, prayed blessing on bent pate . . .
Never once dreaming, the two moony dolts,   (376)
There's nothing moves his Eminence so much
As — far from all this awe at sanctitude —
Heads that wag, eyes that twinkle, modified mirth
At the *closet*-lectures on the Latin tongue
A lady learns so much by, we know where.
Why, body o' Bacchus, you should crave his rule
For *pauses* in the elegiac couplet, *chasms*
Permissible only to Catullus! There!
Now go to duty: brisk, break Priscian's head
By reading the day's office — there's no help.
You've Ovid in your poke to plaster *that*;   (unidiomatic Church Latin)
Amen's at the end of all: then sup with me!"   (amends)
</pre>

After three or four years of this frivolous life, I found myself one night at the theater. "Then she turned, / Looked our
way, smiled the beautiful sad strange smile" (407-8). "That
night and next day did the gaze endure, / Burnt to my brain,
as sunbeam thro' shut eyes, / And not once changed the
beautiful sad strange smile" (430-3). So when my patron
spoke in altered guise, 'Young man, can it be true . . . you
have . . . gone play truant in church all day long? / Are you
turning Molinist?' I quickly answered:

Sir, what if I turned *Christian*? It might be.   (Promethean; 469)
The *fact* is, I am troubled in my *mind*,
Beset and pressed hard by some *novel thoughts*.
This your Arezzo is a limited world:
There's a *strange Pope*, — 't is said, a priest who *thinks*.
Rome is the port, you say: to Rome I go.

One evening I was sitting in a muse over the opened
"Summa," thinking how my life had shaken under me,
broken indeed and shown the gap between what is, what
should be and into what abysm (hell) the "soul" may slip,

Thinking moreover . . . oh, thinking, if you like,   (R.B.'s ellipsis)
How utterly dissociated was I   (487)
A priest and celibate, from the sad strange wife
Of Guido, — just as an instance to the point,
Naught more, — how I had a whole store of *strengths*   (passions)
Eating into my heart, *which craved employ*,
And she, perhaps, need of a finger's help, —
And yet there was no way in the wide world
To stretch out mine and so relieve *myself*, —   (blatant)
How when the page o' the Summa *preached its best*,
Her smile kept glowing out of it, as to mock
The silence we could break by no *one word*.   (Love)

Mysteriously interrupted by Guido's mistress and messenger,
I then received the first of a batch of forged letters, a correspondence which demanded that I ultimately face Guido's
own self for explanation. Instead of Guido, when I went to
the terrace of his establishment, "There at the window stood,
/ Framed in its black square length, with *lamp in hand* [sym-
bolic of Promethean], / Pompilia; the same great, grave, grief-
ful air / As stands i' the dusk, on altar that I know" (690-3).

'You have sent me letters, Sir: . . . / That you a priest, can dare love me, a wife, / Desire to live or die as I shall bid, . . . / Because you saw my face a single time. . . . / Such wickedness were deadly to us both: / But *good true love* would help me now so much' (712-24).

```
'Care only to bestow what I can take,                          (741)
That it is only you in the wide world,                         (fate)
Knowing me nor in thought nor word nor deed,
Who, all unprompted save by your own heart,
Come proffering assistance now, — were strange             (Shelleyan)
But that my whole life is so strange: as strange
It is, my husband whom I have not wronged
Should hate and harm me. For his own soul's sake,
Hinder the harm! But there is something more,
And that the strangest: it has got to be        (Homer Merc 38.1; fated)
Somehow for my sake too, and yet not mine,
— This is a riddle — for some kind of sake     (St Epips 111, Hellas 1083,
Not any clearer to myself than you,                       Faust 2.239)
And yet as certain as that I draw breath, —
I would fain live, not die — oh no, not die!'            (deceptive)
```

Pompilia found that she had become the wife of Count Guido, who waiting not a moment changed into a fury of fire. If once he had been man, his face threw fire at hers. He laid a hand on her that 'burned all *peace*, / All *joy*, all *hope*, and last all *fear* away' (759-78). Of me she said, 'I cannot understand what prompts your *soul*, / I simply needs must see it is so, / Only one *strange* and wonderful thing more.' Of Guido she had told this story and more to *good great* men (PU 4.577) and they had smiled, then frowned or eventually brought despair upon her soul. It was the letter she received from me that morning which woke her from the whole despairing dream, said,

```
'You would die for me: I can believe it now:                   (848)
For now the dream gets to involve yourself.
First of all, you seemed wicked and not good,
In writing me those letters: you came in
Like a thief upon me. I this morning said
In my extremity, entreat the thief! . . .
But now, that you stand and I see your face,                   (859)
Though you have never uttered word yet, — well, I know,
Here too has been dream-work, delusion too, . . .
```

Nor wrote such letters therefore. It is false,   (869)
And you are *true*, have been *true*, will be *true*.
To Rome then, — when is it you take me there?
Each minute lost is mortal. When? — I ask.'

Pompilia spoke and I at once received, "accepted my own *fact*, my *miracle* / *Self*-authorized and *self*-explained, — she chose / To summon me and signify her choice" (904-6; "miracle," Calderon 2.55, Vita Nuova 3):

'As I   (916)
Recognized her, at *potency* of truth,   (Calderon 3.173)
So she, by the *crystalline* soul, knew me,   (Hellas 696-99)
Never mistook the *signs*. Enough of this —   ("seal," Hellas 700)
Let the *wraith* go to *nothingness* again,   (guardian angel; Church)
Here is the *orb*, have only thought for her!'   (PU 4.269, 455, 521)

Thought for her? I dare to say that I have confronted God and man in thought, and my duty to both. But no such faculty helped here:

I put forth no thought, — *power*less, all that night   (930)
I paced the city: it was the *first* Spring.   (Promethean)
By the *invasion* I lay passive to,   (of Love)
In rushed *new* things, the *old* were rapt away;
Alike abolished — the imprisonment
Of the outside air, the inside weight o' the *world*   (Christian)
That pulled me down. *Death* meant to spurn the ground   (cf., 7.1804)
Soar to the sky, — die well and you do that.
The very immolation made the bliss;
Death was the heart of life, and all the harm   (PU 3.3.113-24)
My *folly* had crouched to avoid, now proved a *veil*   (PU 3.3.113)
Hiding all gain my *wisdom* strove to grasp.   ("folly," St Epips 117)

First admonished by the Church to cater to the social and influential elite, to avoid the *ninny* altar service that gabbled Latin and protruded nose "smoothed to a sheep's through no *brains* and much faith," I obeyed. Now the Church changed tone:

Now, when I found out first that *life and death*   (981)
Are means to an end, that *passion* uses both,   (Love)
Indisputably mistress of the man
Whose form of worship is *self-sacrifice*:
Now, from the *stone lungs* sighed the *scrannel* voice   (unmelodious)
"Leave that *live passion*, come be dead with me!"

Sirs, I obeyed but not by ignorantly plucking hips and haws and feasting to satiety while scorning the thing of perfect gold, the *apple's* self (Faust 2.327-34):

Obedience was too strange, —	(to Prom; 995)
This *new* thing that had been struck into me	
By the look o' the lady, — to dare disobey	
The first authoritative word. 'T was *God's.*	(Prometheus'; 10.1544)
I had been *lifted* to the level of her,	(changed)
Could take such sounds into my sense. I said	
"We two are cognizant o' the *Master* now; . . .	(Prometheus)
I thought the *other way* self-sacrifice:	(the Church; 1004)
This is the true, *seals* up the perfect sum."	(Eze 29.12; PU 4.563)

Back home at dawn I weakly changed my resolve, saying that God who created Pompilia would "save her too / Some new way, by *one miracle* the more, / Without me" (1016-8). "Could she but *know* / That, were there *good* in this distinct from God's [Jehovah's], / Really *good* as it reached her, though procured / By a sin of mine, — I should sin: . . . / She knows it is *no fear* withholds me: fear? / Of what?" Yet to prove I did not fear, I returned to the terrace only to hear Pompilia say: 'Why is it you have suffered me to stay / Breaking my heart two days more than was need? / Why delay help, your own heart yearns to give? / You are again here, in the *self-same mind,* / I see here, steadfast in the face of you, — / You grudge to do no one thing that I ask. / Why then is nothing done?' (1050-7). Unavoidable danger, legal and ecclesiastical injunctions notwithstanding, I answered, "Lady, waste no thought, no word / Even to forgive me! Care for what I care — / Only! Now follow me as *I were fate*!"

At the dead between midnight and morn, there was I at the goal, before the gate, with a tune in the ears, low leading up to loud, a *light* in the eyes, faint that would soon be *flare,*

Ever some spiritual witness *new and new*	(1117)
In faster frequence, *crowding solitude*	(both Shelleyan)
To watch the way o' the *warfare,* — till, at last,	(graphic)
When the ecstatic minute must bring birth, . . .	
The white I saw shine through her was *her soul's.*	(1124)

So began the flight with Pompilia, whose very "breath or

look of hers, / Which poured forth would present you one pure *glass*, / *Mirror* you plain, — as God's sea, glassed in gold, / His saints, — the perfect soul Pompilia. Men, / You must know that a man gets drunk with truth / Stagnant inside him!" (1141-6). Truth so intoxicating that when Pompilia asked why I smiled at the great gate with the eagles and the snakes (Islam 193), I replied that I had an impulse, a whim, to say to the residing prelate, one wise in ways of preferment: "What, still at work *so gray and obsolete* [PU 4.31]? / Still rocketed and mitred more or less? / Don't you feel all that *out of fashion now*? / I find out when the day of things is done!" As the hours of heavy travel wore on, however, the joys of being a new Promethean were eclipsed by Pompilia's weariness and bad dreams of Guido, 'Never again with you! / My soul is mine, my body is my soul's.' So instead, "Why in my whole life I have never prayed! / Oh, if the God, that only can [cf., Saul 270], would help! / Am I his priest with *power* to cast out fiends? / Let God [Prometheus] *arise* and all his enemies / Be scattered!" (1279-83). Thus charged, by morn there was "peace," no sigh out of the deep sleep. But by night of the next day all the "calm" was again gone, Pompilia was exhausted and delirious, and I was back at prayer: "Too deep i' the thick of the struggle, [not to] struggle through! / Then *drench* her in repose though death's self pour / The plenitude of quiet, — help us, God [Prometheus], / Whom the *winds carry*!" (1371-4; PU 4.548). "Suddenly . . . / Castelnuovo . . . / Say you are saved, sweet lady!"

Yet not as expected, because "the motionless and breathless pure and pale Pompilia" had swooned and would remain unconscious until waked the following morning. "In they broke / O' the chamber *late my chapel*" and there she lay "wax-white, seraphic, saturate with the sun [Prometheus] / O' the morning that now flooded from the front / And filled the window with a *light like blood*" (1492-4). Facing Guido that "opprobrious blur / Against all *peace* and *joy* and *light* and *life*" (PU 4.592), Pompilia started up and cried, 'I am God's, I love God, God — whose knees I clasp, / Whose *utterly most just reward* [Love, Hope 6] I take, / But bear no more love-making devils: hence!' (1504-6). Pinioned fast I was powerless in the *clutch* of the rabble but Pompilia grasped Guido's loose sword, 'See how God can help at last and worst! . . . / Die, devil, in God's name!' (1517-20). Before she could strike she too was closed round by "the unmanly men, no woman-mother made, / Spawned somehow! Dead-white and disarmed she lay." Being in secular garb though a priest, I first threatened with "slight at your peril," then demanded "that the Church I serve, decide / Between us, right the slandered lady there. . . . bid Rome / Cover the wronged with her *inviolate shield*" (1554-8; Cyclops 273, 179).

It was "the last time *in this life*" (1563) that I saw Pompilia, though I thought that I had saved her: "No, Sirs, I cannot have the lady dead! / That erect form, flashing brow, fulgurant [resembling lightning] eye, / That voice immortal . . . / That vision in the blood-red daybreak — that / Leap to life of the *pale electric sword* [Gisb 124] / Angels go armed with, — that was not the last / O' the lady!" (1573-9). "Though she were dying, a Priest might be of use, / The more when he's a friend too, — she called me / Far beyond 'friend.' Come, let me see her . . . / I never touched her *with my fingertip* / Except to carry her to the couch, that eve, / Against my heart, beneath my head, bowed low, / As we priests carry the paten: that is why / — To get leave and go see her of your grace — / I have told you this whole story over again. / Do I deserve grace?" (1583-97).

For I might lock lips and laugh at your jurisdiction. "She had only you to trust to, you and Rome, / Rome and the Church, and no pert meddling priest / Two days ago, when Guido . . . / Hacked her to pieces" (1604-7). I come as friend of the Court, for pure friendship's sake, yet must tell my tale to the end, leave you no excuse. The papers you produced were a pack of stupid and impure banalities called letters. Pompilia wrote the letter you quoted "when the Holy Father wrote / The bestiality that posts thro' Rome, / Put in his mouth by *Pasquin*" (1631-33; ironic). I wrote the answer to that letter "when Saint John wrote / The tract *'De Tribus*

[*Impostoribus*': Moses, Mahomet, Christ; ironic] ." Thus did
I first stand question, make answer, still with the same results
of smiling disbelief (1681-2), a peccadillo yet by one

Who had not brought disgrace to the order, played	(1687)
Discreetly, ruffled gown nor ripped the cloth	
In a bungling game at romps: I have told you, Sirs —	
If I pretended simply to be pure,	
Honest and *Christian* in the case, — *absurd*!	(ironic)
As well go boast *myself* above the needs	
O' the human nature, careless how meat smells,	
Wine tastes, — a saint above the smack! But once	
Abate my crest, own flaws i' the flesh, agree	(sardonic)
To go with the herd, be *hog* no more or less,	
Why, hogs in common herd have common rights.	

Oh, Sirs, depend on me for much new light, thrown on the
"justice and religion here / By this proceeding, much fresh
food for thought!" (1727-9). Now that I have been recalled
from relegation, I rise in your esteem, sagacious Sirs (1742):

The *officious* priest would personate Saint George	(Cisma 1; 1744)
For a *mock* Princess in *undragoned* days.	
What, the *blood* startles you? What, after all,	
The priest who needs must carry sword on thigh	
May find imperative use for it? *Then, there was*	(pagan days)
A Princess, *was* a dragon belching flame,	
And should have been a Saint George also? *Then,*	(double entente)
There might be worse schemes than to break the bonds	
At Arezzo, lead her by the little hand,	
Till she reached Rome, and let her try to live?	
But you were law and gospel, . . .	(against freedom)
Fools, alike ignorant of *man and God*!	(paganism & Prom; 1757)

What perplexed your wit not to know that Guido "plotted
to plague her into overt sin / And shame, would slay Pompilia
body and soul, . . . / That she and I might take the *taint*, be
shown / To the world and shuddered over, *speckled* so?"
(Cenci 4.1.132; PU 3.4.156).

— That when at the last we did rush each on each,	(1785)
By *no chance* but because *God* willed it so —	(Prometheus)
The *spark of truth* was struck from out our souls —	
Made all of me, descried in the first glance,	
Seem fair and honest and permissible love	(double entente)

O' the good and true — as the first glance told me
There was no duty patent in the world
Like *daring* try be good and true *myself,*   (courage & self-cons'ness)
Leaving the shows of things to the *Lord of Show*   (Jehovah, Alastor
And *Prince* o' the Power of the Air.   711; Jehovah, not Satan)

I have done with being judged. I stand here guiltless in thought, word and deed to the "point" that I apprise you, —

                in [my] *contempt*   (Caponsacchi's; 1834)
For all *misapprehending ignorance*   (gullibility)
O' the human heart, much more [of] the *mind of Christ,* —   (Prom)
That I assuredly did bow, was blessed
By the *revelation* of Pompilia. There!   (of Prometheus)
Such is the final *fact* I fling you, Sirs,
To mouth and mumble and *misinterpret*: there!
"The priest's in love," have it the *vulgar* way!   (not the Promethean)

Nonetheless, "for Pompilia — be advised, / Build [Promethean] churches, go pray! You will find me there, / I know, if you come, — and you will come, I know." Yes, "I conceive . . . / How you will deal with Guido: oh, not death! / Death, if it let her life be: otherwise / Not death — your lights will teach you clearer!" (1872-6). "Why, Sirs, what's this? Why, this is sorry and strange! / Futility, divagation: this from me / Bound to be *rational,* justify an act / Of sober man! — whereas, being moved so much, / I give you cause to doubt the lady's *mind*: / A pretty sarcasm for the world! I fear / You do her *wit* injustice, — all through me! / Like my fate all through, — ineffective help! / A poor rash advocate I prove *myself* [graphic]. / You might be angry with good cause: but sure / At [of] the advocate, — only at the undue zeal / That spoils the *force* of his own plea, I think?" (1926-37).

Love! "We had no thought / Of such *infatuation,* she and I: / There are many points that prove it" (1943-5). "Oh, Sirs, there are worse men than you I say! / More easily duped, I mean: this stupid lie, / [Guido] never dared propound in Rome, / He gets Arezzo to receive, . . . / Rome for me henceforward — Rome, / Where better men are, — most of all, that man / The Augustinian of the Hospital" (2023-31). He writes of her whom he confessed, 'Many a dying person, never one / So *sweet* and *true* and *pure* and *beautiful.*' A *good* man! Will you make him Pope one day? Sirs, I am quiet again. You see, we are

So very pitiable, she and I,	(2041)
Who had *conceivably* been otherwise.	
Forget distemperature and idle heat!	
Apart from truth's sake, what's to move so much?	
Pompilia will be presently with *God*;	(Prometheus)
I am, on earth, *as good as out of it,* . . .	(in spirit)
She and I are mere *strangers* now: . . .	(to the world; 2049)
I do but play with an imagined life . . .	(2052)
To live, and see her *learn,* and *learn* by her,	(2056)
Out of the low obscure and *petty* world — . . .	(ignorant)
To *learn* not only by a *comet's rush*	(Shelleyan; 2065)
But a *rose's* birth, — not by the grandeur, *God* —	(passion; Jehovah)
But the comfort, *Christ.* All this, how far away!	(Prometheus)
Mere delectation, meet for a minute's dream! —	
Just as a drudging *student* trims his *lamp,*	(not priest; Prom's emblem)
Opens his *Plutarch,* puts him in the place	(not St. Thomas or Bible)
Of *Roman, Grecian*; draws the patched gown close,	(paganism)
Dreams, "Thus should I fight, save or rule the world!"	(against dragons)
Then, smilingly, contentedly, awakes	
To the old solitary *nothingness.*	(the Church)
So I, from *such communion pass* content . . .	(depart; R.B.'s ellipsis)

O *great,* just, *good* God! *Miserable* me! (DEMOGORGON. "This, like
thy glory, Titan, is to be / *Good, great* and joyous, beautiful
and free," PU 4.576-7; THE EARTH. "The tongueless
Caverns of the craggy hills / Cried 'Misery!' then; the hollow
Heaven replied, / 'Misery!' And the Ocean's purple waves, /
Climbing the land, howled to the lashing winds, /
And the pale nations heard it, 'Misery!' " PU 1.107-11)

LA SAISIAZ

1878

If Browning did not plan *La Saisiaz* as a swan song, a "summing-up and judgment," he at least never surpassed elsewhere in his poetry its compactness of reasons for being a Promethean and an antagonist of Jehovah. Nor could he have chosen a natural setting dearer to Shelley's heart than the spectacular view of Mont Blanc, gained from the top of Mt. Salève after an inspired climb from the chalet La Saisiaz which to the natives meant The Sun, to the poet Prometheus. Prometheus, Demogorgon and Shelley are simultaneously worshiped. For it is in the poem "Mont Blanc" that Shelley most effectively and beautifully advances his doctrine of Necessity, his rationale for an unthinking ultimate force which, being without will, is unable to determine whether its fateful releases shall be considered good or evil. Like the snow which falls silently and secretly on Mont Blanc, Shelley's Demogorgon acts only as he must act. And as the snow is destructive in its glaciers but life-sustaining in its resulting waters, so Demogorgon's tolerance of Jupiter may seem destructive while his liberation of Prometheus spells freedom and a savior of mankind. The consequences in each instance only seem good or evil, since the whole is unloosed by the same undifferentiating, unchangeable source or potential. Hence Browning's distantly reached "Mute Mont Blanc" (156), dared and done (cf., Abt Vogler 95):

<pre>
                but, the triumph crowning all —   (73)
There's Salève's own platform facing glory which strikes   (PU 1.158)
        greatness small,   ("platform," R of Islam 2129)
— Blanc, supreme above his earth-brood, needles   (PU 4.555, Gisb 51)
        red and white and green,   (thematic)
Horns of silver, fangs of crystal set on edge   (Islam 1691, 4125)
        in his demense.
</pre>

A dozen times Browning exults over having dared to climb Mt. Salève for this uncommon sight of Mont Blanc, and each time he undoubtedly intends to revalidate Demogorgon's "All things thou dar'st demand" (PU 2.4.8) and Prometheus' unquestioned supremacy.

It is also in *La Saisiaz* that Browning's pantheism, which tends to be equated with worship of Prometheus, probably receives its sincerest expression. More than a dozen times he deifies Nature, surprisingly exerting no precaution in "O'er the grandeur and the beauty . . . / Earth's most exquisite disclosure, heaven's own God [Prometheus] in evidence" (4-6) and "set free, / *Stationed* face to face with — Nature? rather with infinitude" (11). Even though Browning had long before locked in his memory every word precious to Shelley's metaphysical poetry, he continued to focus on specific Shelleyan verse for each new undertaking. Thus the diction of this poem may easily be traced to "Mont Blanc," particularly the words dare, marvel, Infinitude, barrier, vale, sight and sound, strange, glory, star, point, new, joyous, pant, dusk, light, spark, Arve and circle. "Stationed" (Shelleyan) at La Saisiaz premeditatively, Browning further gained the advantage of drawing corroborative support for his undiminished confidence in intellect and self-consciousness from renowned residents of the area. There is the wit of Voltaire from Ferney, the knowledge of Gibbon from Lausanne, the pantheism of Rousseau from Bossex and the poetic power of Byron from Diodati, incidentally suggesting that Browning's earlier attacks on Byron in *Fifine at the Fair* and other poems were calculated deceptions. From Shelley and these other brilliant and accomplished artists, Browning drew formidable confirmation for his uncompromising rationalism, for his contempt of the ignorant surmises of Fancy or faith. As he early learned the beguiling power of the paradox from de Mandeville and the coiling, flaking power of wit from Voltaire, he early grasped the monumental gullibility of mankind. Intellectual superiority is the logical tie-in of *La Saisiaz* with the Parleying and the lighthearted *Two Poets of Croisic* which are literally compacted of Shelleyan diction: "Voltaires, can say and unsay, praise and blame, / Prove black white, white black, play at paradox / And when they seem to lose it, win the game" (1170-2). Intellectual superiority is proved in that under the flimsy theme of the brevity of human fame Browning could flaunt his largest array of druidical and pagan allusions, even to the substitution of a fiery cricket for the traditional grasshopper in which the lowest races saw the fire-bringer or Prometheus who ended man's moaning. Desforges, the Croisic poet, had deceived the La Roques, the Voltaires and other eminent literary critics; Browning had deceived the world.

Without question the sudden death of Ann Egerton Smith at La Saisiaz grieved and distressed Browning, but it is evident that the sad event only contributed to a vehicle for summing-up on which the poet had previously been engaged. That Browning had attempted to win his long-time companion to Prometheanism, or that she may have been or have become as ardent a Promethean as Browning, seems implicit in the poem: "Both of us had loved and wondered just the same" (14); "who working ne'er shall know if work bear fruit . . . / We who, *darkling*, timed the [new] day's birth, — struggling, testified to *peace*, — / Earned, by dint of failure, triumph" (191-4); "Grow *transparent*, grow *transfigured* with the sudden light that leapt / At the first word's provocation, from the heart's depth where it slept" (115-6). Beyond Mrs. Smith, however, even beyond the strident belligerency toward Jehovah, Browning wished to persuade all intelligent readers of the power and love of Prometheus, of the injustice and parsimony of Jehovah. As with Shelley — "Man, oh, not men!" (PU 4.394) — so with Browning, self-sacrificing love is unalterably the stipulated warfare, regardless of how fortuitously the circle of devotees may be drawn. In probably the tenderest of Browning's many expressions of love for another human being and quite reminiscent of Asia's self-effacing words (PU 2.5.38-47), the aging poet cannot be faulted for his skill at "lazy love" or at advancing his Shelleyan conviction:

You supposed that few or none had known and loved   (Ann Smith;
    you in the world: 123)
May be! flower that's full-blown tempts the butterfly,

> not flower that's furled.
> *But more learned sense unlocked you,* loosed the sheath   (Mind)
>   and let expand   ("unlocked," Fr Wedded Souls 8)
> *Bud* to bell and outspread flower-shape at the least   (R of Islam 3162)
>   warm touch of hand
> — *Maybe,* throb of heart, beneath which, — quickening
>   farther than it knew, —
> Treasure oft was *disembosomed,* scent all strange and   (Alastor 396)
>   unguessed hue.
> Disembosomed, re-embosomed, — must one memory   (Alastor 423)
>   suffice,
> Prove I knew an Alpine-*rose* which all beside   (red, passion, secrecy)
>   named Edel*weiss*?   (white; "rose," Calderon's Cisma 1-16)

Browning often uses "May be" synonymously with per-adventure and surmise, usually to confirm. The true sadness of these lines emerges earlier in "the terrace [Alastor 632] showed no figure, tall, white, leaning through the wreaths [Naples 17], ... [that] / Interpose between one's love and Nature's loving" (93-5). As Browning emulates the expansiveness of Shelley's love, however, the memory of Elizabeth Barrett modulates his thought. For Browning unfailingly associates the adequacy of love with the inadequacy of faith or Fancy, this time Elizabeth's sighing "We believe":

> I take the cup of *comfort*   (faith; 251)
>   proffered thus,   (cf., "comfort," Fust 16, 20)
> Taste and try each soft *ingredient,* sweet infusion,   (Oedipus 2.2.25)
>   and discuss
> What their blending may accomplish for the cure or [of]
>   doubt, till — slow,
> Sorrowful, *but how decided!* needs must I o'erturn
>   it — so!

Then, confirming that the overturned cup of faith is the one proffered by his departed wife, Browning rejects for himself any attempt at vindication of Jehovah's cruel and jealous ways. Indeed his increasing scorn of dependence upon Christian faith or Fancy is here profoundly intensified by the effects of an earlier (213-5), typically Shelleyan, reversal of Dante's "Thus I believe, thus I affirm, thus I am certain it is, that from this life I shall pass to another better, there, where, that lady lives of whom my soul was enamoured":

no less	(358)

Mine results in "Only grant a second life, I   (R.B.'s verdict)
    acquiesce . . .
Only grant my soul may carry high through death her   (367)
    cup unspilled,
Brimming though it be with *knowledge,* life's loss
    drop by drop *distilled,*   (faith)
I shall boast it mine —

Like his Paracelsus Browning does not pretend to modesty. Characteristically he boasts credit for awakening Elizabeth Barrett to the knowledge of life, credit for the distillation of life's losses from her Christian faith, as unhesitatingly as he boasts credit for establishing self-assurance in the reticent Ann Egerton Smith: "But more learned sense unlocked you." Of course there is a double entente in the Christian-like "Only grant," for Browning was assured that he need only dare (will), dare (demand), before receiving whatever he wished including a second life. Yet one cannot here avoid being more curious about Isa Blagden, Julia Wedgwood, Lady Ashburton, other friends with whom the poet fell out for unknown reasons, and Mrs. Sutherland Orr to whom Browning seems to have revealed his Prometheanism and to whom *La Saisiaz* is dedicated. Never once does Browning devote a thought to the possibility that the imposed hobbling, tethering and hindering of this life could be extended to the next and inhibit his expected freedom. So even at this stage of Browning's life the best reason for thinking that he accepted *Prometheus Unbound* as apocalyptic is his determination to "fight on, fare ever / There as here!" If Prometheus remains impaled until "a diviner day," then why not the spirit Browning?

Comprising in all a small one-third of *La Saisiaz,* the above matter reappears intermittently to the end as do emphases on the Shelleyan doctrines of Progress, Perfection and Unity. But the remaining two-thirds are tenaciously designed as a stepped-up warfare on Jehovah's governance and possibly as a consummate assault on Jehovah's total being. These two-thirds are moreover seductively begun in line 139 with an habitual disquisition between Faith and Reason which Browning formalizes as a debate in line 405. The inescapable repetition, which permits a syncopated assault on faith in Jehovah, not only ridicules hopes and fears, rewards and punishments, but also enables Browning the opportunity to contrast his Promethean courage with Christian cowardice: "If a spirit of the place [Mont Blanc] / Broke the silence, bade me question, promised answer, — *what disgrace* / Did I stipulate 'Provided answer suit my hopes, not fears!'" Undismayed by fearful consequences Browning asks himself, "Is there God's self, no or yes?"

Well, and wherefore shall it daunt me, when 't is
    I *myself* am tasked,   (self-sufficiency; 147)
When, by *weakness weakness* questioned, *weakly* (cf., 135, Epipsy 273)
    answers — *weakly* asked?
Weakness never needs be falseness: truth is truth
    in each degree
— *Thunderpealed* by *God* to Nature, whispered   (Shelleyan; Prom)
    by my soul to me.
Nay, the *weakness* turns to *strength* and triumphs
    in a truth beyond:
Mine is but man's truest answer — how were it   (self-consciousness)
    did *God* respond?   (Prometheus)

Only in "Saul" does Browning approach this directness of allusion to Shelley's reversal of the scriptural "My grace is sufficient for thee: for my strength is made perfect in weakness." And in "Saul" the poet's unadorned and unstressed reversal is much better concealed among Christian overtones and pagan undertones. Observe how freely Browning now paraphrases the Sun-treader's thought:

Resist not the weakness,   (PU 2.3.93-7)
Such *strength* is in meekness   (PU 2.4.44, wisdom)
That the *Eternal*, the *Immortal*,   (Demogorgon, PU 3.1.52)
Must unloose through life's portal
The snake-like Doom coiled underneath his throne
                By *that* alone.   (weakness)

Yet Browning still dared not exploit so openly three helpful Shelleyan glosses which might have been his immediate undoing: Hercules says to Prometheus, "Most glorious among

Spirits, *thus doth strength* / To wisdom, courage, and long-suffering love, / And thee, who art the form they animate, / Minister like a slave" (PU 3.3.1-4); Asia says to Demogorgon, "Then Prometheus / Gave wisdom, *which is strength*, to Jupiter, / And with the law alone, 'Let man be free'" (PU 2.4.43-5); and Panthea says to THE EARTH, "How glorious art thou, Earth! And if thou be / The shadow of some spirit lovelier still, / Though evil stain its work, and it should be / Like its creation, *weak* yet beautiful, / I could fall down and worship that and thee" (PU 2.3.12-6). However one interprets Shelley's pivotal words, the weakness of man is thought converted into strength by wisdom, courage and long-suffering love, that is, by man's talent and effort, never by an infusion of Jesus Christ's strength as enunciated by St. Paul. No tyrannical law-giver, Prometheus stipulated only the freedom of man's mind, gave him all the necessary tools for its development and determined that man's thought, which according to Shelley is Prometheus' thought in small or portion, be "the measure of the universe." Thus Browning, if he had not elected to deceive, could have initiated his latest confirmation of a lifelong acceptance of Shelley's trust in self-awareness (Browning's Myself) and Shelley's reliance upon the Mind as the sole determining factor of existence.

Never elaborating Shelley's subjective idealism in broader details, Browning presupposes two essential points (218): 1) he, Browning, *is*, knows; 2) he, Browning, perceives a force outside himself. Call one soul, he adds; call the other God (the One Mind). Since these are the only Facts for him, all else which may be added is surmise, mere faith or Fancy. Of course he is guided by Shelley's ritualistic "Nothing exists but as it is perceived." So Browning too must distinguish between "perceive," which man can do, and "create," which man cannot do. His sole departure from Shelley seems to be the committing of God's and the soul's existence to the categorical imperative "Fact it is I know I know not something which is fact as much," all because God and soul overpass his power of proving them. He would have a less debatable if less precise premise had he stuck with self-consciousness, spiritual kinship and belief that spirit cannot die or fail to find happiness, its birthright. But Browning is really preparing the way for indorsement of Shelley's conclusions on cause and effect: "What before caused all the causes, what effect of all effects / Haply follows, — these are fancy," "mere surmise not knowledge." Therewith launched into another dialogue of the mind, this time the poet's own, Browning can ask and answer: Why [then], because I doubtless *am*, shall I as doubtless [continue to] *be*, if God be good and wise? Not because God seems powerful, for then right and wrong would not be at strife. Thus, if wrong predominates, death is better than life; if right predominates, there is no need for a double boon. Then why want a second life? Because life, submerged as it is in "triumphant evil," would otherwise be brutish: "Well, what signifies repugnance? ... / Stalwart body idly yoked to stunted spirit, ... / Hindrance is the fact acknowledged" (197-202). Just the bare hope of a better world therefore encourages endurance, in spite of the fact that no single hope has ever reached complete fulfillment. As unwilling as Shelley to admit to the duality of matter and spirit, Browning dispenses with the contention that "the soul is not the body," knowing that belief in a divine Creator, thereby rationalized, results in the gullibility of those who hope and fear, who accept the Christian ethics of reward and punishment:

Cause before, *effect* behind me — blanks! The midway point *I am*,	(Myself; 255)
Caused, itself — *itself efficient*: in that narrow space must cram	
All experience — out of which there crowds *conjecture* manifold,	(faith or Fancy)
But as *knowledge*, this comes only — things may be as I behold,	
Or may not be, but, *without* me and above me, things there are;	(outside & perceived)
I *myself* am what I know not — ignorance which proves no bar	(double talk)
To *the knowledge that I am*, and, since I am, can recognize	

What to me is *pain and pleasure*: this is sure, the
    rest — surmise.
If my fellows are or are not, what may please them
    and what pain, —
Mere surmise: *my own experience — that is knowledge,*
    once again!

Illusory state of earthly life to the contrary, Browning could
have met the traditional watch-watchmaker argument by asking who or what caused the watchmaker. But his purpose,
without being that revealing, is to confirm Shelley's unrelenting insistence that "It is infinitely improbable that the cause
of mind, that is, of existence, is similar to mind." Browning
substitutes the rush for Mont Blanc's snow, and the rush
knows the source of the stream on which it floats no better
than the snow knows the universe in which it falls.

Perhaps the most difficult assignment throughout Browning's long warfare was to find a workable manner of deposing
in the minds of Jehovah's followers a deity whom Demogorgon was destined to depose. Clearly Browning's problem was
as inconclusively presented as was Shelley's search for an
absolute which would not reintroduce the Christian idea of a
divine Governor. Else why, if heaven's kingless throne is already wrapped in lasting night (PU 2.4.149), does Browning
so often and so vehemently protest his fearlessness in opposition to Jehovah? It would have been much easier to operate
on the assumption that the Jehovah who created man and
then enslaved him had ceased to reign: "The tyranny of
heaven none may retain, / Or reassume, or hold, succeeding
thee" (PU 3.1.57-8). It would however have been less provoc-
ative to the poet, altogether fatal to the advancement of
Prometheus' beneficence, to be required to battle a van-
quished yet still worshiped God without representing that
God as immediately existent and vindictively motivated.
Browning knew that with his exceptional talent he could
make Shelley's blasphemous reversals instinctive with Christian prejudice and terminology. As long as he alluded
regularly to the love and might of Jehovah as expounded in
the Old and New Testaments, Browning could count on the

benefit of any and all doubt aroused over imputed anger and vengeance. He had successfully falsified a Christian sympathy which placed him solidly among the faithful. He had gradually been excused his obscurity, prolixity, convolutions and equivocations, not on the proper ground of perversity but of inability to perform otherwise. And his crowning double entente had been accepted for more than a half century without suspicion that his use of GOD was a ploy to evade distinguishing between Prometheus and Jehovah, his use of CHRIST a ploy to conceal Prometheus. Through the one he expected his praise of Prometheus to be attributed automatically to Jehovah by gullible readers; through the other he projected a recognition of Jesus Christ no Christian would be inclined to dispute because of excessive emphasis on love and wisdom. But Browning's patience was wearing thin and in *La Saisiaz* he was resolved to say belligerently, if not for another soul in the world, that he could not defend a God who withheld any favor from man, exactly what he had opposed in Jehovah since the day he decided that love and justice are eternally incompatible, that joys and sorrows, rewards and punishments make no acceptable supreme power.

So the wavering or uncertain immediacy of Jehovah in Browning's poetry is probably due, not to the poet's misunderstanding of the apocalyptic nature of Shelley's new Promethean day, but to the deceptive medium of presenting the immedicable aftereffects of Jehovah's creation, a condition not even Prometheus could change, except slowly through his unsurpassed example of courage, love and wisdom and what he teaches for the expansion of man's mind. Unlike Shelley, Browning had to cast a deceptive doubt over his trust in the absolute power of knowledge. Unlike Shelley, he had to falsify a sympathy for faith and intuitive truth while relying on the mentality of rational creatures, especially that of talented minds. And unlike Shelley, he had to pretend a distrust in man's capability while extolling the efficacy of the arts and science, especially that of poetry and music. To both poets it is the arts and science which provide a two-way communication between Prometheus and man, and it is in Browning's surreptitious eulogies to various art forms that he most genuinely reflects Shelley's demand for freedom. Now it becomes clearer why Browning's aversion to Gothic architecture, a Church product; why his lack of sympathy for the copyist of Virgin, Babe and Saint, Pictor Ignotus; why his praise of Giotto's independence and aspiration, not his quality to adore and glorify; and why his pretense that pagan art perished because it had no farther to reach. The passage in *Prometheus Unbound* to which Browning rarely failed to allude, poem after poem, is probably the nearest thing to law he ever willingly accepted:

The echoes of the human world, which tell   (PU 3.3.44)
Of the low voice of love, almost unheard,
And dove-eyed pity's murmured pain, and music,
Itself the echo of the heart, and all
That tempers or improves man's life, now free;
And lovely apparitions, — dim at first,
Then radiant, as *the mind*, arising bright
From the embrace of beauty (whence the forms
Of which these are the phantoms) casts on them
The gathered rays which are reality —
Shall visit us, *the progeny immortal*   ("Nurslings of immortality,"
Of Painting, Sculpture, and rapt Poesy,   PU 1.749)
And arts, though unimagined, yet to be.
The wandering voices and the shadows these
Of all that man becomes, *the mediators*
Of that best worship love, by him and us
Given and returned; swift shapes and sounds, which grow
More fair and soft as man grows wise and kind,
And, veil by veil, evil and error fall.

All such freedom and happiness of creativity is a gift of Prometheus who resolutely objected to Jupiter's inflicted famine, toil, disease, strife, wounds, fierce want, unreal good, unseasonable frost and fire and ghastly death unknown before. All such suffering results from none other than Jupiter's refusal of "the *birthright* of their [mankind's] being, knowledge, power, / The skill which wields the elements, the thought / Which pierces this dim universe like light, / *Self-empire*, and the majesty of love" (PU 2.4.32-105). Having seen the ruin of man's lair, Prometheus waked the "legioned hopes" (bottom of Pandora's box) that they might hide the shape of death. He sent love to bind the disunited tendrils of the human heart, and he tamed fire, torturing to his will iron and gold and all the subtle forms beneath the mountains and the waves. Prometheus gave man speech, which created thought "the measure of the universe," and science, which shook but did not topple the thrones of heaven and earth. And on being told the hidden power of herbs and springs by Prometheus, man curbed disease and made death more like to sleep. Human hands first mimicked then mocked with molded limbs more lovely than the human form, till marble grew divine. The harmonious human mind then poured itself forth in all-prophetic song (poesy) and music until it walked Godlike exempt from mortal care. Such, the alleviations of his state, Prometheus gave to man.

Shelley's above evaluation of the arts and science, his insistence upon birthright and self-empire in the subsequent abstract and now his severest indictment of Jehovah for restricting man, particularly genius, provide an exceptional insight into the depth of animosity to which Browning vowed a lifetime of support and advancement:

<pre>
                all-prevailing foe!   (Jupiter-Jehovah; PU 1.285)
I curse thee! let a sufferer's curse
Clasp thee, his torturer, like remorse;
Till thine Infinity shall be
A robe of envenomed agony;
And thine Omnipotence a crown of pain,
To cling like burning gold round thy dissolving brain.

Heap on thy soul, by virtue of this Curse,
    Ill deeds, then be thou damned, beholding good;
Both infinite as is the universe, . . .   (evil & good)
             [and] let the hour   (297)
Come, when thou must appear to be
That which thou art internally;   (hell, PU 1.56)
And after many a false and fruitless crime
Scorn track thy lagging fall through boundless space and time.
</pre>

Small wonder, as discouragement encompassed his avowal and long effort, that Browning's animosity against Jehovah became greater and greater. Scholars have not accounted to

their own satisfaction for what Browning terms the pettish-
ness of *La Saisiaz*, what they term the embittered cynicism of
old age. Now it may be seen that Shelley's vivid models and
Browning's most uncontrollable bursts of anger evidence a
common distress at not being more influential in dethroning
Jehovah in the minds of readers and a common tendency to
absolve the failure in the ignorance and sheep-like acquiescence of Jehovah's followers, in the unmitigated nescience of
the masses.

Having lived and suffered, loved and hated, Browning has
"learnt *and taught*" (265) that "there is no reconciling wisdom with a world distraught, / Goodness with triumphant
evil, power with failure in the aim." That is, once barred his
lifelong assumption that earth is merely a pupil's place, that
"life, time — with all their chances, changes" are just probation-space. Knowledge resting solely on his own experience
notwithstanding, Browning does once again extrapolate
human pain and pleasure and once again reach the conclusion
that they are the product of a wicked machine devised by an
unloving and miserly Jehovah. Because mind is all — the
measure of the universe — he has the privilege, indeed the
duty, of proving his forces (talents) every one, and they tell
him to solve the problem: "From thine [Browning's] apprehended scheme of things, deduce / Praise or blame of its [the
machine's] contriver, shown a niggard or profuse / In each
good or evil issue!" (287-9). Many times now Browning has
reached the same angry conclusion, both in judgment of
Jehovah and of his followers. But *La Saisiaz* is the first poem
in which he angrily challenges all of Jehovah's praiseworthy
attributes:

<pre>
            did *He* lack power or was the   (Jehovah)
      will in fault   (Shelleyan; 303)
When he let blue heaven be shrouded o'er by
      vapors of the vault,   (death)
Gay earth drop her *garlands shrivelled at*   (PU 3.4.183-204; Violet 5)
      the first *infecting* breath . . .   (PU 3.4.148)
What, no way but this that man may learn and
      lay to heart how rife
Life were with delights would only *death* allow
      their taste to life?
</pre>

Clearly Browning's personal problem was, like Shelley's, acute, for it is death alone, the last denial of freedom and happiness, to which Browning can make no adjustment unless offered assurance of a second life. Extinction of self-consciousness was one thought Browning would not entertain, and its avoidance may explain his Prometheanism more readily than animosity toward Jehovah: "Can we love but on condition, that the thing we love must die?" Still firmly based on Shelley's early pantheistic postulate that an acceptable God must be "intelligent and *necessarily* beneficent," Browning's belief in spiritual perpetuity, wholeheartedly adopted before *Pauline*, demonstrates how thoughtfully he conceived Pope Innocent's isosceles deficient in Love. Here it is solipsistically blunt: "As the power, expect performance! God's be God's as mine is mine!" (300). Consequently, for himself, Browning will "vindicate *no way* of [Jehovah's] to man" nor relent in his opposition unless granted assurance of a second life.

Plainlier! if this life's conception new life fail to   (326)
    realize, —
Though earth burst and proved a bubble glassing
    hues of *hell*, one *huge*   (cf., M N Post Fr 36,72,78)
Reflex of the devil's doings — *God's work* by   (Pr Athan 129; Jehovah,
    no subterfuge — ...   Cyclops 265)
Still, — with no more Nature, no more Man as
    riddle to be read,   (Hellas 1083; 331)
Only my own joys and sorrows now to reckon real   (self-sufficiency)
    instead, —
I must say — *or choke in silence* — "Howsoever
    came my fate,
Sorrow did and joy did nowise, — life well weighed, —
    preponderate."

Though he possess absolutely no evidence beyond himself, Browning still must report that sorrow did outweigh joy in his life. Yet not by necessity (fate) of "a cause" all-good, all-wise, all-potent do sorrows exceed joys, Browning hastens to add. As he is man, he judges better and knows that to Jehovah wisdom and power are unavailing, or Jehovah would have (fate) to employ them: "Power? 't is just the main assumption *reason* most revolts at!" Even the worm, man's fellow-creature, enjoys a pure perfection bright if brief unbestowed upon man. "No, as I am man," Browning repeats, "I mourn the poverty I must impute: / Goodness, wisdom, power, all bounded, each a *human attribute!*" (347-8; cf., R & B 10.1628, Calderon 1.123-5). So to suspect or to judge that Browning downgrades greatness or perfection gained by the mind and one's talent, condones failure except as a spur to success, is to be hoodwinked by one of Browning's most constant deceptions. Whatever comes near to perfection on earth may perish, but only after its essence is translated to the Cave of Prometheus. Browning may have been embittered by his failure to win sudden or even early renown as a poet, but his worship of the mind never faltered and any hint that he begrudged the brilliance or astuteness of great independent minds must be marked down as deliberate misleading. The same hints at disparagement of fame are to be found in *Pauline*. Yet Browning already imagined world-wide acclaim for his projected mission. Like Shelley, Browning believed profoundly in the return of the Golden Age and this return was to be effected not by faith in Jehovah and dependence upon the dictates of the heart, as the poet dissembled, but by gradual restoration of the power of mind and genius, all of which, as is said at the end of *La Saisiaz*, is simply part of the Promethean whole.

Browning never forgot that Shelley utilizes two characteristic listings under his intellectual philosophy which only seem improperly classified: 1) "And call truth, virtue, love, *genius*, joy"; 2) "This is alone Life, Joy, *Empire*, and Victory" (PU 2.3.6, 4.578). Each poet placed Genius and Self-empire within close range of the absolutes Beauty, Truth and Goodness, well knowing that to "Fate, Time, Occasion, Chance, and Change" all things are subject but eternal Love (PU 2.4.119-20). Thus only in their bluntness are Browning's arguments in *La Saisiaz* different from the studied equivocation of *The Ring and the Book*. In unshakable hope Browning probably exceeded the limits of Shelley's metaphysical reality by imagining individual identity beyond the grave and conscious reunion, in this poem with Ann Egerton Smith: "Grant me (once again) assurance we shall each meet each some day, / *Walk* — but with how bold a footstep! on a way — but what a way!" (387-8; cf., PU 3.4.131-3). Keats, Shelley preferred to think, was in death made one with Nature and became a portion of the loveliness he once had made more lovely.

Browning's oft repeated "grant assurance of a second life" is deeply rooted in Shelley's doctrine of Progress. As Shelley found support for the development of his doctrine in a simultaneous moral and physical melioration, Browning found a similar way to strengthen his cause in the face of moral and intellectual pessimism: "Since time means *amelioration*, tardily enough displayed, / Yet a mainly onward moving, never wholly retrograde. / We know more though we know little, we grow stronger though still weak, / Partly see though all too purblind, stammer though we cannot speak" (415-8). "Call progress toilsome," Browning protests, when reminded of the natural glory of Lake Geneva's lights, new, strange, careless, joyous, all Shelley's words. And though Browning knows and speaks "that somehow every actor, somewhere in this earthly scene, / Fails," he also asserts "This — that somewhere *new* existence led by men and women *new* / Possibly attain *perfection* coveted by me and you" (179, 187-8). This he can do because Prometheus is responsible for the beauty and majesty of nature, Jehovah for all failure, and Time for the unavoidable delay of new life with new men and women. It was however Shelley's inordinate confidence in the metaphysical Unity of all things which provided the ultimate boost for Browning's belief in the eventual removal of imperfection, that of Jehovah (all evil) as well as of man, and restoration of all Good in the One Mind. Certainly for Browning as for Shelley the hope for a perfect existence relates to an hypothesized ancient departure from Nature's pure and happy days by man and a temporary adoption of unnatural ways such as worship of Jehovah. Both poets hoped for and anticipated the return of a new Promethean day, or Golden Age, when men would walk peacefully and joyously like angels in an atmosphere of perpetual spring. This is why Reason, on being told that Death alone offers release from earth's pain and sorrow, rejoins, "I pronounce for man's obtaining at this moment [unity and perfection]. Why delay?" (427).

Disdainful of Fancy's addition of heaven and hell to God, soul and earth as facts or realities, Reason scornfully agrees that there is nothing else to desiderate:

Nothing! Henceforth man's existence bows to
    the monition "*Wait!*   (Ro 8.25; 466)
Take the joys and bear the sorrows — neither
    with extreme concern!
Living here means *nescience* simply: 't is the next life
    that helps to learn.   (Avison 342, 359)

When Browning wrote these lines he knew that with the constant shuffling about of contradictory ideas, unidentified speakers and tricky quotations almost any deduction except the proper one could and probably would be drawn from "the monition." Actually one speaker, Fancy, is an individual who accepts Jehovah's machinery of alternating joys and sorrows, one who hopes for that which he sees not and waits patiently for it. It is he, never Browning the other speaker, who lives a life of nescience simply. In trusting the scriptural promise of heavenly enlightenment he, unlike Browning and his Grammarian (109), discounts this life and passively enters the next, still an infant in thought and deed. To Browning there is no "waiting" to learn. This life is a proving-ground which shall be used to perfect his talent and to launch him into the next well on the way to Godship. His third use of the word Nescience, Browning has conveyed the same import in his regular attacks on Ignorance, always centered in the faith or Fancy of Jehovah's followers. If Shelley's strictures against authoritarian Church and State surpass Browning's in severity, they fall short of the frequency with which Browning exploits their rationale, Ignorance: "Thrones, altars, judgement-seats, and prisons; . . . / Of reasoned wrong, glozed on by ignorance"; "Hard-featured men, or with proud, angry looks, / Or cold, staid gait, or false and hollow smiles, / Or the dull sneer of *self-loved ignorance*" (PU 3.4.164-7, 38). As the postulates Heaven and Hell deny Browning the chance to consider life a probation-space and are thus repudiated, so Good and Evil, the sixth postulate to be submitted by Fancy or faith, deny him the chance to reject rewards and punishments and are summarily repudiated. Without uninhibited choice Browning knows that he could not conceivably be responsible for whatever he does; he might as well be ordered not to breathe: "Liberty of doing evil gave his doing good a grace; / Once lay down the law, ... / Thenceforth neither good nor evil does man, doing what he must" (492-7). While Faith allows no sward firm like Reason's "God there is, and soul there is," whereby Soul is bound to pass probation, prove its powers and exercise sense and thought on fact, Reason may educe that earth affords warrant of future hope (518-24).

Only Weakness and Strength seem more ingrained in Browning's eschatology than Hope; in fact, hope is his ultimate mainstay: "If, supplanting hope, assurance [of a second life] needs must change this life to me. / So, I hope [without assurance] — no more than hope, but hope — no less than hope" (534-5). And Shelley's thought is no less evident than usual or any more explicit: "To suffer woes which Hope thinks infinite; ... to hope till Hope creates / From its own wreck the thing it contemplates" (PU 4.570-4). Whence the good of goodness vanishes when the ill of evil ceases:

Hope the *arrowy* [light], just as constant, comes (Pr Athan 128-9; 543)
       to pierce *its gloom*, compelled   (cloud of laws, cf., 327-8)
By a *power* and by a *purpose* which, if no one   (Demogorgon; Prom)
       else beheld,
I behold in life, so — *hope*!
              Sad summing-up of all to say!
Athanasius contra mundum, why should *he hope*   (Hooker; R.B.)
       more than *they*?   (disbelievers in Prometheus)
So are men made notwithstanding, such *magnetic*
       virtue *darts*
From each head their fancy *haloes* to their
       unresisting hearts!   ("Twin Spheres of light who rule this
          passive Earth, / This world of *love*, this *me* [Myself]; and into
            birth / Awaken all its fruits and flowers, and *dart* / *Magnetic*

> *might* [virtue] into its central heart," Epipsy 345-8;
> "Sheds not a light so mild, *so powerful,* / As that which,
> bursting from the Fairy's form, / Spread a purpureal *halo*
> round the scene, . . . / And the clear silver tones, / As thus she
> spoke, were such / As are unheard by all but *gifted* ear," Q Mab
> 1.100-13; "His hosts of blind and *unresisting* dupes / The
> despot numbers; . . . Scarce living pulleys of a dead *machine,* /
> Mere *wheels* of work and articles of trade," Q Mab 5.69-77)

Browning against the whole world. Why should he dare to hope more than they, the blinded to Prometheus' love and power? Because of the gifted few who dart magnetic might into the earth's central heart, and to four of these geniuses Browning consecrates his favorite imagery which is Promethean fire and light — the stolen fire which was concealed in a *hollow* fennel stalk, the stalk which became a way of carrying light in the Greek isles. Symbolic of wisdom, the light from Rousseau is like a fiery flying serpent; from Byron, a phosphoric fame swathing blackness' self with brightness till putridity looked flame; from Voltaire, a darting wit that sparkles in and out the boughs; and from Gibbon, a central solid knowledge kindled in the core. Browning "thanks" the pine-trees of Makistos which, as well as providing the chain of beacons signaling the fall of Troy, provided the emblematic lamp that "emulous youths / *Bore* to thy [Prometheus'] honor through the divine gloom . . . even as those / Who bear the untransmitted torch of *hope* / Into the grave, across the night of life, / As thou [Prometheus] hast borne it most triumphantly / To this far goal of Time" (PU 3.3.168-74). Thus under Nature's sky for architrave, in trust and not despair, Browning brandishes the dazzling beacon-light, the giant torch fed by the combustible resin of Rousseau, Byron, Voltaire, Gibbon, all concentrated in one mighty flame. Blatantly excessive, flashed, effulgence, terebinth, explosive, resplendency, detonations, fulgurations, flare, fireworks, brand, flamboyant merely delay rather than intensify the move to rainbow (Prometheus' glory), from which Browning deceptively withdraws for an elliptical moment:

O the sorriest of conclusions to whatever *man*
     of sense   (597)
Mid the millions stands the *unit*, takes no
     flare for evidence!   ("'All is not lost! There is some recompense
     / For *hope* whose fountain can be thus profound, . . . / 'Such
     are the thoughts which, like the fires that *flare* / In storm-
     encompassed isles, we cherish yet . . . / The *buds* foreknow their
     life — this *hope* must ever rise," R of Islam 3145-62)
Yet the millions have their portion, live their calm
     or troublous day,
Find significance in *fireworks*: so, by help of   (hell)
     mine, they may
Confidently lay to heart and lock in head their life
     long — *this*:   (belligerent)
"He there with the brand flamboyant, *broad* o'er   (R of Islam 3171)
     night's forlorn abyss,   (R of Islam 1692)
Crowned by *prose and verse*; and wielding, with   (Peter 718)
     Wit's *bauble*, Learning's *rod* . . .   (To Death 17; Oedipus 1.149-
Well? Why, he at least believed in Soul,   62; R.B.'s ellipsis)
     was very sure of God."   (Prometheus)

* * * * *

The thematic conclusion as indicated by Browning and approved by his most thoroughly misled admirers, Browning's surety in Prometheus does not yet satisfy his indebtedness to Shelley. So as Shelley has controlled the poet's thought on Hope during the past hundred lines, he quite unexpectedly controls almost every key word in the remaining fourteen prosaic lines. If Browning had vowed before his career ended to honor every single word used by Shelley, it is doubtful that a better example of his intent could be found, particularly for "a chain of linkéd thought," PU 4.394; "forge / Many a weapon, chain," Men of England 9-10; "'Tis something sadder, sweeter," PU 1.671; "unravelled my entangled will," Cenci 3.1.220; "disinterred," Naples 1; "stock," Devil 76; "uprooting every germ," Q Mab 7.46; "Earthquake, . . . / The torpor of the year," Mont B 87-8; "So much of life and joy is lost," Mont B 117; "resurrection . . . awakened," Hellas 100-13; "With earthquake shock,"

PU 4.379; "evoked, awake, dream," R of Islam 811-9; "The least of which wronged Memory," Fr Home 2; "Let every part depending on the chain / That links it to the whole," Q Mab 7.17-8. Yet Browning was not alone successful in concealing the prodigality of these collations which extract the very substance of their contexts. He was also successful in reverting unnoticed to one of the best known memorials of his poetry: "And there I put inside my breast / A moulded feather, . . . / Well, I forget the rest" (Memorabilia). Having found flawless the chain of Shelleyan thought which he had forged for Ann Egerton Smith and then reexamined atop Mt. Salève without her, he decides, "Not so filmy was the texture, but I *bore* it in my breast / *Safe thus far*" (Q Mab ded 13).

CONCLUSION

The poems heretofore chosen in this study by no means represent the endless struggle Browning waged, but they do constitute the backbone of the poet's effort to replace Jehovah with Prometheus. Truly it is a rare poem in which Browning does not overtly or covertly make a strike for his God Prometheus. Even the least to be suspected — including the dramas which must have disappointed Browning greatly in their unconvincing play on Weakness and Strength — become prime candidates for the exercise of his wit, mockery and lightheartedness. And many of these gain a magic invulnerability when to the habitual machinations Browning adds a topical figure whose conduct provides a double mask for the poet's deceptive scheme. MR. SLUDGE, who is purportedly the object of the most livid anger of Browning's intellectual life, is only a supposed exposure of the current craze in spiritualism. For Mr. Sludge is a genuine Promethean who says what all other Browning masks say in favor of Prometheus and Prometheanism in opposition to Jehovah and Christianity. He gave Browning an ideal opportunity to distract careful analysis from evidences of his own spiritualism and a new springboard from which to advance Prometheanism through a most unlikely and likely mask. The poem is brimful of Shelley's favorite words which in turn became Browning's favorites, even the long and distracting opening part, and in lines 664-1042 Faith (fancy) and Reason (doubt) run the gamut of challenge and support endemic to Browning's sacred avowal to Shelley and Prometheus. Through the "detestable" Mr. Sludge Browning may have made his sharpest thrust at the credulity of his readers: "I've made a spirit squeak / In sham voice for a minute, then outbroke / Bold in my own, defying the *imbeciles* — / Have copied some ghost's pothooks, half a page, / Then ended with my own scrawl undisguised" (592-6; Q Mab 8.152).

Browning could not have avoided marveling at the gullibility attendant on reception of MR. SLUDGE or wincing at the alacrity with which readers detected the atheism of BISHOP BLOUGRAM. Although the Bishop's apology is probably the most nearly transparent of all his attacks on Faith, Browning knew his public well and rightly gauged its animosity toward Roman Catholicism to be far greater than its contempt for a fraudulent medium. But Bishop Blougram not only proves faithless to Jehovah, rejecting his machinery of rewards and punishments, hopes and fears, injunctions against self-fulfillment and self-gratification; he also proves faithful to Prometheus and paganism, living his life to the absolute best of what Jehovah stingily provided (355) and counting its sensuous pleasures preparation for the pure enjoyment of the next life: "Ask him, if this life's all, who wins the game?" With many a twist in thought — notably contingent upon Shelley's chance, check, choice, gifted, lidless, mind, monarch, myself, new, pasturage, points, sheep, slave, sphere, sward, tether, touch, warrant, wheel, wither, worn — Blougram nonetheless underlines the obvious in saying that something had struck Gigadibs in the Outward-bound *another way* than Blougram's purpose" (1007-8). That is, voyaging out to Australia rather than to the greensward surrounding Prometheus' Cave. Like Browning's cozened readers, Gigadibs is especially obtuse in not considering that "the great bishop [honestly] rolled him out *a mind* / Long crumpled, till creased *consciousness* lay smooth." Blougram knew that he could not more openly advocate the inviolability of the Myself: "His power and consciousness and self-delight" (500); the primacy of Promethean Fire: "fire and life / Are all" (557); the supremacy of the Mind and Genius: "such men / Carry the fire, all things grow warm to them" (940-1); and the absolute need of a God: "I, who want, am made for, and must have a God" (845-6). Yet it is not Jehovah about whom this Promethean speaks, for Blougram believed only half he spoke, "some *arbitrary accidental* thoughts, / That crossed his mind, amusing because *new*." "That's better," he knows, "than acquitting God [Jehovah] *with grace* / As some folk do" (710-1).

CLEON is an aristocrat of more ancient days and, apart from his famous concluding jibe which has been thought ironic in a Christian sense, seems to be portrayed as an unregenerate pagan. Whether the Christian "doctrine could be held by no sane man" appears less important to Browning than Cleon's inability to believe in Prometheus. Cleon had written three books to disprove what was written on the Soul, throwing all back to ignorance again, and he had imaged out a fiction of the God whom Shelley and Browning saw as self-sacrificing, loving and beneficent (115-38). Still as his mis-known soul vainly cries out to Zeus to vindicate his purpose in human life, Cleon cannot believe that it is for Zeus to boast that his happiness is gained at the expense of man's happiness. If that were true, he could not thank his Lord as hearts beat on to doing. So it is neither malice nor carelessness. Yet if it is care, Cleon has not observed the sign. By the same process of reasoning, if there were a future state unlimited in capability for joy as Cleon's life is unlimited in desire for joy, Zeus would have revealed it: "I ask / And get no answer, and agree in sum, / O king, with thy profound discouragement, . . . / Most progress is most failure." Thus perhaps the dilemma of modern man and Browning's disappointment in his intellectual peers. They had been granted freedom from Jehovah and Zeus, both unloving and without benevolence, but they remained indifferent to the overpowering love of Prometheus. In spite of his being a feeling, thinking, acting man who loved his life over-much and was horrified at the thought of extinction, Cleon apparently could no more surrender belief in Zeus than Paulus could surrender faith in Jehovah. The true irony in Cleon's prideful rejection seems to be, not that Christianity met all the unfulfilled longings of his superb mind, but that Prometheanism offered the unlimited capability for joy for which he unavailingly yearned.

Neither Browning nor Shelley could have approved of the tyranny, sycophancy and slavery made so prominent in Cleon's life. These trappings must be evaluated as disapproval of Cleon or as artful deception of the reader. Yet the poem has the same generous sprinkling of Shelleyan words which Browning wished to codify, and it advances through the complexity of Cleon's thought some of Shelley's most cherished ideas. Death of the soul Cleon stubbornly disavows and indirectly opposes despite his books (138), since he is convinced that works of art — magnificent tower or morning chant — are lost less to Death than to the minds of the artists' survivors. In fact, Cleon understands the Shelleyan points, point by point (PU 2.3.41-63), as fully as the theory that admiration grows as knowledge grows, that imperfection means perfection reserved to grace the after-time (182-6). Thus Shelley's doctrine of perfectability and Prometheus' care for Genius are both extensively implied in Cleon's contradictory words, adding proof to the evidence that Browning successfully misled readers into believing that he preferred the modern to the ancient or classic. As Cleon is misinterpreted though he implies what Abt Vogler makes explicit — "There shall never be one lost good!" — so Browning's parleying with GERARD DE LAIRESSE is misinterpreted through a similarly imposed design. For there Browning exults in "'Walk,' [cf., La S 388] come what come may, / No measure [PU 4.135] of steps on this our globe / Shall ever match for marvels." Since Browning read Lairesse with the greatest delight of his childhood and forever worshipped every pagan marvel unfurled on the vivid walks, it is not improbable that Lairesse magically broke the soil of Browning's mind for Shelley's fruitful planting. Browning had now waited more than fifty years before daring to pay specific homage to certain people of importance as well as to speak out boldly in his own name. So if Lairesse first introduced him to Prometheus, the parleying would also have satisfied a longing to unite (PU 4.80-8) the three in commemoration of Prometheus' self-sacrifice:

Thunders on thunders, doubling and redoubling   (Jupiter's; 181)
Doom o'er the mountain, while a sharp white fire
Now shone, now sheared its *rusty* herbage, troubling   (Q Mab 9.120)
Hardly the fir-boles, now discharged its *ire*   (Q Mab 7.189)
Full where some pine-tree's *solitary* spire   (Alastor 43, Q Mab 9.31)

Crashed down, defiant to the last: till — lo,
The motive of the malice! — all a-glow,   (Q Mab 7.112, 180, 248)
Circled with flame there *yawned* a sudden rift   (Q Mab 7.88)
I' the rock-face, and I saw *a form erect*   (Prometheus)
Front and defy the outrage, while — as checked,
Chidden, beside him dauntless in the drift —
Cowered a heaped *creature*, wing and wing outspread   (Jupiter's eagle)
In deprecation o'er the crouching head
Still hungry for the feast foregone awhile.
O thou, of *scorn's unconquerable smile*,   (PU 1.473-4)
Was it when this — Jove's feathered fury — slipped
Gore-glutted from the *heart's* core whence he ripped —   (PU 1.579)
This eagle-hound — neither reproach nor prayer —
Baffled, in one more fierce attempt to tear
Fate's secret from thy safeguard, — was it then   (Jupiter's downfall)
That all these thunders rent earth, ruined air
To reach thee, pay thy *patronage* of men?   (fire & wisdom)
He thundered, — to withdraw, as *beast* to lair,   (PU 1.581)
Before the triumph on thy *pallid brow.*   (PU 1.565, 598)
Gather the night again about thee now,
Hate on, love ever! Morn is *breaking* there —   (PU 1.393-5)
The granite ridge pricks through the mist, turns gold
As wrong turns right. O *laughters manifold*   (PU 1.611)
Of oceans' ripple at *dull earth's* despair!   (Two Spirits 1-48)

A critic has written that Browning was probably thinking of "winged hound" in Elizabeth Barrett's translation of THE PROMETHEUS BOUND when he coined "eagle-hound." Yet why not Shelley's "wingèd hound" for both? Every word in these twenty-nine lines appears in Shelley's PROMETHEUS UNBOUND and, save for the typically impassioned "Hate on" which only Aeschylus supplies, their essence is lifted from Act I, particularly lines 1-58 and 597-615.

Because the negative, implicit Christian elements of Browning's contradictory lines have been followed rather than the positive, explicit pagan elements, critics have naturally decided that Cleon complements not only Browning's Karshish but also Matthew Arnold's Empedocles. Consequently Cleon, like Empedocles, is thought to be representative of Hellenistic failure, as perhaps best confirmed in OLD PICTURES IN FLORENCE. But in such an analysis the overwhelming quantity of references to Greek literature in

Browning's poetry has been ignored. Even Browning's importunate appeals for republication of Arnold's poem substantiate the poet's wish to ally Cleon and Empedocles in their intellectual despair but surely not as examples of the disastrous effects of paganism or the failure of Hellenism. Browning's more likely purpose was to enunciate by conformity with Arnold the blindness of two great pagan intellects in not recognizing that what their minds had accomplished should be attributed to Prometheus' gifts alone and was to be rewarded by his enduring love. Only if the doctrine of the imperfect is not identical with Shelley's doctrine of perfectability, only if the thought of CLEON, OLD PICTURES and the parleying with LAIRESSE is not overweighted with the inevitability of Progress, can these poems possibly fail to be all of one piece.

"What's come to perfection perishes," the best known pronouncement of OLD PICTURES, was undoubtedly concocted as a double entente or a deliberate contradiction to the theme of the poem. Since there can now be no confusion about either the possessor of "the ineffable Name" in ABT VOGLER (7, 65) or "the race of Man / That receives life in part to live a whole [hereafter] , / And grow here according to God's clear plan" in OLD PICTURES (110-2), it is easier to observe the similarity of these two poems. The Prometheus who whispers in Vogler's ear is the Prometheus who inspires Browning's most sacredly held belief: "When this life is ended, begins / New work for the soul in another state, / Where it strives and gets weary, loses and wins: / Where the strong and weak, this world's *congeries,* / Repeat in large what they practised in small, / Through life after life in unlimited series" (OLD PICTURES 162-8). To Browning as to Shelley Progress was everything, was indeed Life, and there could never have been a tilt in either's mind over modern and ancient art. For if the art of great ancients reached perfection, it perished only because it was instantly translated to Prometheus, the talented artists being "the mediators / Of that best worship love, by him [man] and us [Prometheus & Asia] / Given and returned" (PU 3.3.58-60). Each sufferer has his scheme of the weal and woe, but "God has a few of us whom he whispers in the ear" (ABT VOGLER 86-7), and only those "of the little wit" (OLD PICTURES 52, 60) could doubt that the Michaelangelos and Rafaels now see Prometheus face to face.

With his epistle relatively free of deceptive tactics, KARSHISH is almost openly Promethean. He avidly explains the phenomenon of Lazarus' trance according to an accumulated knowledge which was originally a gift from Prometheus: "He told the hidden power of herbs and springs, / And disease drank and slept" (PU 2.4.85-6). Of this gift both Karshish and Abib had learned through "our lord the sage / Who lived there in the pyramid alone" and was, as calculated by the earthquake, prefigured by the learned leech Jesus in "the loss / To occult learning." Thus when the risen Lazarus encounters "*Demand* / The reason why — ''t is but a word,' *object* — 'a gesture'," he is said by Karshish to regard thee as curiously as our lord the sage looked at us. That is, when young Abib and Karshish would unadvisedly recite the beginning of a charm able to bid the sun throb wide and burst all into stars! Locked in Karshish's vocabulary are learning's crumbs, allsagacious, scholar, sage, inquisitive, skill, wit and wisdom. Forefront in his mind is the entrapment of the soul by the flesh, which despite stress and strain is aptest under the contrivance of Jehovah to prevent the wily vapor to "slip / Back and rejoin its source before the term." And surpassing all else is Karshish's consternation at finding that not he or his sage or his lord in the cave but of all people the Jew Lazarus had truly seen Prometheus:

The very God! *think*, Abib; dost thou *think*?
So, the All-Great, were the All-Loving too —
So, through the thunder comes a human [-like] *voice*   (Prometheus')
Saying, "O heart I made, a heart beats here!
Face, my hands fashioned, see it in *myself*!   (cf., Saul 310)
Thou hast *no power* nor mayst conceive of mine,   (weakness)
But love I gave thee, with *myself* to love,
And thou *must* love me who have *died* for thee!"   (Will; suffered)

Illustrative of how completely Browning exploited Christian terminology which had been emptied of its original integrity by Shelley, these famous lines and the following ones now form a comprehensive pattern in their Shelleyan lucidity: "The man's fantastic *will* is the man's law"; "he knows / God's secret, . . . the especial marking of the man / Is prone submission to the heavenly [Prometheus'] will"; "So long as God [Prometheus] please, and just how God please. / He even seeketh not to please God [Jehovah] more / (Which meaneth, otherwise) than as God please"; "Should his child sicken unto *death*, — why, look / For scarce abatement of his cheerfulness"; "Thou [Abib] and the child have each a *veil* alike / Thrown o'er your heads, from under which ye both / Stretch your blind hands and trifle with a match / Over a mine of Greek *fire*, did ye know?" Expectedly Lazarus, now a pantheist, would gaze with stupor at the ignorant who with opened eyes saw not what he saw and Karshish, despite a distrustful Syrian messenger, would discover "an *itch* I had, a *sting* to write, a *tang*!" (OEDIPUS 1.44; 241, 271; 375). Even though Karshish "must hold [on to] his *peace*" of mind in a profession "accused, — our learning's fate, — of wizardry, / *Rebellion*," he is no less practiced at saying "what harms not" on the surface than his fellow Prometheans Rabbi Ben Ezra and the Grammarian.

Also committed to Reason and the increase of Knowledge, work for the sake of progress — not mere work — and ultimate perfection, the RABBI and the GRAMMARIAN explain their abounding energy in terms of a radiant Death which will not end but complete the same. And they exhibit total assurance that their work both in and out of human existence is assigned, cooperated in and completed by Prometheus. So if Edward FitzGerald was responsible for Browning's Ben Ezra, it was because Omar's nihilism was a denial of Prometheanism not Christianity. What better historical figure than a Jewish scholar could Browning have selected to round out his imaginary Renaissance scholar and forward the cause of Culture against "the vulgar mass" and "the common crofts," each either held fast in the tether of Jehovah or the unlettered herd of the plain? The same aristocracy of mind which prompts Cleon and Karshish prompts Ben Ezra and the Grammarian, but the former do not seem to fall victim to the condescending platitudes of the Rabbi or the disproportionate pedantry of the Grammarian. Too often Browning builds his thought around specific Shelleyan words and theories, as in these two poems, and the insufficiency of his own thought is more an exposure than the barriers he deceptively erects. Thus Browning's continuing distaste for BEN KARSHOOK'S WISDOM, the surname of which is a rather childish play on Shelley's use of the thistle.

Probably the most difficult of Browning's poems to which to assign a true recipient are those which deal unreservedly with the subject of love. Yet, since the poems on art, music, questing, faith and doubt are all shared with and culminate in Prometheus, it seems likely that Elizabeth Barrett will now have to share Browning's protestations of love with Love the absolute, with Prometheus and possibly with Asia and Panthea if not others as well. O LYRIC LOVE, which has always defied rational interpretation, may indeed be a double entente addressed in the main to Shelley's eternal Love (PU 2.4.118-20) but disguised as if directed solely to Elizabeth. For read in conformity with Browning's uninterrupted emphasis on love, the dedication of THE RING AND THE BOOK no longer need be considered unintelligible: "When the first summons from the darkling earth / Reached thee [Prometheus] amid thy chambers, blanched their blue, / And bared them of the glory — to drop down, / To toil for man, to suffer or to die." Nor does "Hail then, and harken from the realms of help" seem less directly addressed to eternal Love as symbolized in Asia and materialized in the self-sacrificing love of Prometheus who taught Browning the gift of song and forever won his loyalty. And surely love's gifts of all hope, all sustainment and all reward are as ambiguously directed to Elizabeth Barrett as are the famous lines in PROSPICE: "Then a *light*, then thy [Prometheus] breast, / *O thou* soul of my soul! I shall clasp thee again, / And with God [Prometheus] be the rest!"

If one human soul is absorbed by another, or if all human

souls are eventually absorbed by Prometheus the One Soul, what occurs to the indestructible self-awareness of the absorbed? To Shelley absorption by Prometheus in this regard seems to have become a moot question, the other to have been avoided by such an act as "mingling." Not so to Browning, however, for beyond death he saw himself, and other individuals, journeying from new world to new world throughout eternity. To the urge of earthly lovers to become one, Browning's thought was so regularly attuned that its consideration broke into the most unexpected poems, as witness the lesson given the Duchess by the gipsy Queen on the difference between blending or unifying souls and knowing one is a distinct portion of the One Soul. Such a conflict or irresolution may even be the chief reason for Browning's many poems on love and his frequent use of Love as a double entente to represent the absolute but to imply his departed wife. As the lovers in the CAMPAGNA stray in spirit, unashamed of soul or love, that which tantalizes the lover is an inability or desire of his soul to surrender its will. Despite the momentary fire the lover has experienced, the greater and more lasting yearning is for infinite, not finite, passion. Thus the mystery of the soul's identity and its wish to be reabsorbed by the One Soul or One Mind are symbolized in the pervasive thread of thought which vanishes like the anchorage of the spider's web. It is believed that the lovers BY THE FIRESIDE exemplify Browning's perfect or heavenly marriage, but they may only illustrate his most serious attempt to surmount the inviolability of the Myself. Described in Shelleyan diction and enshrined closest to Prometheus "when Alps meets heaven in snow," that experience too is momentary; the true test of earthly oneness arrives in the maturity of love: "At first, 't was something our two souls / Should mix [mingle] as mists do; *each is sucked / In each now*" (PU 3.3.102). As unique and inexplicable as the poem becomes, the contradictory innuendoes are distinct enough to hint that for the good moment the oneness was gained by way of Prometheus in Nature, that for more than the moment the absolute oneness is reserved for the next life (cf., Jane, Recoll):

Oh, moment, one and infinite! . . .

A moment after, and *hands* unseen   (Prometheus')
   Were hanging the night around us fast;
But we knew that a bar was broken between
   Life and life: we were mixed at last   (Shelleyan Life, earthly life)
In spite of the mortal *screen*.   (flesh)

The forest had done it; there *they* stood;   (the trees, the deities)
   We caught *for a moment* the powers at play:
They had mingled us so, for once and good,   (the deities)
   Their work was done — *we might go or stay,*   (divertive)
They relapsed to their ancient mood.   (the trees)

Whether ONE WORD MORE helps or hinders in explaining the momentary mingling of souls, it provides Browning another chance to subvert Dante's best known lines on Beatrice: "Thus I believe . . . that lady lives of whom my soul was enamoured." As Shelley's inversion of Boccaccio's Demogorgon leaves a false impression, so Browning's inversion of Dante's Christian faith leaves an impression that Beatrice is in the keeping of Prometheus. Oddly — since Dante was interrupted while drawing an angel — Browning chooses to report "Then I stopped my painting"; Dante writes, "Another was with me just now, and because of that I was abstracted." Unusually bouncy as the tension of deception mounts, Browning's thought seems less on Elizabeth than on the outcome for his MEN AND WOMEN. Despite his pretentious candor the poet does not, as will be seen, speak "this once" in his true person. But he does reveal that Elizabeth saw him enter fifty masks and "use their service, / Speak from every mouth, — the speech, a poem. / Hardly shall I tell my [own] joys and sorrows, / Hopes and fears, belief and disbelieving: . . . Where my heart lies, let my brain lie also! / Poor the speech; *be how I speak, for all things. / Not but that you know me!*" Like the moon which reserves one side for moonstruck mortal, Elizabeth reserves one side of her nature for Robert alone:

Proves *she* as the paved work of a *sapphire*   (the moon; Islam 604; 172)
Seen by Moses when he *climbed* the mountain? ("went up," Ex 24.9-10,
Moses, Aaron, Nadab and Abihu   "climb," PU 3.1.14, Islam 2656)
Climbed and was the very God, the Highest,
Stand upon the *paved work* of a *sapphire* [emerald]   (Ex 24.10, PU
Like the *bodied* heaven in his clearness   3.3.13; Q Mab 1.144-51)
Shone the stone, the *sapphire* of that *paved work*, ("paved," PU 3.3.13)
When they ate and drank and saw *God* also! . . .   (Jehovah)

                    yourself my moon of poets!   (Elizabeth, Love)
Ah, but that's the world's side, *there's the wonder,*   (Q Mab 1.144-51)
Thus they see you, praise you, *think they know you!*
There, in turn I stand with them and praise you —
Out of *my own self,* I dare to phrase it.
But the best is when I *glide* from out them,   (R of Islam 622)
Cross a step or two of *dubious twilight*   ("doubtful light," PU 3.3.17;
Come out on the other side, the *novel*   PU 1.662; Dante Conv 9)
Silent silver lights and *darks undreamed of,*   (PU 2.3.21, 3.3.16, 71,
          4.70, R of Islam 620; "supernatural night," R of Islam 621)
Where I *hush* and bless *myself* with silence.   ("'Hush! hark! Come they
        yet? *Just Heaven* [Prometheus]! thine hour is near!'" Islam 4188)

Having prepared the way for Moses in the bold emphasis of
his disobedient moment of glory, his latitude at love-making
and his rejection by a powerless, ignorant and bickering
people, Browning knew that he could easily camouflage his
own "climb" to Prometheus and Elizabeth-Love with allu-
sions to the memorable face-to-face encounter of Moses with
Jehovah. But if only lines 595-666 of THE REVOLT OF
ISLAM and 6-17, Act III, Scene III of PROMETHEUS UN-
BOUND are collated with the above lines, it becomes clear
that being reunited with Elizabeth in death is less than all of
Browning's projected "wonder." For it is in Prometheus'
Cave or a restored Temple nearby that he will sit among "the
Great, who had departed from mankind, / A mighty Senate."
And on the jasper walls he will see "Paintings, the poesy of
mightiest thought, / Which did the Spirit's history display; /
A tale of passionate change, divinely taught, / Which in their
wingèd dance, unconscious *Genii* wrought" (R of Islam 600).
    One cannot forget Browning's confidence in LA SAISIAZ
when, on recalling the loss of Elizabeth and her love, he asks,
"Only grant my soul may carry high through death her cup

unspilled, / Brimming though it be with knowledge, life's loss drop by drop distilled, / I shall boast it mine." The questions are inescapable: Did Prometheus bring the Brownings together? Did Robert win Elizabeth to Prometheus? She did make the overture for friendship on a note as odd as Browning's fascination with the pomegranate legend and, some six years older, she did write: "I believe in what is divine and floats at highest, in all these different theologies — and because the really Divine draws together souls, and tends so to a unity, I could pray anywhere and with all sorts of worshippers." Their 1845 letters which turn quickly to Elizabeth's retranslation of THE PROMETHEUS BOUND present a tantalizing referendum, especially since Browning's extraordinary help immediately involved thoughtful consideration of Prometheus' "I did restrain besides / My mortals from premeditated death. ... I set *blind hopes* to inhabit in their house." Nor could Browning refrain from adding that to Aeschylus (thus to himself) it was cruel to plant undying yearnings, restless longings, instinctive desires in men unless they were eventually to be indulged. "Like a sigh from the admitted *Eleusinian* AEschylus" is the poet's way of reminding Elizabeth that her master, "the divinest of divine Greek souls," was an initiate in the most famous of pagan Mysteries. So one may assume that she was cognizant of Browning's delight in religious rites which entailed the earth-mother, the sacred way, mystic drama, the torch, magic formulae, the goddess' cup, mesmerism, terrorless judgment, unoppressive dogmatism, higher happiness, death a blessing and Zagreus if not Promethean fire in the hollow corn-stalk of still another god — what Browning apparently wanted to commemorate in MANSOOR THE HIEROPHANT but decided to dilute in the renamed THE RETURN OF THE DRUSES. Is it unlikely that the beautiful lyric, written independently of IN A GONDOLA but appropriately attached, was at first addressed to Prometheus alone?

> I send my heart up to thee, all my heart
>   In this my singing.
> For the stars help me, and the sea bears part;

> The very night is clinging
> Closer to Venice's streets to leave one space
> Above me, whence thy face
> May light my joyous heart to thee its dwelling-place.

Before one concludes that the greater part of Browning's life was as tense and lonely as the record implies, it is well to remember that at first there were his father's library and Shelley, though ironically his mother gave him the inflammable QUEEN MAB. The early headaches were undoubtedly real, but Browning soon found an emotional outlet for his pent-up secret in theater groups. And then there was Landor to be followed by Elizabeth, both of whom could talk knowledgeably about Browning's beloved pagan literature. Supposedly Robert and Elizabeth did not see each other's work in progress, but it is difficult to believe that she could honor this unreasonable privacy as completely as his family had honored the youthful poet's inviolable desk — haven of the destroyed INCONDITA. And though Browning is said not to have discussed himself or his poetry in the presence of a third person, he discusses both quite freely if often elliptically with Elizabeth in their letters: his work being all on the "inside" and largely unpublished, his focus on self-consciousness, his thought of giving up secrecy; her use of "Life," her references to mesmerism and clairvoyance, her "Christianity is a worthy myth"; their cooperative use of "Myself" and "God bless you, my dearest friend" (1.117-46) — all leading to a caution against "comment" (1.313) which may or may not refer to a Promethean brotherhood. One would at least surmise that Elizabeth was early alerted to Browning's "I don't think I shall let you hear, after all, the *savage* things about . . . imaginative religions that I *must* say" (1.6). But with all of Browning's work sheets and possibly helpful correspondence destroyed, it is idle to speculate on what passed between the poet and Landor, J. S. Blackie, the skeptical and cynical ex-Jesuit F. S. Mahony and many other irregular intimates. Yet the time came in 1883, if the Epilogue to FERISHTAH'S FANCIES is not a deceptive act, when Browning's unparalleled will and industry needed support. Still trusting the famous ones of old who smilingly ask, "What, our names, our deeds so soon erases / Time upon his tablet where Life's glory lies enrolled," Browning nonetheless there resigns the field's fortune to "our leader" Prometheus (TRIUMPH 293). Still knowing that his courage has endured, that his heart and soul applaud nothing less than perfection, he yet recoils with "only, at heart's utmost joy and *triumph*, terror / Sudden turns the blood to *ice* [TRIUMPH 78]: ... What if all be error — / If the halo *irised* [TRIUMPH 440ff] round my head were, Love, thine arms?"

If Browning's expressed terror is as genuine and stark as that of his Cleon is convincingly made, it vanishes remarkably fast. More in accord with an earlier Epilogue (DRAMATIS PERSONAE), his favorite spot for speaking out, Browning's last two volumes are a pyrotechnic of rebellion against Jehovah and justification for Prometheus. In that epilogue he had angrily denounced the witless Jehovah worshipers and the witless rationalist Renan for not recognizing Nature as their cathedral and Prometheus as the Face which truly restores. "I am glad it is written," Browning told a friend of Renan's LIFE OF JESUS; "if he thinks he can prove what he says, he has fewer doubts on the subject than I, *but mine are none of his.*" And "That Face," he told Mrs. Orr in explanation of the last stanza, "is the face of Christ [Prometheus]. That is how I feel him." That is, still unaltered from the Face promised by David to receive King Saul, the Face unrecognized by either Renan or Strauss. Now in the last two volumes Browning utilizes unpublished poems or miraculously pulls all the stops, daringly casting to his conditioned readers an unbelievably concerted effort before death to strike one blow more at the arch foe. Whether REPHAN and REVERIE are late creations or from unpublished poems of Browning's creative prime, they are powerful protests among what may now scarcely be considered a tedious lot and to be compared with the deceptive genius of CHILDE ROLAND TO THE DARK TOWER CAME. Every idea Browning had garnered from Shelley is present, and the directness of thought as well as the imitative diction now lies wide open. How Browning's true purpose in these poems could for so long be missed embarrasses less only because IXION, Browning's angriest denunciation of Jehovah, also went undetected in full. Now all that IXION requires for clarity, once the double entente is seen in the mythical account, is the substitution of the name Robert Browning for Ixion, the speaker, and of Jehovah for Zeus, the deity whose malicious jealousy of man's potential under Prometheus' love caused all the torture. So when Browning again turns to the business of defending man whatever the weakness or mistake, it is still the fault of Jehovah who made him: "Zeus who madest man — flawless or faulty, thy work!" (cf., TRIUMPH 201). Whatever the punishment man wills to endure against such a vengeful God, it is bitterly intensified by rejection of false promise of reward to other sufferers who blindly worship and idolize Jehovah. Indeed IXION is an amazing replica of Shelley's Jupiter-Jehovah sacrilege and probably the climactic height of the unrelenting warfare which was promised and initiated in PAULINE. The object of Ixion's scorn is the same God whom Browning parades through the resistance of all his heroes, the creator of an evilly constructed machinery of alternating pain and pleasure, hope and fear, joy and sorrow, ever therefore to be opposed with the gifts which made Prometheus' self-sacrifice so glorious. IXION thus begins and ends with a prediction of man's triumph, each time symbolized by a Promethean rainbow juxtaposed to spasms of pain once ghastly borne, now glorified. The variations on "made for a purpose of hate," "flesh became vapor thro' pain," "foiled by my senses I dreamed," "good was the evil that seemed," "made false things seem true," "never so baffled but" and "hell's sad triumph suspended" are dramatically arranged to justify "Arrogant thought, word, deed, — mere man who conceited me godlike." So it is blind faith in man and pitiless power in Jehovah which introduce Browning's most exposed proselytical appeal, itself a paraphrase of Demogorgon's ringing last words: "Strive, mankind, though strife endure through endless obstruction ["Destruction"], /

Stage after stage, each rise marred by as certain a fall!''

Almost totally dependent on THE TRIUMPH OF LIFE, Browning employs a language which in the first eighty-eight lines of IXION permits a selective collation with the following Shelleyan words and thoughts: suspended 395, old yet young 248, agonies 143, rainbow 357, 440, ghastly 171, 540, glorified 245, wheel 171, sparklike 388, 201, vesture 449, sense 341, 160, pierce 103, star 256, pore 59, pain's 258, pleasure 319, 143, slave 259, atom 446 (thematic), rush 87, wonder 471, 95, 41, shade 30 (thematic), good 231, sight 410 (thematic), torture 143, taught 307, blind 78, 101, pure 202, dreamers 42 (thematic), low 127, folly 73, melts 513, murderous 285, expiate 255, touch 404, 130 (thematic), lie 174, play 449, people 45, 483, weakling 226, deed 281, palm 361, athwart 25, 380, flame 130, vision 40, 411, 233, root 182, stem 24, lay 41, laying 126, doom 244, face 520, circle 454, limbs 24, misery's 121, 280, glow 152 (thematic), 513. All of which are followed by an interweaving whose intricacy is unsurpassed in Browning's self-imposed obscurity:

So did *a man* conceive of *your* passion, you	(R.B.; Jehovah's; 89)
passion-*protesters*!	(Triumph 275)
So did he trust, so love — being *the truth*	(the opposite)
of *your* lie!	(Jehovah's)
You to aspire to be Man! Man made you who	
vainly would ape him:	(cf., Death in Desert 561)
You are the *hollowness*, he — filling you,	(PU 1.56,299,442,768,
falsifies *void*.	Gisb 256; PU 3.1.76, 2.10)
Even as — witness the *emblem*, Hell's sad	(PU 1.594, 3.4.177)
triumph *suspended*,	(Triumph 395)
Born of my tears, sweat, blood — *bursting*	(Triumph 410)
to vapor above —	
Arching my torment [Mab 7.249], an *iris ghostlike*,	(Triumph 439; 357,
startles the *darkness*,	385ff; 60, 428; 4)
Cold white — jewelry *quenched* — justifies,	(Triumph 35,71,468; 81,
glorifies pain.	186,473,490; 102,292,400; 2,245,350; 258)
Strive, mankind, though strife *endure* through	(PU 4.559-78)
endless *obstruction*, . . .	("Destruction," PU 4.564)
Whatsoever the medium, flesh or *essence*, —	Ixion's (Q Mab 3.215; 101)
Made for a purpose of *hate*, —	(Triumph 176-275,319,475)
clothing the entity *Thou*,	(Q Mab 1.182; R.B.)
— *Medium* whence that entity strives for the	("means of good," Tri 231)

Not-Thou beyond it,   (Prometheus)
  Fire elemental, free, frame unencumbered,
    the *All*, —   (Triumph 128)
Never so baffled but — when, on the verge of
    an *alien* existence,   (Prometheus' Cave)
  Heartened to press, by pangs *burst* to the   (Triumph 68)
    infinite *Pure*,   ("Spirit of Nature," Q Mab 3.214-5)
Nothing is reached but the ancient *weakness* still that   (Jehovah)
    arrests strength [& freshness],   (Q Mab 8.191,184-204; Tri 521)
  Circumambient [darkness] still, still the poor   (Q Mab 2.37)
    human *array*,   (Triumph 504, Q Mab 5.21)
Pride and revenge and hate and cruelty — all it
    has *burst* through,   (Triumph 68)
  Thought to escape, — *fresh formed*,   (Tri 211,521; Q Mab 4.154)
    found in the fashion it fled, —
Never so baffled but — when Man pays the price
    of *endeavor*,   (Epipsy 14)
  Thunderstruck, downthrust, Tartaros-*doomed* (Hellas 1020; Tri 244)
    to the wheel, —
Then, ay, then, from the tears and sweat and
    blood of his torment,
  E'en from the *triumph of Hell*, up let   (of Jehovah, 11., 1,93,114)
    him look and *rejoice*!
What is the *influence*, high o'er Hell, that turns   (PU 3.3.120)
    to a *rapture*   (Skylark 65, 88)
  Pain — and despair's *murk mists* blends in a   (Alastor 660)
    rainbow of hope?   (symbolic of Prometheus)
What is beyond the *obstruction*, stage by   ("Destruction," PU 4.564)
    stage tho' it baffle?
  Back must I fall, confess "Ever the *weakness*
    I fled"?
No, for beyond, far, far is a *Purity all*   ("Never," Q Mab 9.189)
    unobstructed!   ("naked purity," Q Mab 1.132, 182)
  Zeus [Jehovah] was Zeus [Jehovah] — not Man: wrecked
    by *his weakness*, I whirl   (Jehovah's)
Out of the wreck I rise — past *Zeus* to the   (Ch Ist 2.108; Jehovah)
    Potency o'er him! . . .   (Will, Prom; Power, Demogorgon)
  Thither I *rise*, whilst thou — *Zeus*,   (cf., Tri 206ff; Jehovah)
    keep the godship and sink!

In remarkable ways IXION is Browning's PROMETHEUS
UNBOUND, for there he re-lives both Prometheus' curse of
Jupiter-Jehovah and Demogorgon's fulfillment of that curse,
even to use of the symbolic Rise which indicates the restoration of Prometheus and the symbolic Sink which indicates

the lagging fall of Jehovah. IXION is also Browning's TRIUMPH OF LIFE — which is Death — and possibly his truest swan song. It seems to have gone unnoted that STRAFFORD, Browning's first play, was in all likelihood inspired by Shelley's fragmentary CHARLES THE FIRST. So "Out of the wreck" is probably a premeditated return to thematic Weakness which the poet now transfers to Jehovah who jealously and vengefully conveyed it to man. Unconcerned by the distortion of their metaphysics neither poet could believe that Jehovah possessed a soul. Shelley's Prometheus says that at Jupiter's fall his "soul, cloven to its depth with terror" shall "gape like a hell within." Browning believed it and never once grew weary of enunciating it. Like his own Lazarus the man's fantastic will was the man's law. "Shall I, with sight [knowledge] thus gained," Ixion (Browning) asks, "by torture be taught I was blind once?" "What were the need" of anything less than perfection but of pitying power to touch and disperse it? Love should be absolute love, which means a slave, or it is no love at all. If the spark with which Heaven lit his spirit had been with purer nutriment supplied (TRIUMPH 201, 207), the rebellious Ixion (Browning) too would ignite a thousand beacons not unlike the beacons lifted high by genius of old. In making Good and the means of good irreconcilable Jehovah willed his fate and shall eventually sink with the godship. Ixion (Browning) shall rise to a "Purity all unobstructed!"

Had Browning believed more in action and less in words, pursuit of his avowal might have had a far greater impact through creation of more Lippos, old bishops and Andreas. Fra Lippo, a pure pagan, has been thought his most fascinating character by countless impressionable minds, the Old Bishop is a perfect exponent of the vanity of all things except self-gratification, and Andrea satisfies both those who enter into his plight and those who are repulsed by his colorless life. Yet Browning's self-awareness and his avowal were so fully in command that every means of the poet's existence bowed thereto. He misapplied the greatest opportunity of his life when he was unable to take advantage of Macready's backing in the drama, and even when his characters take control by the strength of their own reality, Browning was unwilling to permit their actions alone to justify his appeals for paganism. Perhaps his wisest move was to take up residence in Italy. At least he was farther removed from prying eyes and nearer to Shelley's grave, Shelley's beloved mountains and Shelley's volcanoes. Browning lived always in two worlds which to him were inseparable — pagan and Christian. One he loved as much as he hated the other. Nonetheless he determined that he know as much about Christianity as one can learn from the outside, and that was enough to persuade the Christian world he was one with it. Thus where the implicit warrant was to believe that Pope Innocent honored Jehovah, Browning deceptively honored Prometheus: "Within whose circle of experience burns / The central truth, Power, Wisdom, Goodness, — God." For Browning himself says "plainlier" of Jehovah: "No, as I am man, I mourn the poverty I must impute: / Goodness, wisdom, power, all bounded, each a *human attribute*!" (La S 347-8; Calderon 115-25). And "if ye demur," Browning's St. John had warned, "this judgment on your head, / Never to reach the *ultimate*, angel's law, / Indulging every instinct of the soul / There where law, life, joy, impulse are one thing!" (630; Q Mab 2.76, 8.200, PU 4.578). Is there any wonder that Browning could not refrain from introducing Prometheus and Shelley's triple goddess into FIFINE AT THE FAIR?

> As I mean, did he mean, (2212)
> The poet whose bird-phrase sits, singing in my ear
> A mystery not unlike? What through the dark and drear
> Brought comfort to the Titan? Emerging from the lymph,
> "God, man, or mixture" proved only to be a nymph: . . .
> "Impulsively she rushed, no slippers to her heels,"
> And "Fear not, friends we flock!" soft smiled the sea-Fifine —
> Primitive of the veils (if he meant what I mean)
> The poet's Titan learned to lift, ere "Three-formed Fate,
> *Moirai Trimorphoi*" stood unmasked the *Ultimate*.

In truth, the Epilogue now epitomizes Browning's philosophy and metaphysics: "Love is all and Death is naught!"